The New Eight Steps
to Happiness

Also by Venerable Geshe Kelsang Gyatso Rinpoche

Meaningful to Behold
Clear Light of Bliss
Universal Compassion
Joyful Path of Good Fortune
The Bodhisattva Vow
Heart Jewel
Great Treasury of Merit
Introduction to Buddhism
Tantric Grounds and Paths
Ocean of Nectar
Essence of Vajrayana
Living Meaningfully, Dying Joyfully
Transform Your Life
The New Meditation Handbook
How to Solve Our Human Problems
Mahamudra Tantra
Modern Buddhism
The New Heart of Wisdom
The New Guide to Dakini Land
How to Understand the Mind
The Oral Instructions of Mahamudra

Profits from the sale of this book are designated to the
NKT-IKBU International Temples Project Fund
according to the guidelines in *A Money Handbook*
(Nonprofit 501(c)3 Organization ID 14-1822928, USA)
A Nonprofit Buddhist Organization
Building for World Peace
www.kadampa.org/temples

VENERABLE GESHE KELSANG
GYATSO RINPOCHE

The New Eight Steps to Happiness

THE BUDDHIST WAY OF
LOVING KINDNESS

THARPA PUBLICATIONS
US · UK · CANADA
AUSTRALIA · ASIA

21 20 19 18 17 16   1 2 3 4 5 6

Tharpa Publications US   Tharpa Publications UK
47 Sweeney Road   Conishead Priory
Glen Spey, NY 12737   Ulverston, Cumbria
USA   LA12 9QQ, England

Tharpa Publications has offices around the world,
and our books are published in most major languages.
See page 349 for more information.

The cover image is of Buddha White Tara, and the frontispiece images are
Buddha Amitabha and Bodhisattva Langri Tangpa.

ISBN 978-1-61606-049-7 paperback
ISBN 978-1-61606-050-3 ePub
ISBN 978-1-61606-051-0 kindle

Library of Congress Control Number: 2009939211

Printed in the United States of America. Paper supplied from well-man-
aged forests and other controlled sources, and certified in accordance with
the rules of the Forest Stewardship Council.

Contents

Illustrations

*The illustrations depict the lineage Gurus
of the stages of the path to enlightenment*

(included at the request of faithful disciples)

Acknowledgements

This book, *The New Eight Steps to Happiness*, gives a detailed and practical commentary to the revered Mahayana Buddhist poem *Eight Verses of Training the Mind*, written by Bodhisattva Langri Tangpa (AD 1054–1123). The poem expresses the essential methods for developing universal love and compassion, and does so in a way that has inspired generations of practitioners for almost a thousand years.

The book is based upon transcripts of two courses of oral teachings given by the author at Manjushri Kadampa Meditation Center. The transcripts were carefully checked and substantially augmented by the author during intensive editing retreats in 1998 and 1999.

We are deeply grateful to Venerable Geshe Kelsang Gyatso Rinpoche for his great kindness in preparing a commentary that brings alive the full meaning of this celebrated text for the benefit of all worldwide. The power and lucidity of the commentary show clearly that the author writes with full personal realization of the subject matter.

We would also like to thank all those dedicated senior Dharma students who assisted the author with the editing and who prepared the final manuscript for publication.

Roy Tyson,
Administrative Director,
Manjushri Kadampa Meditation Center,
August 1999

Introduction

*E*veryone, whether religious or non-religious, is looking for happiness all the time and wants to be free from problems and suffering permanently. We can fulfill these wishes through understanding and practicing the instructions given in this book.

This book is based on the widely renowned *Eight Verses of Training the Mind* (*Lojong Tsig Gyema* in Tibetan), which was composed by Bodhisattva Langri Tangpa, an eleventh-century Buddhist Master from Tibet. Though comprising only eight four-line verses, this remarkable text reveals the essence of the Buddhist path to enlightenment, showing how we can transform our mind from its present confused and self-centered state into the perfect wisdom and compassion of an enlightened Buddha.

Every living being has the potential to become a Buddha, someone who has completely purified his or her mind of all faults and limitations and has brought all good qualities to perfection. Our mind is like a cloudy sky, in essence clear and pure but overcast by the clouds of delusions. Just as the thickest clouds eventually disperse, so too even the heaviest delusions can be removed from our mind. Delusions such as hatred, greed and ignorance are not an intrinsic part of the mind. If we apply the appropriate methods they can be

Buddha Shakyamuni

completely eliminated, and we will experience the supreme happiness of full enlightenment.

Everyone wants to be happy and no one wants to suffer, but very few people understand what is the real cause of happiness and what is the real cause of suffering. We tend to look for happiness outside ourself, thinking that if we had the right house, the right car, the right job and the right friends that we like, we would be truly happy. We spend almost all our time adjusting the external world, trying to make it conform to our wishes. All our life we have tried to surround ourself with people and things that make us feel comfortable, secure or stimulated, yet still we have not found pure and lasting happiness. Even when we succeed in fulfilling our desires, it is not long before our desires change and we want something else. We may find the house of our dreams, but a few months later we feel that we need a bigger kitchen, an extra bedroom or a larger yard, and we begin to think of moving. Or perhaps we meet the "perfect" partner, fall in love and move in together. At the beginning our partner seems to be the most wonderful person in the world, but before long we begin to see faults in him or her. We discover that we are no longer in love, and soon we are looking for someone else to fulfill our desires.

Throughout history human beings have sought to improve their external situation, yet despite all our efforts we are no happier. It is true that from the point of view of material development many countries are making progress. Technology is becoming more and more sophisticated, and worldly knowledge has increased dramatically. We know so many things we did not know before and can do things we never even dreamed of. Superficially it looks as if our world is improving, but if we look a little more deeply we will see that there are now many problems that never existed before. Terrifying weapons have been invented, our environment is being poisoned and new diseases are appearing. Even simple pleasures like eating or lying in the sun are becoming more dangerous.

The result of an unbridled pursuit of happiness from external sources is that our planet is being destroyed and our lives are becoming more complicated and dissatisfying. It is time we sought happiness from a different source. Happiness is a part of the mind that experiences inner peace, or peace of mind, so the real source of happiness must lie within the mind, not in external conditions. If our mind is pure and peaceful we will be happy, regardless of our external circumstances, but if it is impure and unpeaceful we will never be happy, no matter how hard we try to change our external conditions. We could change our home or our partner countless times, but until we change our restless, discontented mind we will never find real happiness.

If we have to walk across rough and thorny ground, one way of protecting our feet is to cover the whole ground with leather, but this is not very practical. We can achieve the same result in a much simpler way—by covering our feet. Similarly, if we wish to protect ourself from suffering we can either try to change external conditions to make them conform to our wishes, or we can change our mind. Until now we have been trying to change the external conditions, but this clearly has not worked. Now we need to change our mind.

The first step toward changing our mind is to identify which states of mind produce happiness and which produce suffering. States of mind that are conducive to peace of mind and happiness are called "virtuous minds," whereas those that destroy our peace of mind and cause us suffering are called "delusions." We have many different types of delusion, such as uncontrolled desire, also known as desirous attachment, anger, jealousy, pride, laziness and ignorance. These are known as "inner enemies" because they are continually destroying our inner peace, our happiness, from within. Their only function is to cause us harm.

Delusions are distorted ways of looking at ourself, other people and the world around us. The way a deluded mind views these phenomena does not accord with reality. The deluded mind of hatred, for example, views another person as intrinsically bad, but there is no such thing as an intrinsically bad person. Desirous attachment, on the other hand, sees its object of desire as intrinsically good and as a true source of happiness. If we have a strong craving to eat chocolate, chocolate appears to us to be an intrinsically desirable object. However, once we have eaten too much of it and start to feel sick, it no longer seems so desirable and may even appear repulsive. This shows that in itself chocolate is neither desirable nor repulsive. It is the mind of attachment that projects onto it all kinds of desirable qualities and then relates to it as if it really did possess those qualities.

All delusions function like this, projecting onto the world their own distorted version of reality and then relating to this projection as if it were true. When our mind is under the influence of delusions we are out of touch with reality and are, in a sense, hallucinating. Since our mind is under the influence of at least subtle forms of delusion all the time, it is not surprising that our lives are so often filled with frustration. It is as if we are continually chasing mirages, only to be disappointed when they do not give us the satisfaction for which we had hoped.

The source of all delusions is a distorted awareness called "self-grasping ignorance," which grasps phenomena as inherently, or independently, existent. In reality all phenomena are dependent arisings, which means that their existence is utterly dependent upon other phenomena, such as their causes, their parts and the minds that apprehend them. Objects do not exist from their own side, in and of themselves; what they are depends upon how they are viewed. Our failure to realize this is the source of all our problems.

The type of self-grasping that harms us most is grasping our own self, or I, as inherently or independently existent. We instinctively feel that we possess a completely real and objective self or I that exists independently of all other phenomena, even our body and mind. One consequence of grasping at our self as an independent entity separate from the world and other people is that we develop self-cherishing, a mind that regards ourself as supremely important. Because we cherish ourself so strongly, we are drawn to the people and things we find attractive, we want to separate ourself from the people and things we find unattractive and we are uninterested in the people and things we find neither attractive nor unattractive. In this way attachment, anger and indifference are born. Because we have an exaggerated sense of our own importance we feel that others' interests are in conflict with our own, and this in turn gives rise to competitiveness, jealousy, arrogance and lack of consideration for others. By acting under the influence of these and other delusions we engage in destructive behavior, such as killing, stealing, sexual misconduct, lying and hurtful speech. The result of these negative actions is suffering for both ourself and others.

Even though our delusions are deeply ingrained, they are not an intrinsic part of our mind and so they can definitely be removed. Delusions are just bad mental habits, and like all habits they can be broken. Through making a sincere and consistent effort to become familiar with constructive states of mind, we can eliminate even the most stubborn delusions and replace them with the opposite virtues. For example, we can weaken our anger by familiarizing our mind with patience and love, our attachment by familiarizing our mind with non-attachment and our jealousy by rejoicing in others' good fortune.

To eradicate delusions completely, however, we must destroy their root—the mind of self-grasping. To do this we need to familiarize our mind with the true nature of reality, or ultimate truth. This is explained in detail in the chapter on training in ultimate bodhichitta. If we destroy self-grasping, all other delusions cease naturally, just as the leaves and branches of a tree die if we destroy its roots. Once we have completely eradicated our delusions it will be utterly impossible for us to experience unpeaceful states of mind. As we will no longer have the internal causes of suffering, external causes of suffering, such as sickness or death, will have no power to disturb our mind. This permanent cessation of delusion and suffering is known as "liberation," or "nirvana" in Sanskrit.

Although attaining our own liberation from suffering is a wonderful achievement, it is not enough. We are not isolated individuals but part of the family of all living beings. Everything we own, everything we enjoy, all our opportunities for spiritual development and even our very body come from the kindness of others. Are we to make our own escape from suffering and then abandon everyone else to their fate? This would be like a young man imprisoned together with his aged parents who makes his own escape but leaves his parents behind. We would not admire such a person. We definitely need to make an effort to liberate ourself from the mental prison of our deluded minds, but our ultimate aim must be to help everyone else do the same.

Thus our final goal is the attainment of full enlightenment, or Buddhahood. The Sanskrit term "Buddha" means "Awakened One," and refers to anyone who has awakened from the sleep of ignorance and is free from the dream of mistaken appearance. Because ordinary beings like us have not yet awakened from the sleep of ignorance, we continue to live in a dream-like world of mistaken appearances and do not see the true nature of things. This is the fundamental reason why we experience suffering and are of limited benefit to others. Through completely removing all traces of the darkness of ignorance from their minds, Buddhas attained omniscient wisdom and the limitless ability to help all living beings.

Their boundless and all-encompassing compassion gives Buddhas the energy to work without interruption for the sake of others. They understand the real causes of happiness and suffering, and they know exactly how to help living beings in accordance with their individual needs and inclinations. Buddhas have the power to bless the minds of all living beings, causing them to experience inner peace and they also have the ability to emanate innumerable forms for the benefit of others. Of all the ways in which Buddhas help living beings, the most effective is to teach them how to control their minds and follow the spiritual path to liberation and enlightenment.

The founder of Buddhism in this world was Buddha Shakyamuni. After attaining enlightenment, Buddha gave eighty-four thousand teachings, all of which are advice on how to subdue and overcome delusions by cultivating virtuous states of mind. Buddha's teachings, as well as the inner realizations achieved through putting these teachings into practice, are known as "Dharma."

In the text on which this book is based, Bodhisattva Langri Tangpa has condensed the very essence of Buddhadharma into eight short verses. Through contemplating the meaning of these verses we will see that they contain a step-by-step path to complete inner peace and happiness. If we sincerely put these teachings into practice we will gradually subdue our destructive and self-centered habits of mind and replace them with the positive minds of unconditional love and compassion. In particular, by practicing the instructions given in the chapter on training in ultimate bodhichitta, we will be able to overcome the fundamental delusion of self-grasping ignorance, together with its imprints, and thereby experience the bliss of full enlightenment. Through putting the instructions given in this book into practice, we will develop and maintain a peaceful mind all the time so that we will be happy all the time. This is the real meaning of seeking happiness from a different source.

Although *Eight Verses* was written over nine hundred years ago, it is as relevant today as it was then. Whether Buddhist or not, anyone with a genuine wish to overcome their daily problems and achieve permanent inner peace and happiness can benefit from Langri Tangpa's advice. As mentioned above, happiness is a part of the mind that experiences peace of mind. It does not exist outside of ourself. Similarly, our problems and suffering are part of the mind that experiences unpleasant feelings. They do not exist outside ourself. If our car is broken, this is an outer problem, and we need to solve this problem by applying external methods. But our problems are internal problems, and we need to solve these problems by developing and maintaining a peaceful mind. It is only when living beings experience a peaceful mind that they are happy. Generally, by themselves alone they have no power to develop a peaceful mind. It is only through receiving Buddha's blessings upon their mind that they will develop and maintain a peaceful mind. This is why Buddha is the source of the happiness of all living beings.

REBIRTH AND KARMA

Our sleeping is like death, our dreaming is like the intermediate state and our waking up is like rebirth. The cycle of these three shows us the existence of future rebirth. Since some background knowledge of rebirth and karma is useful for understanding the main practices explained in this book, there now follows a brief introduction to these topics.

The mind is neither physical, nor a by-product of physical processes, but a formless continuum that is a separate entity from the body. When the body disintegrates at death, the mind does not cease. Although our superficial conscious mind ceases, it does so by dissolving into a deeper level of consciousness, called "the very subtle mind." The continuum of our very subtle mind has no beginning and no end, and it is this mind which, when completely purified, transforms into the omniscient mind of a Buddha.

Every action we perform leaves an imprint, or potential, on our very subtle mind, and each karmic potential eventually gives rise to its own effect. Our mind is like a field, and performing actions is like sowing seeds in that field. Positive or virtuous actions sow the seeds of future happiness, and negative or non-virtuous actions sow the seeds of future suffering. This definite relationship between actions and their effects—virtue causing happiness and non-virtue causing suffering—is known as the "law of karma." An understanding of the law of karma is the basis of Buddhist morality.

After we die our very subtle mind leaves our body and enters the intermediate state, or "bardo" in Tibetan. In this subtle dream-like state we experience many different visions that arise from the karmic potentials that were activated at the time of our death. These visions may be pleasant or terrifying depending on the karma that ripens. Once these karmic seeds have fully ripened they impel us to take rebirth without choice.

It is important to understand that as ordinary samsaric beings we do not choose our rebirth but are reborn solely in accordance with our karma. If good karma ripens we are reborn in a fortunate state, as either a human or a god, but if negative karma ripens we are reborn in a lower state, as an animal, a hungry spirit or a hell being. It is as if we were blown to our future lives by the winds of our karma, sometimes ending up in higher rebirths, sometimes in lower rebirths.

This uninterrupted cycle of death and rebirth without choice is called "cyclic existence," or "samsara" in Sanskrit. Samsara is like a Ferris wheel, sometimes taking us up into the three fortunate realms, sometimes down into the three lower realms. The driving force of the wheel of samsara is our contaminated actions motivated by delusions, and the hub of the wheel is self-grasping ignorance. For as long as we remain on this wheel we will experience an unceasing cycle of suffering and dissatisfaction, and we will have no opportunity to experience pure, lasting happiness. By practicing the Buddhist path to liberation and enlightenment, however, we can destroy self-grasping, thereby liberating ourself from the cycle of uncontrolled rebirth and attaining a state of perfect peace and freedom. We will then be in a position to help others to do the same. A more detailed explanation of rebirth and karma can be found in the books *Introduction to Buddhism* and *Joyful Path of Good Fortune.*

Bodhisattva Langri Tangpa

*T*he author of *Eight Verses of Training the Mind* is the Kadampa Buddhist Master, or Geshe, Bodhisattva Langri Tangpa. Reading about his life and good qualities will help us to develop faith in him and to appreciate the authenticity of *Eight Verses*, and this will strengthen our determination to put these instructions into practice.

Bodhisattva Langri Tangpa was born in central Tibet in the eleventh century AD. His actual name was Dorje Senge, but he became known as Langri Tangpa after Lang Tang, the area in which he lived. He was a disciple of Geshe Potowa, who was one of the principal disciples of the Buddhist Master Atisha, the founder of Kadampa Buddhism in Tibet.

Geshe Potowa was renowned throughout Tibet as a great scholar who showed an immaculate example to other practitioners, emphasizing the practice of bodhichitta, the altruistic mind of enlightenment. He wrote many profound scriptures of Kadampa Buddhism, in particular a text called *The Scripture of Examples* in which he used everyday experiences to illustrate the meaning of Dharma. In this text he recounted a story about a thief who had broken into a house, found a barrel of chang, or Tibetan beer, and proceeded to get drunk. The family was woken by his singing, "How happy

Maitreya

I am to be drinking from the mouth of the barrel of chang, but how much more wonderful it would be if I were drinking from the bottom of the barrel!" Geshe Potowa used the thief's song as a parable, changing the words to, "How happy we are to be practicing Dharma from the mouth, but how much more wonderful it would be if we were practicing it from the bottom of our hearts!" There was a saying in Tibet that Geshe Potowa's disciples were as numerous as stars in the sky, and that his two principal disciples, Geshe Langri Tangpa and Geshe Sharawa, were like the sun and the moon.

Bodhisattva Langri Tangpa was widely respected throughout Tibet as a holy person, and was recognized by many great meditators as an emanation of Buddha Amitabha. Although others regarded him as special, he always behaved in a humble manner and viewed others as important and worthy of respect. Completely indifferent to wealth, status and other worldly attainments, for many years he was very poor, living almost like a beggar. Inwardly, however, he was engaged in the practice known as "accepting defeat and offering the victory to others"—happily accepting whatever difficulties and adverse conditions he encountered, and offering his happiness and good conditions to others. His willing acceptance of poverty and hardship was a good example to other spiritual practitioners.

Bodhisattva Langri Tangpa's demeanor was very different from that of most people. We tend to be overly concerned that others like us, and so make a great effort to present a cheerful aspect, no matter how we feel inside. Langri Tangpa was the opposite. He maintained such a stern, unsmiling expression that he was nicknamed "Grim Face." His assistant once said to him, "People are calling you 'Grim Face.' When they come to receive blessings from you, it would be good if you could smile sometimes and speak gently to them." Langri Tangpa replied, "What you say is true, but I find it difficult to find anything in samsara to smile about. Whenever I see someone I think of their suffering, and instead of laughing I feel like crying." It was due to his deep compassion for all living beings that Langri Tangpa found it difficult to smile. It is important not to misunderstand this. Langri Tangpa was not unhappy; his compassion and other spiritual realizations protected him from ever feeling depressed and caused him to experience great joy. However, he saw clearly that there is no true happiness in samsara, and that confusing worldly pleasure with real happiness serves only to bind us more tightly to samsara. His stern manner challenged people to confront their actual samsaric situation and to enter into spiritual paths.

Langri Tangpa rarely laughed, and when he did it was so unusual that his assistant made a note of it. On one occasion Langri Tangpa was meditating in a cave on a hillside overlooking a river. It was mid-winter and the river was completely iced over. A traveling potter was crossing the river, but laden with pots, he kept slipping and breaking them. As the potter knew that Langri Tangpa was somewhere up on the hillside, whenever he slipped he would call out, "O Langri Tangpa, Grim Face!" in much the same way as some people in the West say, "O God!" or "O Jesus!" in similar situations. Langri Tangpa heard him and thought it was so funny that he started laughing.

On another occasion, after Langri Tangpa had been offered a large piece of turquoise he saw a mouse trying to steal it from his meditation table. Unable to move the stone, the mouse went away and returned with four other mice. The first mouse, which was the smallest, lay on its back, and the other mice pushed the turquoise onto its stomach. They each took one of its legs, and, pushing and pulling, managed to drag the turquoise to their mouse hole. However, when they got there they found that the stone was too large to fit through the hole, and so they had to leave it behind. Langri Tangpa found this so amusing that he laughed out loud.

Despite his stern appearance, through his actions people gradually came to understand that Bodhisattva Langri Tangpa's real nature was very special. Recognizing him to be a holy being, they made many offerings to him, but as soon as anyone gave him anything he would immediately offer it to his Spiritual Guide, Geshe Potowa, and to the community of Geshe Potowa's disciples. Just before Geshe Potowa passed away, Langri Tangpa made two promises in front of him: to give away all his own possessions, and not to remain in any one place for long. From then on, whenever he traveled to a new place he would give away any possessions he had accumulated and move on empty-handed. By happily accepting poverty and continuously practicing generosity, Langri Tangpa accumulated a vast amount of merit. As a result of all this merit, later in his life he received so many offerings that he was able to establish a large monastery, support two thousand monks and help many poor people. Without engaging in any business activities or making any effort to acquire wealth, he nevertheless became rich simply through accumulating merit. Every month he would give away all he owned, but the next month he would be given even more!

Although Langri Tangpa's generosity initially made him poor, the merit he accumulated through his practice of giving later made him very wealthy.

Langri Tangpa was also a great scholar and practitioner. His main practices were exchanging self with others, accepting defeat and offering the victory and bodhichitta—all of which are explained in this book. By teaching these practices to others he led many thousands of disciples to enlightenment. Even the area of Lang Tang in which he lived was blessed by his presence, such that the local people became peaceful and friendly, and the animals and birds lived in harmony. He also had a special power to cure sickness and pacify obstacles, and on one occasion was able to protect the lives of many people by causing dangerous floods to recede.

Langri Tangpa practiced accepting defeat and offering the victory to others all the time, both in meditation and in daily life. Once a young woman living nearby had a child who became seriously ill. She had already lost her first child, and fearing that this child might die too, she consulted a Lama who told her that the way to save her daughter was to give her to Geshe Langri Tangpa. "But how can a monk look after a baby?" she asked. The Lama replied, "Geshe Langri Tangpa is a Bodhisattva. His nature is to accept all hardship and give all good conditions to others, and so he will definitely agree to look after your child."

The woman went to Langri Tangpa with her baby but found him sitting on a throne teaching a large audience. Still not really believing that he would accept the baby, yet convinced that if she did not give her to him the baby would surely die, she strode up to him and placed the baby in his lap, saying, "Here is your baby. I cannot feed her. You look after her." To the surprise of his disciples, Langri Tangpa accepted the child. Although some people assumed that he really was the father and began to develop doubts about him, Langri Tangpa was unconcerned. Tenderly wrapping the child in his yellow robe, he carried on with the discourse. When he had finished he took the child home, fed her and blessed her. He cared for her for two years, and through his blessings she was completely cured. After two years the mother returned to see if her daughter was well. When she saw how healthy the child was, she asked Langri Tangpa if she could have her daughter back, and the kind Geshe immediately complied. From this and many other examples of his selfless behavior, everyone came to understand that Langri Tangpa was a very special, holy person.

It was not only in that life that Langri Tangpa worked extensively to benefit living beings and spread Buddhadharma in Tibet; he had done the same in many previous incarnations and continued to do so in subsequent lives. In a previous life, as the translator Gowa Pagtse, he had traveled to India, learned Sanskrit and translated many Buddhist texts into Tibetan. Later he reincarnated as Je Tsongkhapa's principal disciple Khedrubje, as Gyalwa Ensapa, and as the first and second Panchen Lamas.

When I was in Lhasa I met my Spiritual Father, Vajradhara Trijang Rinpoche, for the first time, and just seeing him reminded me of Bodhisattva Langri Tangpa. I felt great devotion toward him and often thought that he must be an emanation of Langri Tangpa. A senior monk later gave me a small book that listed the names of Trijang Rinpoche's previous incarnations, and among these was the name "Geshe Langri Tangpa." I was so happy to find my previous belief confirmed!

Because Langri Tangpa is Buddha Amitabha, and a Buddha's compassion is unlimited, there are definitely emanations of Langri Tangpa throughout the world even though we do not recognize them. We can be certain that his emanations are working in the West to benefit living beings and to spread Buddhadharma. The only reason we do not recognize them is that our minds are clouded by ignorance.

Through sincerely practicing the instructions on training the mind, Bodhisattva Langri Tangpa found ultimate happiness and helped many others to do the same. He then explained the essence of his experience of Dharma in *Eight Verses of Training the Mind*. Based on this text, later Kadampa Lamas such as Geshe Chekhawa spread the study and practice of Kadam Lojong, or training the mind, throughout Tibet. We should consider ourself very fortunate to have met such precious teachings.

The Pre-Eminent Qualities of These Instructions

Since *Eight Verses of Training the Mind* comes from the wisdom of a fully enlightened being, it is a blessed instruction and very precious. To develop deep appreciation of its value I will explain some of its benefits. In general, by putting this instruction into practice we will experience both temporary and ultimate happiness. This is because through this practice we can eliminate the ignorant mind of self-cherishing and self-grasping, the root of all suffering and problems.

Especially, this teaching shows us how to transform adverse conditions into the spiritual path, through which we will experience pure and everlasting happiness. From the point of view of spiritual development this present time is extremely degenerate, with many conditions hindering spiritual progress. However, by putting these instructions into practice we can make use of all these adversities and transform them into opportunities for spiritual growth.

The minds of human beings today are less pure than they were in the past, and delusions and wrong views are more prevalent. Because human beings in the past had purer minds it was relatively easy for them to see pure beings such as

Asanga

Buddhas and Bodhisattvas, but nowadays it is difficult for people even to believe in the existence of holy beings. In the past people were less prone to distracting thoughts, and so it was easier for them to attain tranquil abiding and other advanced levels of meditative concentration. With the mind of tranquil abiding they could achieve various types of clairvoyance, such as the ability to see forms beyond the scope of ordinary vision or to hear subtle and distant sounds. Many gained the power to know the minds of others, or to look into past and future lives; and miracle powers, such as the ability to fly in the sky or emanate various forms, were quite common. In addition to these mundane attainments, countless people achieved liberation and full enlightenment.

Gradually these attainments became less and less common. These days very few people can see Buddhas directly, and it has become extremely difficult to attain tranquil abiding, clairvoyance and other spiritual realizations. This is a clear indication that we are living in spiritually degenerate times. Not only is it more difficult to gain spiritual realizations but we also experience many difficulties and dangers that did not exist before. The political situation in the world is now very unstable, and with the proliferation of increasingly destructive weapons human life is more precarious than ever. Despite the advances of modern medicine, new diseases are appearing and old ones are returning. Every year more and more people die as a direct or indirect result of environmental pollution, and even the conditions that we generally regard as helpful, such as cars, electricity or medicine, are potential causes of untimely death.

People in the past generally had a more spiritual outlook, but nowadays the worldview of most people is increasingly gross and materialistic. It is very difficult to find people who hold pure and correct views; nearly everyone harbors views that are incompatible with spiritual development. Some people have a natural inclination toward wrong views, while others pick them up from their family or close friends or in the course of their education. Very few people manage to escape the influence of wrong views completely.

Our delusions are now very strong and difficult to control. We have so little inner peace that it is rare to enjoy a peaceful mind even for just a few hours. If we check our mind we will see that we are living in a state of almost constant discomfort and anxiety. As soon as we stop worrying about one thing, something else starts to bother us. Our delusions give us no rest. We have uncomfortable minds and experience very little real happiness. Our lives nowadays are extremely busy and complicated, filled with an ever-increasing variety of distractions. Even when we have the time to relax we tend to switch on the television or radio and are subjected to a multitude of ever-changing images and sounds. We are so used to being stimulated from the outside that we find it difficult to be quiet and enjoy the stillness of our own mind. Our attention span is decreasing all the time, and it is becoming more and more difficult to concentrate on internal development, such as cultivating pure views and pure intentions.

Our world is becoming increasingly dangerous and polluted, while internally our minds are becoming rougher and more uncontrolled. Although such conditions make conventional spiritual practice very difficult, if we practice the instructions contained within *Eight Verses* we can transform all these adversities into the path to enlightenment and live happily in the midst of this impure world. Rather than being an obstacle to our spiritual progress, the impurities of this present age can become fuel for our spiritual practice. Without practicing these teachings I think it is now very difficult to find true peace and happiness.

Atisha's Teacher, Dharmarakshita, compared samsara to a forest of poisonous plants, because we are constantly surrounded by attractive and unattractive objects that stimulate the mental poisons of attachment and anger. He compared those who are unable to transform their adversities into the spiritual path to crows, which cannot eat poisonous plants. Practitioners of training the mind, however, are like peacocks, which are said to thrive on plants that are poisonous to other birds, because they can transform both attractive and unattractive objects into the spiritual path. They are able to enjoy attractive objects without developing attachment, and they can happily accept unattractive objects, such as sickness and other adverse conditions, without becoming angry or discouraged. Whatever circumstances arise, practitioners of training the mind can enjoy and make good use of them. Since in these degenerate times we are constantly surrounded by objects of attachment and aversion, we definitely need to learn how to transform them into the spiritual path by training our mind.

Through practicing Langri Tangpa's Lojong, or mind training, teachings we have a wonderful opportunity to find true inner peace by destroying our self-grasping and self-cherishing, the main causes of all our suffering. This is very difficult to achieve through any other method. For this reason, at the beginning of *Training the Mind in Seven Points*, a commentary to *Eight Verses*, Geshe Chekhawa compares the instructions of training the mind to a diamond, to the sun and to a medicinal tree. They are like a diamond because just as a small fragment of a diamond is valuable, so putting even a small part of the instructions of training the mind into practice has great power to change our mind from unhappiness to happiness. They are like the sun because just as the first few rays of the rising sun lighten the early morning darkness, so even superficial experience of a part of these teachings reduces the inner darkness of our ignorance; and just as full sunlight completely dispels all darkness, so deep experience of the entire practice of training the mind overcomes our ignorance completely. They are like a medicinal tree because just as every part of a medicinal tree has curative properties, so every part of these teachings has the power to cure the internal disease of our delusions.

I could continue for many more pages to explain the good qualities of these teachings, but the only way that you will be able to appreciate them fully is by putting them into practice and experiencing their benefits for yourself. As Geshe Chekhawa says, "The meaning of this text should be known," by which he means that it is only by understanding the meaning of these instructions and putting them into practice that we will come to appreciate all their excellent qualities. For example, a salesperson might try to persuade us of the excellence of a particular brand of tea, but the only way we can know for sure whether the tea is as good as he or she says is by tasting it ourself.

We know from our own experience that we can never derive pure peace and happiness from material things. No matter how perfectly we arrange our external situation, for as long as we remain in samsara problems will continue to trouble us. Indeed, it often seems that the more emphasis we place on material development, the more problems we encounter. Pure happiness can only be attained through developing our mind. Through improving our qualities of love, compassion and wisdom, we can gradually eliminate all our suffering and problems, and eventually attain the everlasting joy of full enlightenment. I guarantee that if you put the instructions of training the mind into practice in your daily life you will find the inner peace and joy that everyone is looking for. Understanding this, you should develop a strong determination to practice these instructions.

Vasubandhu

The Preliminary Practices

Inner realizations do not arise magically from the earth, nor do they fall from the sky. Gaining deep experience of the practices explained in *Eight Verses* depends upon certain inner conditions, which we can create by engaging in the preliminary practices. Just as a farmer needs to prepare the ground before he plants his crop, so we need to prepare our mind before we can hope to harvest a crop of spiritual realizations. There are many people who are very interested in meditation but who, not understanding the importance of the preliminary practices, neglect them and consequently are disappointed when their efforts in meditation do not yield results. They are like a farmer who fails to weed, fertilize or water his field, yet still expects his crop to flourish. The more conscientiously we practice the preliminaries, the more easily we will gain realizations from our practice of training the mind.

The preliminary practices perform three functions: they purify our mind of negativity; they accumulate merit, good fortune or good luck; and they help us receive the blessings of the Buddhas and Bodhisattvas. Purifying our mind is like removing rocks and weeds from a field before sowing the seeds. At the moment our mind is polluted by the imprints of negative thoughts and the potentials left by all the non-virtuous actions that we have performed in the past. Until we remove this negativity from our mind through the practice of purification, it will obstruct the growth of virtuous qualities and our meditation will not produce results.

Secondly, we need to endow our mind with the strength to support the growth of Dharma realizations by accumulating merit. Merit is the positive energy of virtuous actions. Just as well-fertilized soil will produce an abundant harvest, so if our mind is enriched with merit we will harvest a bountiful crop of spiritual realizations.

Thirdly, we need to receive the blessings of the holy beings. Unless our mind is watered by a rain of blessings, or inspiring energy, from the Buddhas and Bodhisattvas, it will remain like a dry field in which the seeds of spiritual realizations sown through meditation are unable to grow. The way to receive blessings is to develop strong faith and devotion in the holy beings and request them to bless our mind. Just as rain can bring a desert to life, so if our mind receives the blessings of the holy beings our virtuous potentials will be activated and spiritual realizations will grow in our mind.

If we prepare our mind well by purifying negativity, accumulating merit and receiving blessings, our meditations will be very successful. A simple way of doing this is to begin each meditation session on training the mind by reciting the prayers entitled *Essence of Good Fortune*, found in Appendix III, while contemplating their meaning and engaging in the appropriate visualizations. For those with less time, a more condensed practice called *Prayers for Meditation* can also be found in Appendix III. Both sets of prayers contain the six preparatory practices for successful meditation. These are:

1. Cleaning the meditation room and setting up a shrine
2. Arranging beautiful offerings
3. Sitting in the correct meditation posture, going for refuge and generating bodhichitta
4. Visualizing the Field for Accumulating Merit
5. Offering the seven limbs and the mandala
6. Requesting the holy beings to bestow their blessings

The instructions on the six preparatory practices are based on the *Perfection of Wisdom Sutras*. Atisha received these instructions from his Guru, Lama Serlingpa, and subsequently this tradition flourished throughout the Kadampa world.

Both *Essence of Good Fortune* and *Prayers for Meditation* include the practice of Guru yoga, which is the gateway to receiving the blessings of all the Buddhas and Bodhisattvas. In this particular practice we visualize Buddha Shakyamuni in the space in front of us, surrounded by all the Buddhas and Bodhisattvas. Focusing on Buddha Shakyamuni, who is seen as one with our Guru, or Spiritual Guide, we develop faith and request his blessings. When reciting these prayers as a preparation for meditation on *Eight Verses* it is auspicious to make a minor alteration to the visualization. At the heart of Guru Buddha Shakyamuni we visualize Buddha Amitabha, who has a red-colored body and sits with his two hands in the gesture of meditative equipoise. Alternatively we can visualize Buddha Amitabha instead of Buddha Shakyamuni. The reason for making this slight alteration is to strengthen our connection with Bodhisattva Langri Tangpa, who, as already explained, is an emanation of Buddha Amitabha. Visualizing in this way helps us to develop greater faith in the author of these verses and in his instructions, and this will help us to receive his inspiring blessings more quickly.

Buddha Amitabha is known as the "Vajra Speech Buddha," which indicates that he is the manifestation of the speech of all Buddhas. In the future all living beings will meet this Buddha in the aspect of an ordinary being who will guide them along the path to enlightenment. Buddha Amitabha, Buddha Amitayus and Buddha Vajradharma are the same in nature, differing only in aspect. On the crown of Avalokiteshvara, the Buddha of Compassion, Buddha Amitabha, his Spiritual Guide, is always present. In the same way, on the crowns of all faithful disciples, Buddha Amitabha, their Spiritual Guide, will always be present.

Apart from this change in the visualization, the remaining preparatory practices are exactly the same. A brief explanation of the six preparatory practices will now be given.

CLEANING THE MEDITATION ROOM AND SETTING UP A SHRINE

Cleaning practice

We know from our own experience that dirty and untidy surroundings tend to bring our mind down and drain our energy, while a clean and tidy environment uplifts our mind, making it clear and vibrant. When people invite special guests into their home it is natural that they show their respect by making an effort to clean the house beforehand. In our meditation session we invite all the Buddhas and Bodhisattvas to appear before us, accept our offerings and prayers and help us in our meditation, so it is only natural that before we begin our session we should spend some time cleaning our meditation room.

Having physically cleaned our room, we should imagine that our environment transforms into the Pure Land of Buddha. We feel that all the enlightened beings are delighted to come into our meditation, and that our mind becomes lucid and concentrated. It is very helpful to recall the story of Lam Chung, whose sole practice was sweeping the floor of the temple. Imagining that he was sweeping away his delusions, Lam Chung spent all his time cleaning the temple, and by doing so he purified his karmic obstructions, received Buddha's profound blessings and spontaneously developed high realizations. This story is explained in detail in the book *Joyful Path of Good Fortune*.

Setting up a shrine

If our circumstances permit, it is very beneficial to set up a shrine with representations of Buddha's body, speech and mind. A shrine provides a focus for our faith, serving as a continual reminder of the Buddhas, through whose kindness living beings have the opportunity to attain permanent inner peace and the supreme happiness of enlightenment.

In the center of our shrine, to represent Buddha's body, we place a picture or statue of Buddha Shakyamuni, and of any other holy beings who have a special connection with our daily practice. On the left side of the shrine, to represent Buddha's speech, we can place a Dharma book; and on the right side of the shrine, to represent Buddha's mind, we can place a stupa.

When we go for refuge to the Three Jewels, we make commitments to regard all images of Buddha as actual Buddhas and all Dharma books as actual Dharma Jewels. It is therefore very important to treat Buddha images and Dharma books with respect. We should arrange them beautifully in a place that is clean and elevated, and not put them down casually like a cup of tea. Dharma books are a principal means for dispelling our ignorance, the source of all our problems, but if we treat such books with disrespect it only causes our ignorance to increase. We should therefore not leave Dharma books on the floor, step over them or mix them with ordinary books or magazines.

One of the best methods to increase our faith in the Buddhas and to receive their blessings is to gaze at an image of a Buddha again and again, regarding it as an actual Buddha who is supremely kind to all living beings. When we see a Buddha statue, for example, instead of thinking of it as an object made of metal or stone, or focusing on its artistic faults or merits, we should feel that we are in the presence of a real living Buddha and develop deep faith. By viewing images of Buddhas in this way, it is as if we are opening a window in our mind through which the blessings of the holy beings can enter. This special way of viewing Buddha images is based on wisdom, not ignorance, and serves to increase our faith and receive blessings.

The representations of Buddha's body, speech and mind are so blessed that, even if we have no faith, just seeing them blesses our mind. There was once a man called Shri Datta, who had committed many extremely negative actions such as trying to poison Buddha. Many years later, when he was an old man, Shri Datta became interested in Dharma and requested Buddha to grant him ordination. It is said that to receive ordination we need at least some small virtuous potentiality that is a cause of liberation; but when clairvoyant disciples of Buddha examined Shri Datta they were unable to find a single such potentiality, and so they declared him unfit for ordination. However, these disciples could not see the subtle karmic potentialities that are seen only by enlightened beings. When Buddha looked into Shri Datta's dark mind he saw a tiny potentiality for virtue, and he told his disciples, "Many eons ago Shri Datta was a fly who landed on some horse dung near the stupa of a Buddha. It was raining heavily and the water carried the dung, together with the fly, around the stupa. Although the fly had no intention of circumambulating the stupa, it nevertheless received Buddha's blessings just by seeing the stupa, and this left on its mind a virtuous potentiality to attain liberation." Buddha then granted the ordination. As a result, Shri Datta's positive potentiality increased and he attained liberation in that lifetime.

In the Lamrim teachings it says that just seeing an image of a Buddha places a potentiality on the mind that is a definite cause of enlightenment, and which nothing can destroy. This potentiality is likened to a tiny wisdom nectar pill that is swallowed and passes through our body intact, uncorrupted by all bodily impurities. Because Buddha is a completely pure object wholly beyond samsara, the imprint of seeing a Buddha image has a special quality that does not belong to samsara, and even if it is placed in a mind filled with delusions it can never be corrupted or destroyed. This imprint or potentiality is also compared to a spark with the power to ignite a fire that in time consumes a haystack the size of the world. We have seen how, due to the imprint of seeing a stupa, Shri Datta was able to generate the wish to enter the path to liberation, and by practicing Dharma, burn away all the delusions in his mind.

From these examples we can understand how seeing images of Buddha has the same function as seeing actual living Buddhas. In a similar way, making offerings and prostrations in front of Buddha images has the same function as making offerings and prostrations in front of living Buddhas, and accumulates the same amount of merit. This is why it is considered so important to have a large and beautiful statue of Buddha in Buddhist temples, because then anyone who visits the temple and sees the statue is creating the cause to attain liberation and enlightenment.

ARRANGING BEAUTIFUL OFFERINGS

In front of the images of Buddha on the shrine we can arrange beautiful offerings such as flowers, incense, light and food, as well as bowls of water, regarding the water as pure nectar. We can also imagine that all the objects of enjoyment of humans and gods, such as gardens, palaces, mountains and lakes, are transformed into pure and precious offerings to the Buddhas.

The purpose of making offerings is not because the Buddhas need anything from us, but for the effect it has on our own mind. There are many people who place beautiful flowers on the graves of their loved ones, and even though the dead person is not there and cannot benefit from their offerings we cannot say that these actions are meaningless. How much more meaningful it is then, to arrange beautiful offerings with a mind of faith in front of Buddha images, because the Buddhas are actually present and can take delight in our offerings.

Having attained omniscient wisdom, a Buddha knows when we are making offerings to him or her. Moreover, a Buddha's body and mind are the same nature, and wherever his mind exists so does his body. Our mind and body are different natures, and while our mind is not obstructed by physical obstacles, our body is. Our mind can easily roam the universe, but our body has to remain on the ground. A Buddha's body, on the other hand, is no more obstructed by matter than his or her mind, and can travel just as freely. Because a Buddha's mind is mixed with the ultimate nature of all phenomena and is free from the obstructions to omniscience, it pervades all phenomena; and because his body and mind are the same nature, his body is also all-pervasive. From this we can understand that Buddhas are present everywhere and that there is no place where Buddha does not exist. Buddhas are like the sun and our ignorance is like the clouds that obscure the sun. When clouds disperse we see that in reality the sun has been shining all along, and in a similar way, when we remove the clouds of ignorance from our mind we will see that the Buddhas have always been present all around us.

SITTING IN THE CORRECT MEDITATION POSTURE, GOING FOR REFUGE AND GENERATING BODHICHITTA

Sitting in the correct meditation posture

Although meditation is an action of mind, rather than of body or speech, as our mind and body are closely related it is important to sit in a correct posture when we engage in meditation because this will help us to maintain a clear and concentrated mind. If we are sitting on a cushion we should try to sit cross-legged, ideally in the vajra posture with each foot resting on the opposite thigh, but if this is too difficult we should sit in a posture as close to this as possible while remaining comfortable. If we are sitting on a chair we should have our feet resting on the floor. Our back should be straight, and the right hand should be placed on the left hand with the palms facing upward and the tips of the thumbs slightly raised and just touching at the level of the navel. The mouth should be gently closed, with the tongue touching the back of the upper teeth. The head should be inclined slightly forward, the eyes slightly open and the shoulders level. We should try to adopt this posture during formal meditation sessions, but in general we can meditate in any position and at any time—while we are resting, eating, cleaning and so forth.

Once we are in the correct meditation posture we should try to calm our mind, because with a busy and distracted mind neither our preparatory practices nor our actual meditations on training the mind will be successful. To dispel our distractions we can engage in the following simple breathing meditation. As we exhale we imagine that we are breathing out all our distracting thoughts in the form of dark smoke, which disappears into space; and as we inhale we imagine that we are breathing in the blessings of all the Buddhas in the aspect of white light, which enters our body and dissolves into our heart. We focus single-pointedly on this process of exhalation and inhalation, breathing out our distractions and breathing in Buddha's blessings, until our mind has become clear and peaceful. At this stage our mind is like a clean white cloth that we can now color with a virtuous motivation such as compassion or bodhichitta.

Going for refuge

Having calmed our mind, we now go for refuge to the Three Jewels. The Three Jewels are the Buddha Jewel—all fully enlightened beings; the Dharma Jewel—the spiritual realizations developed through practicing Buddha's teachings; and the Sangha Jewel—the Superior practitioners who have realized ultimate truth directly. Understanding that it is only these Three Jewels that have the actual power to protect living beings from fear, danger and suffering, we imagine and believe that in the space before us is the living Buddha Shakyamuni surrounded by all other Buddhas and Bodhisattvas, like the full moon surrounded by stars. Then with strong fear of samsaric rebirth and with deep faith in the power of the Three Jewels to protect us, we recite the refuge prayer and make a strong determination to rely upon Buddha, Dharma and Sangha until we attain enlightenment.

Generating bodhichitta

We then generate the motivation of bodhichitta. The value of our meditation, and indeed of any virtuous action, depends primarily upon the motivation with which we engage in it. If we meditate with the motivation just to relax and improve our physical health, our meditation may accomplish these goals but it can hardly be considered a spiritual practice. The highest motivation of all is bodhichitta, the wish to attain full enlightenment to help all living beings. If we meditate with this motivation the merit of our meditation will be limitless. To generate bodhichitta we think:

Each and every living being trapped in the prison of sam-
sara is experiencing danger, fear and suffering, life after
life, endlessly. If I myself attain enlightenment my emana-
tions will pervade all worlds and protect every living being.
I must become a Buddha for the benefit of all living beings.

With this motivation we recite the bodhichitta prayer three
times.

Going for refuge to the Three Jewels is the gateway
through which we enter Buddhism in general, and generating
bodhichitta motivation is the gateway through which we enter
Mahayana Buddhism. Since the strength of our bodhichitta
depends upon the strength of our love and compassion, we
then recite the following prayer from the depths of our heart:

May everyone be happy,
May everyone be free from misery,
May no one ever be separated from their happiness,
May everyone have equanimity, free from hatred and
    attachment.

With bodhichitta motivation we then engage in the
practices of accumulating merit, purifying negative karma,
receiving the blessings of the Buddhas and contemplating and
meditating on *Eight Verses of Training the Mind.*

VISUALIZING THE FIELD FOR ACCUMULATING MERIT

We imagine that in the space in front of us is the living Buddha
Shakyamuni, who is one nature with our Spiritual Guide, surrounded by the lineage Gurus, Buddhas, Bodhisattvas and
other holy beings. At the heart of Buddha Shakyamuni is

Buddha Amitabha, who is the same nature as Bodhisattva Langri Tangpa, the author of *Eight Verses of Training the Mind*. We focus on the assembly of these enlightened beings, and when we perceive a rough mental image we meditate on this for a short while. This assembly is called the "Field for Accumulating Merit" because just as external crops grow from seeds sown in an external field, so the internal crops of merit or good fortune grow from the seeds of faith and devotion sown in the field of all enlightened beings.

Although these holy beings are in reality present in front of us, because of our ignorance and negative karma we cannot see them. Even so, we can communicate with them by means of visualization. If we find it difficult to visualize the Buddhas, or if we do not develop any special feelings when we do so, this is because in the depths of our heart we do not believe that they are actually there. However, as already explained, Buddhas are everywhere. Visualizing Buddhas is not like a children's game of make-believe, but a way of opening our mind to what is already there. Buddha Shakyamuni said, "Whenever anyone with faith visualizes me, I am there." On an overcast day, although we cannot see the sun directly we have no problem imagining it shining behind the clouds because we know that it is there. In the same way, even if our visualization of the Buddhas is very unclear we should have no doubt that they are really present before us. If we engage in visualization with full confidence that the living Buddhas are in front of us, our mind will definitely make a connection with them, and gradually the clarity of our visualization will improve.

At the beginning we do not need to visualize the Buddhas in detail; instead we should simply believe that they are present in front of us and develop strong faith. Through the power of our faith and familiarity, visualizing the Buddhas will eventually become effortless. We do not find it hard to visualize our mother, because we know her so well. In a similar way, when through studying and developing faith in Dharma teachings we come to understand the nature, functions and good qualities of Buddhas, it will be easier for us to visualize them. It is also important to understand how we too can become a Buddha, for when we are confident that enlightenment is a possibility for us we will naturally feel much closer to those who have already attained enlightenment.

OFFERING THE SEVEN LIMBS AND THE MANDALA

To accumulate merit and purify negativity we now offer the practice of the seven limbs and the mandala. The seven limbs are: prostration, offering, confession, rejoicing, beseeching the holy beings to remain, requesting the turning of the Wheel of Dharma and dedication.

Prostration

Focusing on the assembly of Buddhas in the space before us, with a mind of deep faith and respect we press the palms of our hands together at our heart and recite the appropriate line from the prayer of seven limbs.

Offering

To empower our mind with the positive energy needed to attain full enlightenment for the sake of all living beings, we make extensive offerings to the assembly of holy beings. We make not only the offerings we have arranged on our shrine, but also use our imagination to offer all objects of enjoyment existing throughout the universe, such as beautiful gardens, lakes, trees and mountains, as well as the sun, the moon and the stars.

Confession

In the presence of the great Compassionate Ones, the assembly of Buddhas, we confess with a mind of great regret all the non-virtues and negative actions that we have accumulated in this life and in countless previous lives, and we promise that from now on we will not commit them again. In this way we purify our mind of our burden of negative karma and remove the principal obstacles to spiritual development.

Rejoicing

To rejoice means to appreciate and take delight in the good fortune, virtue and happiness of others. If we rejoice in others' good qualities, this will create the cause for us to develop similar qualities ourself. Overcoming all feelings of jealousy and competitiveness, we should rejoice in the virtues of all beings—those still in samsara and those who have completed the spiritual path to enlightenment. All those who are now Buddhas once wandered the painful paths of samsara, just as we still do now. However, through their great effort they entered the Bodhisattva's path, and progressing through all its stages, attained complete enlightenment. From the depths of our heart we rejoice in their virtuous attainments and pray to become just like them.

Beseeching the holy beings to remain

Without Spiritual Guides, who are manifestations of Buddha's compassion, to lead sentient beings on the path to liberation, this world would be plunged into spiritual darkness. From the depths of our heart we request Buddha's emanations to remain with us until samsara ceases.

Requesting the turning of the Wheel of Dharma

As a result of the gods Brahma and Indra requesting Buddha to turn the Wheel of Dharma, Buddha taught many methods for curing the disease of the delusions, which have led countless beings to liberation from suffering. To ensure that these teachings remain in this world we request the holy beings to teach the precious Dharma.

Dedication

At the end of any virtuous action we should dedicate the merit that we have created toward the complete and perfect happiness of all living beings. If we do not dedicate our merit in this way, it can easily be destroyed by anger or other strong delusions, or dissipated through the fulfillment of our self-centered wishes. By dedicating our merit toward our own and others' enlightenment, however, we safeguard it and thereby ensure that it will never be exhausted. In particular we dedicate all our virtuous actions, both past and present, toward gaining the realizations of *Eight Verses of Training the Mind*, and thereby to attaining the supreme happiness of full enlightenment.

These seven practices are called "limbs" because they support our meditation just as limbs support our body. Without bodily limbs we cannot accomplish much in the way of physical actions, and in a similar way, without the limbs of accumulating merit and purifying negativity we cannot accomplish much in the way of meditation. The practices of prostration, offering, beseeching and requesting accumulate merit; the practices of rejoicing and dedication multiply merit; and the practice of confession purifies negative karma. A detailed explanation of the seven limbs can be found in the book *Joyful Path of Good Fortune*.

Offering the mandala

The word "mandala" in this context means "universe." When we offer a mandala to the holy beings we are offering everything—the whole universe and everyone in it. Since the merit we create when we make an offering accords with the nature of that offering, instead of offering an ordinary, impure universe we mentally transform the whole universe into a Pure Land filled with precious objects and inhabited by pure beings. Imagining that we are holding this pure universe in our hands, we offer it to all the enlightened beings. In this way we are offering everything that we have or could wish for. Making mandala offerings is very powerful, and if we wish for good fortune and spiritual attainments we should offer a mandala every day. A detailed explanation on making mandala offerings can be found in the book *The New Guide to Dakini Land.*

REQUESTING THE HOLY BEINGS
TO BESTOW THEIR BLESSINGS

Requesting blessings

The word for blessing in Tibetan is "jin gyi lob," which literally means "to transform." When we request blessings we are asking for our mind to be transformed from a non-virtuous state to a virtuous state, and from an unhappy state to a happy state. Most importantly, we need to transform our mind into the mind of an enlightened being, and it is for this purpose that we request the holy beings to bestow their blessings upon our mind so that we may attain the realizations of the stages of the path to enlightenment. To do this we recite the *Prayer of the Stages of the Path* while concentrating on its meaning.

Receiving blessings

We then imagine that due to our heartfelt requests the holy beings bestow their blessings, which descend from their hearts in the form of lights and nectars. These enter our body and mind, pacifying our negativity and obstacles and increasing our merit, lifespan, inner peace and Dharma realizations. We meditate on this experience for a short while.

Having received the blessings of all the holy beings we now imagine that all the holy beings surrounding Guru Buddha Shakyamuni dissolve into light and gather into him. He dissolves into Buddha Amitabha at his heart, who comes to the crown of our head. We mentally prostrate and make a short mandala offering to our Spiritual Guide in the aspect of Buddha Amitabha at our crown, and pray to him by reciting *Eight Verses of Training the Mind*:

With the intention to attain
The ultimate, supreme goal
That surpasses even the wish-granting jewel,
May I constantly cherish all living beings.

Whenever I associate with others,
May I view myself as the lowest of all;
And with a pure intention,
May I cherish others as supreme.

Examining my mental continuum throughout all my
    actions,
As soon as a delusion of self-cherishing develops
Whereby I or others would act inappropriately,
May I firmly face it and avert it.

Whenever I see unfortunate beings
Oppressed by evil and violent suffering,
May I cherish them as if I had found
A rare and precious treasure.

Even if someone I have helped
And of whom I had great hopes
Nevertheless harms me intentionally,
May I see him or her as my holy Spiritual Guide.

When others out of jealousy or anger
Harm me or insult me,
May I take defeat upon myself
And offer them the victory.

In short, may I directly and indirectly
Offer help and happiness to all my mothers,
And secretly take upon myself
All their harm and suffering.

Furthermore, through all the above practices,
Together with a mind undefiled by stains of conceptions
  of the eight extremes
And that sees all phenomena as illusory,
May I and all living beings be released from the bondage of
  mistaken appearance and conception.

We recite *Eight Verses* with deep faith in Guru Amitabha, repeating three times the particular verse on which we are going to meditate. We then imagine that through the power of our prayer, streams of light and nectar descend from Guru Amitabha's body, purifying our body and mind of all negativities, delusions and obstructions and ripening our potential to gain the realization of the meditation. We then engage in the meditation and finish with the appropriate dedication prayers.

Learning to Cherish Others

With the intention to attain
The ultimate, supreme goal
That surpasses even the wish-granting jewel,
May I constantly cherish all living beings.

What is the "ultimate, supreme goal" of human life? We should ask ourself what we consider to be most important—what do we wish for, strive for or daydream about? For some people it is material possessions, such as a large house with all the latest luxuries, a fast car or a well-paid job. For others it is reputation, good looks, power, excitement or adventure. Many try to find the meaning of their life in relationships with their family and circle of friends. All these things can make us superficially happy for a short while, but they can also cause us much worry and suffering. They can never give us the pure and everlasting happiness that all of us, in our heart of hearts, long for. Since we cannot take them with us when we die, if we have made them the principal meaning of our life they will eventually let us down. As an end in themselves worldly attainments are hollow; they are not the real meaning of human life.

Of all worldly possessions the most precious is said to be the legendary wish-granting jewel. It is impossible to

Manjushri

find such a jewel in these degenerate times, but in the past, when human beings had abundant merit, there used to be magical jewels that had the power to grant wishes. These jewels, however, could only fulfill wishes for contaminated happiness—they could never bestow the pure happiness that comes from a pure mind. Furthermore, a wish-granting jewel only had the power to grant wishes in one life—it could not protect its owner in his or her future lives. Thus, ultimately even a wish-granting jewel is deceptive.

The only thing that will never deceive us is the attainment of full enlightenment. It is only by attaining enlightenment that we can fulfill our deepest wish for pure and lasting happiness, for nothing in this impure world has the power to fulfill this wish. Only when we become a fully enlightened Buddha will we experience the profound and lasting peace that comes from a permanent cessation of all delusions and their imprints. We will be free from all faults and mental obscurations, and will possess the qualities needed to help all living beings directly. We will then be an object of refuge for all living beings. Through this understanding we can clearly see that the attainment of enlightenment is the ultimate, supreme goal and real meaning of our precious human life. Since our main wish is to be happy all the time and to be completely free from all faults and suffering, we must develop the strong intention to attain enlightenment. We should think, "I need to attain enlightenment because in samsara, the cycle of impure life, there is no real happiness anywhere." Enlightenment is the inner light of wisdom that is completely free from mistaken appearance and whose function is to bestow mental peace upon each and every living being every day. It is the source of all living beings' happiness.

The main cause of enlightenment is bodhichitta, and the root of bodhichitta is compassion. Since the development of compassion depends upon cherishing others, the first step to the sublime happiness of enlightenment is learning to cherish others. A mother cherishes her children, and we may cherish our friends to a certain degree, but this cherishing is not impartial and is usually mixed with attachment. We need to develop a pure mind that cherishes all living beings without bias or partiality.

Each and every living being has within them the seed or potential to become a Buddha—this is our Buddha nature. In Buddha's teachings we have found the best method to realize this potential. What we need to do now is to put these teachings into practice. This is something that only human beings can do. Animals can gather resources, defeat their enemies and protect their families, but they can neither understand nor engage in the spiritual path. It would be a great shame if we were to use our human life only to achieve what animals can also achieve, and thereby waste this unique opportunity to become a source of benefit for all living beings.

We are faced with a choice: either we can continue to squander our life in pursuing worldly enjoyments that give no real satisfaction and disappear when we die, or we can dedicate our life to realizing our full spiritual potential. If we make the effort to practice Buddha's teachings we will definitely attain enlightenment, but if we make no effort enlightenment will never happen naturally, no matter how long we wait. To follow the Buddhist path to enlightenment there is no need to change our external lifestyle. We do not need to abandon our family, friends or enjoyments, and retire to a mountain cave. All we need to do is change the object of our cherishing.

Until now we have cherished ourself above all others, and for as long as we continue to do this our suffering will never end. However, if we learn to cherish all beings more than ourself we will soon enjoy the bliss of Buddhahood. The path to enlightenment is really very simple—all we need to do is stop cherishing ourself and learn to cherish others. All other spiritual realizations will naturally follow from this.

Our instinctive view is that we are more important than everyone else, whereas the view of all enlightened beings is that it is others who are more important. Which of these views is more beneficial? In life after life, since beginningless time, we have been slaves to our self-cherishing mind. We have trusted it implicitly and obeyed its every command, believing that the way to solve our problems and find happiness is to put ourself before everyone else. We have worked so hard and for so long for our own sake, but what do we have to show for it? Have we solved all our problems and found the lasting happiness we desire? No. It is clear that pursuing our own selfish interests has deceived us. After having indulged our self-cherishing for so many lives, now is the time to realize that it simply does not work. Now is the time to switch the object of our cherishing from ourself to all living beings.

Bodhisattva Langri Tangpa and countless other enlightened beings discovered that by abandoning self-cherishing and cherishing only others they came to experience true peace and happiness. If we practice the methods they taught, there is no reason why we should not be able to do the same. We cannot expect to change our mind overnight, but through practicing the instructions contained within *Eight Verses* patiently and consistently, while at the same time accumulating merit, purifying negativity and receiving blessings, we can gradually replace our ordinary self-cherishing attitude with the sublime attitude of cherishing all living beings.

To achieve this we do not need to change our lifestyle, but we do need to change our views and intentions. Our ordinary view is that we are the center of the universe and that other people and things derive their significance principally from the way in which they affect us. Our car, for example, is important simply because it is *ours*, and our friends are important because they make *us* happy. Strangers, on the other hand, do not seem so important because they do not directly affect our happiness, and if a stranger's car is damaged or stolen we are not that concerned. As we will see in later chapters, this self-centered view of the world is based on ignorance and does not correspond to reality. This view is the source of all our ordinary, selfish intentions. It is precisely because we think, "I am important, I need this, I deserve that," that we engage in negative actions, which result in an endless stream of problems for ourself and others.

By practicing the instructions contained within *Eight Verses* we can develop a realistic view of the world, based on an understanding of the equality and interdependence of all living beings. Once we view each and every living being as important we will naturally develop good intentions toward them. Whereas the mind that cherishes only ourself is the basis for all impure, samsaric experience, the mind that cherishes others is the basis for all the good qualities of enlightenment.

Cherishing others is not so difficult—all we need to do is to understand why we should cherish others and then make a firm decision to do so. Through meditating on this decision we will develop a deep and powerful feeling of cherishing for all beings. We then carry this special feeling into our daily life.

There are two main reasons why we need to cherish all living beings. The first is that they have shown us immense kindness, and the second is that cherishing them has enormous benefits. These will now be explained.

THE KINDNESS OF OTHERS

All living beings deserve to be cherished because of the tremendous kindness they have shown us. All our temporary and ultimate happiness arises through their kindness. Even our body is the result of the kindness of others. We did not bring it with us from our previous life—it developed from the union of our father's sperm and mother's ovum. Once we had been conceived our mother kindly allowed us to stay in her womb, nourishing our body with her blood and warmth, putting up with great discomfort and finally going through the painful ordeal of childbirth for our sake. We came into this world naked and empty-handed and were immediately given a home, food, clothes and everything else we needed. While we were a helpless baby our mother protected us from danger, fed us, cleaned us and loved us. Without her kindness we would not be alive today.

Through receiving a constant supply of food, drink and care, our body gradually grew from that of a tiny helpless baby to the body we have now. All this nourishment was directly or indirectly provided by countless living beings. Every cell of our body is therefore the result of others' kindness. Even those who have never known their mother have received nourishment and loving care from other people. The mere fact that we are alive today is a testimony to the great kindness of others.

It is because we have this present body with human faculties that we are able to enjoy all the pleasures and opportunities of human life. Even simple pleasures such as going for a walk or watching a beautiful sunset can be seen to be a result of the kindness of innumerable living beings. Our skills and abilities all come from the kindness of others; we had to be taught how to eat, how to walk, how to talk and how to read and write. Even the language we speak is not our own invention but the product of many generations. Without it we could not communicate with others or share their ideas. We could not read this book, learn Dharma or even think clearly. All the facilities we take for granted, such as houses, cars, roads, shops, schools, hospitals and movie theaters, are produced solely through others' kindness. When we travel by bus or car we take the roads for granted, but many people worked very hard to build them and make them safe for us to use.

The fact that some of the people who help us may have no intention of doing so is irrelevant. We receive benefit from their actions, so from our point of view this is a kindness. Rather than focusing on their motivation, which in any case we do not know, we should focus on the practical benefit we receive. Everyone who contributes in any way toward our happiness and well-being is deserving of our gratitude and respect. If we had to give back everything that others have given us, we would have nothing left at all.

We might argue that we are not given things freely but have to work for them. When we go shopping we have to pay, and when we eat in a restaurant we have to pay. We may have the use of a car, but we had to buy the car, and now we have to pay for gas, tax and insurance. No one gives us anything for free. But from where do we get this money? It is true that generally we have to work for our money, but it is others who employ us or buy our goods and so indirectly it is they who provide us with money. In addition, the reason we are able to do a particular job is that we have received the necessary training or education from other people. Wherever we look, we find only the kindness of others. We are all interconnected in a web of kindness from which it is impossible to separate ourself. Everything we have and everything we enjoy, including our very life, is due to the kindness of others. In fact, all the happiness there is in the world arises as a result of others' kindness.

Our spiritual development and the pure happiness of full enlightenment also depend upon the kindness of living beings. Buddhist centers, Dharma books and meditation courses do not arise out of thin air but are the result of the hard work and dedication of many people. Our opportunity to read, contemplate and meditate on Buddha's teachings depends entirely upon the kindness of others. In addition, as explained later, without living beings to give to, to test our patience or to develop compassion for, we could never develop the virtuous qualities needed to attain enlightenment.

In short, we need others for our physical, emotional and spiritual well-being. Without others we are nothing. Our sense that we are an island, an independent, self-sufficient individual, bears no relation to reality. It is closer to the truth to picture ourself as a cell in the vast body of life, distinct yet intimately bound up with all living beings. We cannot exist without others, and they in turn are affected by everything we do. The idea that it is possible to secure our own welfare while neglecting that of others, or even at the expense of others, is completely unrealistic.

Contemplating the innumerable ways in which others help us, we should make a firm decision: "I must cherish all living beings because they are so kind to me." Based on this determination we develop a feeling of cherishing—a sense that all living beings are important and that their happiness matters. We try to mix our mind single-pointedly with this feeling and maintain it for as long as we can without forgetting it. When we arise from meditation we try to maintain this mind of love, so that whenever we meet or remember someone we naturally think: "This person is important, this person's happiness matters." In this way we can make cherishing living beings our main practice.

THE BENEFITS OF CHERISHING OTHERS

Another reason for cherishing others is that it is the best method to solve our own and others' problems. Problems, worry, pain and unhappiness are types of mind; they are feelings and do not exist outside the mind. If we cherish everyone we meet or think about, there will be no basis for developing jealousy, anger or other harmful thoughts, and our mind will be at peace all the time. Jealousy, for example, is a state of mind that cannot bear another's good fortune, but if we cherish someone how can his or her good fortune disturb our mind? How can we wish to harm others if we regard everyone's happiness to be of paramount importance? By genuinely cherishing all living beings we will always act with loving kindness, in a friendly and considerate way, and they will return our kindness. Others will not act unpleasantly toward us, and there will be no basis for conflict or disputes. People will come to like us, and our relationships will be more stable and satisfying.

Cherishing others also protects us from the problems caused by desirous attachment. We often become strongly attached to another person who we feel will help us to overcome our loneliness by providing the comfort, security or excitement we crave. However, if we have a loving mind toward everyone, we do not feel lonely. Instead of clinging onto others to fulfill our desires we will want to help them fulfill their needs and wishes. Cherishing all living beings solves all our problems because all our problems come from our mind of self-cherishing. For example, at the moment if our partner left us for someone else we would probably feel very upset, but if we truly cherished them we would want them to be happy, and we would rejoice in their happiness. There would be no basis for us to feel jealous or depressed, so although we might find the situation challenging, it would not be a problem for us. Cherishing others is the supreme protection from suffering and problems, and enables us to remain calm and peaceful all the time.

Cherishing our neighbors and the people in our local area will naturally lead to harmony in the community and society at large, and this will make everyone happier. We may not be a well-known or powerful figure, but if we sincerely cherish everyone we meet we can make a profound contribution to our community. This is true even for those who deny the value of religion. There are some people who do not believe in past or future lives or in holy beings but who nevertheless try to give up self-concern and work for the benefit of others.

This is a very positive attitude that will lead to good results. If a schoolteacher cherishes his or her students, and is free from self-concern, they will respect him and learn not only the subject he teaches but also the kind and admirable qualities he demonstrates. Such a teacher will naturally influence those around him in a positive way, and his presence will transform the whole school. It is said that there exists a magic crystal that has the power to purify any liquid in which it is placed. Those who cherish all living beings are like this crystal—by their very presence they remove negativity from the world and give back love and kindness.

Even if someone is clever and powerful, if he does not love others, sooner or later he will encounter problems and find it difficult to fulfill his wishes. If the leader of a country does not cherish his or her people but is concerned only with his own interests, he will be criticized and mistrusted, and eventually lose his position. If a Spiritual Teacher does not cherish and have a good relationship with his or her students, then the Teacher cannot help the students and the students will not gain any realizations.

In *Guide to the Bodhisattva's Way of Life,* the Buddhist Master Shantideva makes the point that if an employer is concerned only with his own interests and does not look after the welfare of his employees, the employees will be unhappy. They will probably work inefficiently, and will certainly not be enthusiastic about fulfilling their employer's wishes. Thus the employer will suffer from his own lack of consideration toward his employees. Similarly, if the employees are concerned only with what they can get out of the company, this will anger their employer, who may reduce their wages or ask them to leave. The company may even go bankrupt, causing them all to lose their jobs. In this way the employees will suffer from their lack of consideration toward their employer. In every field of activity the best way to ensure success is for the people involved to reduce their self-cherishing and to have a greater sense of consideration for others. There may sometimes appear to be short-term advantages to self-cherishing, but in the long term there are always only problems. The solution to all the problems of daily life is to cherish others.

All the suffering we experience is the result of negative karma, and the source of all negative karma is self-cherishing. It is because we have such an exaggerated sense of our own importance that we frustrate other people's wishes in order to fulfill our own. Driven by our selfish wishes we think nothing of destroying others' peace of mind and causing them distress. Such actions only sow the seeds for future suffering. If we sincerely cherish others we will have no wish to hurt them and will stop engaging in destructive and harmful actions. We will naturally observe pure moral discipline and refrain from killing or being cruel to other living beings, stealing from them or interfering with their relationships. As a result we will not have to experience the unpleasant effects of these negative actions in the future. In this way cherishing others protects us from all future problems caused by negative karma.

By cherishing others we continuously accumulate merit, and merit is the main cause of success in all our activities. If we cherish all living beings we will naturally perform many virtuous and helpful actions. Gradually all our actions of body, speech and mind will become pure and beneficial, and we will become a source of happiness and inspiration for everyone we meet. We will discover through our own experience that this precious mind of love is the real wish-granting jewel, because it fulfills the pure wishes of both ourself and all living beings.

The mind that cherishes others is the supreme good heart. Keeping such a good heart will result only in happiness for ourself and all those around us. This good heart is the very essence of the Mahayana path and the main cause of great compassion, the wish to protect all living beings from fear and suffering. Through improving our great compassion we will eventually achieve the universal compassion of a Buddha, which actually has the power to protect all living beings from suffering. In this way cherishing others leads us to Buddhahood. It is for this reason that Langri Tangpa begins *Eight Verses* with the prayer to cherish all living beings in order to attain the ultimate, supreme goal of full enlightenment.

Through contemplating all these advantages of cherishing others we arrive at the following determination:

> *I will cherish all living beings without exception because this precious mind of love is the supreme method for solving all problems and fulfilling all wishes. Eventually it will give me the supreme happiness of enlightenment.*

We meditate on this determination single-pointedly for as long as possible and develop a strong feeling of cherishing each and every living being. When we arise from meditation we try to maintain this feeling and put our resolution into practice. Whenever we are with other people we should be continuously mindful that their happiness and wishes are at least as important as our own. Of course we cannot cherish all living beings right away, but by training our mind in this attitude, beginning with our family and friends, we can gradually extend the scope of our love until it embraces all living beings. When in this way we sincerely cherish all living beings we are no longer an ordinary person but have become a great being, like a Bodhisattva.

Nagarjuna

Enhancing Cherishing Love

Whenever I associate with others,
May I view myself as the lowest of all;
And with a pure intention,
May I cherish others as supreme.

In the first verse Bodhisattva Langri Tangpa explains how to cherish all living beings, and in this verse he now shows us how to enhance this mind of love. The best way to do this is to familiarize ourself with cherishing all living beings by putting our determination to cherish them into practice day and night. To help strengthen this determination Langri Tangpa gives us further instructions on enhancing cherishing love.

We all have someone whom we regard as especially precious, such as our child, our partner or our mother. This person seems to be imbued with unique qualities that make him or her stand out from others. We treasure and want to take special care of this person. We need to learn to regard all living beings in a similar way, recognizing each and every one as special and uniquely valuable. Although we already cherish our family and close friends, we do not love strangers, and we certainly do not love our enemies. For us the vast majority of living beings are of no particular significance. By practicing Langri Tangpa's instructions we can remove this bias and come to treasure each and every living being, just as a mother regards her dearest child. The more we can deepen and enhance our love in this way, the stronger our compassion and bodhichitta will become, and the quicker we will attain enlightenment.

RECOGNIZING OUR FAULTS IN
THE MIRROR OF DHARMA

The main reason why we do not cherish all living beings is that we are so preoccupied with ourself, and this leaves very little room in our mind to appreciate others. If we wish to cherish others sincerely we have to reduce our obsessive self-concern. Why is it that we regard ourself as so precious, but not others? It is because we are so familiar with self-cherishing. Since beginningless time we have grasped at a truly existent I. This grasping at I automatically gives rise to self-cherishing, which instinctively feels, "I am more important than others." For ordinary beings, grasping at one's own I and self-cherishing are like two sides of the same coin: I-grasping grasps at a truly existent I, whereas self-cherishing feels this I to be precious and cherishes it. The fundamental reason for this is our constant familiarity with our self-cherishing, day and night, even during our sleep.

Since we regard our self or I as so very precious and important, we exaggerate our own good qualities and develop an inflated view of ourself. Almost anything can serve as a basis for this arrogant mind, such as our appearance, possessions, knowledge, experiences or status. If we make a witty remark we think, "I'm so clever!", or if we have traveled around the world we feel that this automatically makes us a fascinating person. We can even develop pride on the basis of things we should be ashamed of, such as our ability to deceive others, or on qualities that we merely imagine we possess. On the other hand we find it very hard to accept our mistakes and shortcomings. We spend so much time contemplating our real or imagined good qualities that we become oblivious to our faults. In reality our mind is full of gross delusions but we ignore them and may even fool ourself into thinking that we do not have such repulsive minds. This is like pretending that there is no dirt in our house after sweeping it under the rug.

It is often so painful to admit that we have faults that we make all manner of excuses rather than alter our exalted view of ourself. One of the most common ways of not facing up to our faults is to blame others. For instance, if we have a difficult relationship with someone we naturally conclude that it is entirely his fault—we are unable to accept that it is at least partly ours. Instead of taking responsibility for our actions and making an effort to change our behavior, we argue with him and insist that it is he who must change. An exaggerated sense of our own importance thus leads to a critical attitude toward other people and makes it almost impossible to avoid conflict. The fact that we are oblivious to our faults does not prevent other people from noticing them and pointing them out, but when they do we feel that they are being unfair. Instead of looking honestly at our own behavior to see whether or not the criticism is justified, our self-cherishing mind becomes defensive and retaliates by finding fault with them.

Another reason why we do not regard others as precious is that we pay attention to their faults while ignoring their good qualities. Unfortunately we have become very skilled in recognizing the faults of others, and we devote a great deal of mental energy to listing them, analyzing them and even meditating on them! With this critical attitude, if we disagree with our partner or colleagues about something, instead of trying to understand their point of view we repeatedly think of many reasons why we are right and they are wrong. By focusing exclusively on their faults and limitations we become angry and resentful, and rather than cherishing them we develop the wish to harm or discredit them. In this way small disagreements can easily turn into conflicts that simmer for months.

Nothing good ever comes from dwelling on our own qualities and others' faults. All that happens is that we develop a highly distorted, self-important view of ourself, and an arrogant, disrespectful attitude toward others. As Shantideva says in *Guide to the Bodhisattva's Way of Life*:

> If we hold ourself in high esteem, we shall be reborn
>   in the lower realms
> And later, as a human, experience low status and a
>   foolish mind.

As a result of regarding ourself as superior and others as inferior we perform many negative actions that will later ripen as rebirth in the lower realms. Due to this haughty attitude, even when we finally take rebirth again as a human being we will be of a low social status, living like a servant or slave. Out of pride we may regard ourself as highly intelligent, but in reality our pride makes us foolish and fills our mind with negativity. There is no value in viewing ourself as more important than others and thinking only of our own qualities. It neither increases our qualities nor reduces our faults, and it does not cause others to share our exalted opinion of ourself.

If instead we focus on the good qualities of others, our deluded pride will decrease and we will come to regard them as more important and precious than ourself. As a result, our love and compassion will increase and we will naturally engage in virtuous actions. Due to this we will be reborn in the higher realms, as a human or god, and we will gain the respect and friendship of many people. Only good can come from contemplating the good qualities of others. Therefore, while ordinary beings look for faults in others, Bodhisattvas look solely for good qualities.

In *Advice from Atisha's Heart*, Atisha says:

> Do not look for faults in others, but look for faults in yourself, and purge them like bad blood.

> Do not contemplate your own good qualities, but contemplate the good qualities of others, and respect everyone as a servant would.

We need to think about our own faults because if we are not aware of them we will not be motivated to overcome them. It was through constantly examining their minds for faults and imperfections, and then applying great effort to abandon them, that those who are now enlightened were able to release their minds from delusions, the source of all faults. Buddha said that those who understand their own faults are wise, while those who are unaware of their own faults yet look for faults in others are fools. Contemplating our own qualities and others' faults serves only to increase our self-cherishing and diminish our love for others; and yet all enlightened beings agree that self-cherishing is the root of all faults, and cherishing others is the source of all happiness. The only people who disagree with this view are those who are still in samsara. We can keep our ordinary view if we wish, or we can adopt the view of all the holy beings. The choice is ours, but we would be wise to adopt the latter if we wish to enjoy real peace and happiness.

Some people argue that one of our main problems is a lack of self-esteem, and that we need to focus exclusively on our good qualities in order to boost our self-confidence. It is true that to make authentic spiritual progress we need to develop confidence in our spiritual potential, and to acknowledge and improve our good qualities. However, we also need a keen and realistic awareness of our present faults and imperfections. If we are honest with ourself we will recognize that at the moment our mind is filled with defilements such as anger, attachment and ignorance. These mental diseases will not go away just by our pretending they do not exist. The only way we can ever get rid of them is by honestly acknowledging their existence and then making the effort to eliminate them.

One of the main functions of Dharma teachings is to serve as a mirror in which we can see our own faults. For example, when anger arises in our mind, instead of making excuses we need to say to ourself: "This anger is the inner poison of delusion. It has no value or justification; its only function is to harm. I will not tolerate its presence in my mind." We can also use the mirror of Dharma to distinguish between desirous attachment and love. These two are easily confused, but it is vital to discriminate between them, because love will bring us only happiness while the mind of attachment will bring us only suffering and bind us ever more tightly to samsara. The moment we notice attachment arising in our mind we should be on our guard—no matter how pleasant it may seem to follow our attachment, it is like licking honey off a razor's edge, and in the long run invariably leads to more suffering.

Although we need to be acutely aware of our faults we must never allow ourself to become overwhelmed or discouraged by them. We may have a lot of anger in our mind but this does not mean that we are an inherently angry person. No matter how many delusions we may have or how strong they are, they are not an essential part of our mind. They are defilements that temporarily pollute our mind but do not soil its pure, essential nature. They are like mud that dirties water but never becomes an intrinsic part of it. Just as mud can always be removed to reveal pure, clear water, so delusions can be removed to reveal the natural purity and clarity of our mind. While acknowledging that we have delusions we should not identify with them, thinking, "I am a selfish, worthless person" or "I am an angry person." Instead we should identify with our pure potential and develop the wisdom and courage to overcome our delusions.

When we look at external things we can usually distinguish those that are useful and valuable from those that are not. We must learn to look at our mind in the same way. Although the nature of our root mind is pure and clear, many conceptual thoughts arise from it, like bubbles arising within an ocean or rays of light arising from a single flame. Some of these thoughts are beneficial and lead to happiness both now and in the future, while others lead to suffering and the extreme misery of rebirth in the lower realms. We need to keep a constant watch over our mind and learn to distinguish between the beneficial and harmful thoughts that are arising moment by moment. Those who are able to do this are truly wise.

Once an evil man who had killed thousands of people met a Bodhisattva called King Chandra, who helped him by teaching him Dharma and showing him the error of his ways. The man said, "Having looked into the mirror of Dharma I now understand how negative my actions have been, and I feel great regret for them." Motivated by deep remorse he engaged sincerely in purification practices and eventually became a highly realized Yogi. This shows that by recognizing one's own faults in the mirror of Dharma and then making a concerted effort to remove them, even the most evil person can become a completely pure being.

In Tibet there was once a famous Dharma practitioner called Geshe Ben Gungyal, who neither recited prayers nor meditated in the traditional meditation posture. His only practice was to observe his mind very attentively and counter delusions as soon as they arose. Whenever he noticed his mind becoming even slightly agitated, he was especially vigilant and refused to follow any negative thoughts. For instance, if he felt self-cherishing was about to arise he would immediately recall its disadvantages, and then he would stop this mind from manifesting by applying its opponent, the practice of love. Whenever his mind was naturally peaceful and positive, he would relax and allow himself to enjoy his virtuous states of mind.

To gauge his progress he would put a black pebble down in front of him whenever a negative thought arose, and a white pebble whenever a positive thought arose, and at the end of the day he would count the pebbles. If there were more black pebbles he would reprimand himself and try even harder the next day, but if there were more white pebbles he would praise and encourage himself. At the beginning the black pebbles greatly outnumbered the white ones, but over the years his mind improved until he reached the point when entire days went by without any black pebbles. Before becoming a Dharma practitioner Geshe Ben Gungyal had had a reputation for being wild and unruly, but by watching his mind closely all the time, and judging it with complete honesty in the mirror of Dharma, he gradually became a very pure and holy being. Why can we not do the same?

The Kadampa Geshes taught that the function of a Spiritual Guide is to point out his or her disciples' faults, because then the disciple has a clear understanding of these shortcomings and the opportunity to overcome them. These days, however, if a Teacher were to point out his or her disciples' faults they would probably become upset, and may even lose their faith, and so the Teacher usually has to adopt a gentler approach. However, even though our Spiritual Guide may tactfully be refraining from directly pointing out our faults, we still need to become aware of them by examining our mind in the mirror of his or her teachings. By relating our Spiritual Guide's teachings on karma and delusions to our own situation, we will be able to understand what we need to abandon and what we need to practice.

A sick person cannot be cured of his illness just by reading the instructions on a bottle of medicine, but he can be cured by actually taking the medicine. Similarly Buddha gave

Dharma instructions as supreme medicine to cure the inner disease of our delusions, but we cannot cure this disease just by reading or studying Dharma books. We can only solve our daily problems by taking Dharma into our heart and practicing it sincerely.

VIEWING ALL LIVING BEINGS AS SUPREME

Bodhisattva Langri Tangpa prays:

And with a pure intention,
May I cherish others as supreme.

If we wish to attain enlightenment, or to develop the superior bodhichitta that comes from exchanging self with others, we must definitely adopt the view that others are more precious than ourself. This view is based on wisdom and leads us to our final goal, whereas the view that regards ourself as more precious than others is based on self-grasping ignorance and leads us along the paths of samsara.

What exactly does it mean to say that something is precious? If we were asked which was more precious, a diamond or a bone, we would say a diamond. This is because a diamond is more useful to us. However, for a dog a bone would be more precious because he can eat a bone whereas he cannot do anything with a diamond. This indicates that preciousness is not an intrinsic quality of an object but depends upon an individual's needs and wishes, which in turn depend upon his or her karma. For someone whose main wish is to achieve the spiritual realizations of love, compassion, bodhichitta and great enlightenment, living beings are more precious than a universe filled with diamonds or even wish-granting jewels.

Why is this? It is because living beings help that person to develop love and compassion and to fulfill his or her wish for enlightenment, which is something that a whole universe filled with jewels could never do.

No one wants to remain an ordinary, ignorant being forever; indeed, all of us have the wish to improve ourself and to progress to higher and higher states. The highest state of all is full enlightenment, and the main road leading to enlightenment is the realizations of love, compassion, bodhichitta and the practice of the six perfections. We can only develop these qualities in dependence upon other living beings. How can we learn to love with no one to love? How can we practice giving with no one to give to, or patience with no one to irritate us? Whenever we see another living being we can increase our spiritual qualities such as love and compassion, and in this way we come closer to enlightenment and the fulfillment of our deepest wishes. How kind living beings are to act as the objects of our love and compassion. How precious they are!

When Atisha was in Tibet he had an Indian assistant who was always criticizing him. When the Tibetans asked him why he kept this assistant when there were many faithful Tibetans who would be more than happy to serve him, Atisha replied, "Without this man, there would be no one with whom I could practice patience. He is very kind to me. I need him!" Atisha understood that the only way to fulfill his deepest wish to benefit all living beings was to achieve enlightenment, and that to do this he needed to perfect his patience. For Atisha, his bad-tempered assistant was more precious than material possessions, praise or any other worldly attainment.

Chandrakirti

Our spiritual realizations are our inner wealth for they help us in all situations and are the only possessions we can take with us when we die. Once we learn to value the inner wealth of patience, giving, love and compassion above external conditions we will come to regard each and every sentient being as supremely precious, no matter how they treat us. This will make it very easy for us to cherish them.

In our meditation session we contemplate the reasons given above until we reach the following conclusion:

Sentient beings are extremely precious because without them I cannot gather the inner wealth of spiritual realizations that will eventually bring me the ultimate happiness of full enlightenment. Since without this inner wealth I will have to remain in samsara forever, I will always regard sentient beings as supremely important.

We meditate on this determination single-pointedly for as long as possible. When we arise from meditation we try to maintain this determination all the time, recognizing how much we need each and every sentient being for our spiritual practice. By maintaining this recognition our inner problems of anger, attachment, jealousy and so forth will subside, and we will naturally come to cherish others. In particular, whenever people interfere with our wishes or criticize us we should remember that we need these people in order to develop the spiritual realizations that are the true meaning of our human life. If everyone treated us with the kindness and respect our self-cherishing feels we deserve, this would only reinforce our delusions and deplete our merit. Imagine what we would be like if we always got what we wanted! We would be just like a spoiled child who feels that the world revolves around him, and who is unpopular with everyone. In fact, we all need someone like Atisha's assistant, because such people give us the opportunity to destroy our self-cherishing and train our mind, thereby making our life truly meaningful.

Since the above reasoning is the exact opposite of our normal way of thinking, we need to contemplate it very carefully until we are convinced that each and every sentient being is indeed more precious than any external attainment. In reality Buddhas and sentient beings are equally precious—Buddhas because they reveal the path to enlightenment, and sentient beings because they act as objects of the compassion that we need in order to attain enlightenment. Because their kindness in enabling us to attain our supreme goal, enlightenment, is equal, we should regard Buddhas and sentient beings as equally important and precious. As Shantideva says in *Guide to the Bodhisattva's Way of Life*:

> Since living beings and enlightened beings are alike
> In that the qualities of a Buddha arise in dependence
>   upon them,
> Why do we not show the same respect to living
>   beings
> As we do to the enlightened beings?

LIVING BEINGS HAVE NO FAULTS

We might object that while it is true that we depend upon sentient beings as the objects of our patience, compassion and so forth, it is nevertheless impossible to see them as precious when they have so many faults. How can we regard as precious someone whose mind is pervaded by attachment, anger and ignorance? The answer to this objection is quite profound. Although sentient beings' minds are filled with delusions, sentient beings themselves are not faulty. We say that sea water is salty. However, the real nature of water is not salty because salt can be removed from it. Similarly, all the faults we see in people are actually the faults of their delusions, not of the people themselves. Buddhas see that delusions have many faults but they never see people as faulty, because they distinguish between people and their delusions. If someone is angry we think, "He is a bad and angry person," whereas Buddhas think, "He is a suffering being afflicted with the inner disease of anger." If a friend of ours were suffering from cancer we would not blame him for his physical disease, and, in the same way, if someone is suffering from anger or attachment we should not blame him for the diseases of his mind.

Delusions are the enemies of sentient beings, and just as we would not blame a victim for the faults of his attacker, why should we blame sentient beings for the faults of their inner enemies? When someone is temporarily overpowered by the inner enemy of anger it is inappropriate to blame him, because he and the anger in his mind are two separate phenomena. Just as a fault of a microphone is not that of a book, and a fault of a cup is not that of a teapot, so the faults of delusions are not those of a person. The only appropriate response to those who are driven by their delusions to harm others is compassion. Sometimes it is necessary to restrain those who are behaving in very deluded ways, both for their own sake and to protect other people, but it is never appropriate to blame or become angry with them.

We normally refer to our body and mind as "my body" and "my mind," in a similar way to which we refer to our other possessions. This indicates that they are different from our I. The body and mind are the basis upon which we establish our I, not the I itself. Delusions are characteristics of a person's mind, not of the person. Since we can never find faults in sentient beings themselves, we can say that in this respect sentient beings are like Buddhas.

Just as we distinguish between a person and his or her delusions, so we should also remember that the delusions are only temporary, adventitious characteristics of that person's mind and not its real nature. Delusions are distorted conceptual thoughts that arise within the mind, like waves on the ocean—just as it is possible for waves to die down without the ocean disappearing, so it is possible for our delusions to end without our mental continuum ceasing.

It is because they distinguish between delusions and persons that Buddhas are able to see the faults of delusions without ever seeing a single fault in any sentient being. Consequently their love and compassion for sentient beings never diminish. Failing to make this distinction, we on the other hand, are constantly finding fault with other people but do not recognize the faults of delusions, even those within our own mind.

There is a prayer that says:

This fault I see is not the fault of the person
But the fault of delusion.
Realizing this, may I never view others' faults,
But see all beings as supreme.

Focusing on other people's faults is the source of much of our negativity and one of the main obstacles to viewing others as supremely precious. If we are genuinely interested in developing cherishing love we need to learn to discriminate between a person and his or her delusions, and realize that it is the delusions that are to blame for all the faults we perceive.

There may appear to be a contradiction between this and the earlier section where we are advised to recognize our own faults. Surely if we have faults, so too do other people! But there is no contradiction. For the effectiveness of our purification practice we need to recognize our own faults, which are our delusions and our non-virtuous actions. This also applies to others. And for the effectiveness of the practice of loving kindness toward all living beings, we need to understand that the faults that we see in the actions of living beings are not the faults of living beings, but the faults of their enemy—their delusions. We should practically appreciate these teachings; we do not need meaningless debate.

When a mother sees her child throwing a tantrum she knows that the child is acting in a deluded way, but this does not diminish her love for him or her. Although she is not blind to the anger in her child, this does not lead her to the conclusion that the child is evil or intrinsically angry. Distinguishing between the delusion and the person, she continues to see her child as beautiful and full of potential. In the same way, we should regard all sentient beings as supremely precious, while clearly understanding that they are afflicted by the sickness of delusion.

We can also apply the above reasoning to ourself, recognizing that our faults are really the faults of our delusions and not of our self. This prevents us from identifying with our faults and thus feeling guilty and inadequate, and it helps us to view our delusions in a realistic and practical way. We need to acknowledge our delusions and take responsibility for overcoming them, but to do this effectively we need to distance ourself from them. For example, we can think: "Self-cherishing is presently in my mind, but it is not me. I can destroy it without destroying myself." In this way we can be utterly ruthless with our delusions but kind and patient with ourself. We do not need to blame ourself for the many delusions we have inherited from our previous life, but if we wish for our future self to enjoy peace and happiness it is our responsibility to remove these delusions from our mind.

As mentioned before, one of the best ways to regard others as precious is to remember their kindness. Once again we may object, "How can I see others as kind when they engage in so many cruel and harmful actions?" To answer this we need to understand that when people harm others they are controlled by their delusions. Delusions are like a powerful hallucinogenic drug that forces people to act in ways that are contrary to their real nature. A person under the influence of delusions is not in his right mind, because he is creating terrible suffering for himself and no one in their right mind would create suffering for himself. All delusions are based on a mistaken way of seeing things. When we see things as they really are, our delusions naturally disappear and virtuous minds naturally manifest. Minds such as love and kindness are based on reality and are an expression of our pure nature. Thus when we view others as kind we are seeing beyond their delusions and are relating to their pure nature, their Buddha nature.

Buddha compared our Buddha nature to a gold nugget in dirt, for no matter how disgusting a person's delusions may be, the real nature of their mind remains undefiled, like pure gold. In the heart of even the cruelest and most degenerate person exists the potential for limitless love, compassion and wisdom. Unlike the seeds of our delusions, which can be destroyed, this potential is utterly indestructible, and is the pure, essential nature of every living being. Whenever we meet other people, rather than focusing on their delusions we should focus on the gold of their Buddha nature. This will not only enable us to regard them as special and unique, but also help to bring out their good qualities. Recognizing everyone as a future Buddha, out of love and compassion we will naturally help and encourage this potential to ripen.

Because we are so familiar with cherishing ourself more than others, the view that all sentient beings are supremely important does not arise easily and we need to train our mind patiently for many years before it becomes natural. Just as an ocean is formed by many tiny drops of water gathering over a long period of time, so the realizations of love and compassion of advanced practitioners are the result of constant training. We should begin by trying to cherish our parents, family and close friends and then extend this feeling to the people in our community. Gradually we can increase the scope of our cherishing until it includes all sentient beings.

It is important to begin with our immediate circle because if we try to love all sentient beings in a general way, while neglecting to cherish the specific individuals with whom we associate, our cherishing will be abstract and inauthentic. We may develop some good feelings in meditation, but these will quickly disappear once we arise from meditation, and our mind will remain basically unchanged. However if at the end of each meditation session we make a special determination to cherish those with whom we are going to spend our time, and then put this determination into practice, our cherishing will be grounded and sincere. Through making a concerted effort to love our immediate circle, even when they are making life difficult for us, our self-cherishing will be continuously eroded and we will gradually build in our mind a firm foundation of cherishing others. With this foundation it will not be difficult to extend our love to more and more sentient beings until we develop the universal love and compassion of a Bodhisattva.

Our ability to help others also depends upon our karmic connection with them from this and previous lives. We all have a close circle of people with whom we have a special karmic connection in this life. Though we need to learn to cherish all living beings equally, this does not mean that we have to treat everyone in exactly the same way. For example, it would be inappropriate to treat our employer in the same way that we treat our close friends and family. There are also people who just want to be left alone or who dislike any display of affection. Loving others is principally an attitude of mind, and the way in which we express it depends upon the needs and wishes of each individual as well as our karmic connection with them. We cannot physically care for everyone, but we can develop a caring attitude toward all beings. This is the main point of training the mind. By training our mind in this way we will eventually become a Buddha with the actual power to protect all sentient beings.

Through carefully contemplating all the above points we arrive at the following conclusion:

Because all sentient beings are very precious for me, I must cherish them and hold them dear.

We should regard this determination as a seed and hold it continuously in our mind, nurturing it until it grows into the spontaneous feeling of cherishing ourself and all sentient beings equally. This realization is called "equalizing self and others." Just as we value our own peace and happiness, so too should we value the peace and happiness of all living beings; and just as we work to free ourself from suffering and problems, so too should we work to free others.

DEVELOPING HUMILITY

Whenever I associate with others,
May I view myself as the lowest of all.

Here Langri Tangpa is encouraging us to develop the mind of humility and to see ourself as lower and less precious than others. As mentioned before, preciousness is not an inherent quality of an object but depends upon an individual's karma. It is due to a mother's special karmic connection with her children that they naturally appear precious to her. For a practitioner of training the mind all sentient beings are equally precious, both because they are immensely kind and because they act as supreme objects for developing and increasing his or her spiritual realizations. For such a practitioner no single being is inferior or less important, not even an insect. We may wonder, if preciousness depends upon karma, is it because a practitioner of training the mind has a karmic connection with all beings that he sees them as precious? The practitioner of training the mind develops this special view through contemplating correct reasons that cause to ripen his karmic potential to see all beings as his precious mother. In reality all sentient beings are our mothers, so of course we have a karmic connection with them; but due to our ignorance we have no idea that they are our precious mothers.

In general we would all prefer to enjoy high status and a good reputation, and we have little or no interest in being humble. Accomplished practitioners of training the mind, such as Langri Tangpa, are the complete opposite. They actually seek out subordinate positions and wish for others to enjoy the happiness of higher status. There are three reasons why practitioners of training the mind strive to practice humility. Firstly, by practicing humility we are not using up our merit on worldly attainments but saving it for the development of internal realizations. We only have a limited supply of merit, so if we waste it on material possessions, reputation, popularity or power there will not be enough positive energy left in our mind to effect deep spiritual realizations. Secondly, by practicing humility and wishing for others to enjoy higher status we accumulate a vast amount of merit. We should understand that now is the time to accumulate merit, not to waste it for worldly enjoyments. Thirdly, we need to practice humility because there is no self or I that we normally see. We should view our self or I—the object of our self-cherishing—as the lowest of all, as something we need to neglect or forget. In this way our self-cherishing will become weaker and our love for others will increase.

Although all accomplished practitioners of training the mind practice humility, they will nonetheless accept whatever social position enables them to benefit the most sentient beings. Such a practitioner may become a wealthy, powerful and respected member of society, but his or her motivation for doing so would be solely for the benefit of others. Worldly attainments do not attract him in the least, because he recognizes them as deceptive and a waste of his merit. Even if he were to become a king he would consider all his wealth as belonging to others, and in his heart would continue to view others as supreme. Because he would not grasp at his position or possessions as his own, they would not serve to exhaust his merit.

We need to practice humility even when we associate with those who according to social conventions are equal or inferior to us. Because we cannot see others' minds we do not know who is actually a realized being and who is not. Someone may not have a high position in society, but if in his heart he maintains loving kindness toward all living beings, in reality he is a realized being. Moreover, Buddhas are able to manifest in any form to help living beings, and unless we are a Buddha ourself we have no way of knowing who is an emanation of a Buddha and who is not. We cannot say for sure that our closest friend or worst enemy, our mother or even our dog, is not an emanation. The fact that we feel we know someone very well and have seen him or her behaving in deluded ways does not mean that he or she is an ordinary person. What we see is a reflection of our own mind. An ordinary, deluded mind will naturally perceive a world filled with ordinary, deluded people.

Only when we purify our mind will we be able to see pure, holy beings directly. Until then we cannot know for sure whether or not someone is an emanation. Perhaps everyone we know is an emanation of a Buddha! This may seem unlikely, but only because we are so used to seeing people as ordinary. We simply do not know. All we can realistically say is that maybe someone is an emanation, maybe he or she is not. This is a very useful way of thinking, because if we think that someone may be an emanation of a Buddha we will naturally respect him and avoid harming him. From the point of view of the effect it has on our mind, thinking that someone may be a Buddha is almost the same as thinking that he or she is a Buddha. Since the only person we know for sure is not a Buddha is ourself, through training in this way of thinking we will gradually come to regard everyone else as superior to and more precious than ourself.

Viewing ourself as the lowest of all is not easy to accept at first. When we meet a dog, for example, are we supposed to view ourself as lower than the dog? We can consider the story of Asanga, who came across a dying dog that in reality turned out to be an emanation of Buddha Maitreya. The dog before us may appear to be an ordinary animal, but the fact is that we do not know its real nature. Perhaps it too has been emanated by Buddha to help us develop compassion. Since we cannot know for sure one way or another, rather than wasting our time speculating whether the dog is an ordinary animal or an emanation, we should simply think, "This dog may be an emanation of Buddha." From this point of view we can think that we are lower than the dog, and this thought will protect us against any feelings of superiority.

One of the advantages of humility is that it enables us to learn from everyone. A proud person cannot learn from other people because he feels he already knows better than they. On the other hand, a humble person who respects everyone and recognizes that they may even be emanations of Buddha has the openness of mind to learn from everyone and every situation. Just as water cannot collect on mountain peaks, so good qualities and blessings cannot gather on the rocky peaks of pride. If, instead, we maintain a humble, respectful attitude toward everyone, good qualities and inspiration will flow into our mind all the time, like streams flowing into a valley.

Vajradhara

Exchanging Self with Others

Examining my mental continuum throughout all my
*   actions,*
As soon as a delusion of self-cherishing develops
Whereby I or others would act inappropriately,
May I firmly face it and avert it.

While the first two verses explain the practice of equalizing self and others—cherishing ourself and all other living beings equally—the third verse shows us how to exchange self with others. This means that we give up our self-cherishing and come to cherish only others. Because the main obstacles to gaining this realization are our delusions, Bodhisattva Langri Tangpa now explains how we can overcome our delusions, and in particular our self-cherishing.

Normally we divide the external world into that which we consider to be good or valuable, bad or worthless or neither. Most of the time these discriminations are incorrect or have little meaning. For example, our habitual way of categorizing people as friends, enemies and strangers depending on how they make us feel is both incorrect and a great obstacle to developing impartial love for all living beings. Rather than holding so tightly to our discriminations of the external world, it would be far more beneficial if we learned to discriminate between valuable and worthless states of mind.

To overcome a particular delusion we need to be able to identify it correctly and distinguish it clearly from other states of mind. It is relatively easy to identify delusions such as anger or jealousy and to see how they are harming us. Delusions such as attachment, pride, self-grasping and self-cherishing, however, are more difficult to recognize and can easily be confused with other states of mind. For instance, we have many desires but not all of these are motivated by desirous attachment. We can have the wish to sleep, to eat, to meet our friends or to meditate, without being influenced by attachment. A desire that is attachment necessarily disturbs our mind, but since it may affect us in subtle, indirect ways we may find it difficult to recognize when it arises in our mind.

WHAT IS SELF-CHERISHING?

Of all the innumerable conceptual thoughts that arise from the ocean of our root mind, the most harmful is self-cherishing and the most beneficial is the mind of cherishing others. What exactly is self-cherishing? Self-cherishing is our mind thinking "I am important" while neglecting others. It is defined as a mind that considers oneself to be supremely important and precious, and that develops from the appearance of true existence of the self. The delusion of self-cherishing is functioning in our mind almost all the time, and is at the very core of our samsaric experience.

It is our self-cherishing that makes us feel that our happiness and freedom are more important than anyone else's, that our wishes and feelings matter more, and that our life and experiences are more interesting. Because of our self-cherishing we find it upsetting when we are criticized or insulted, but not when a stranger is criticized, and we may even feel happy when someone we dislike is insulted. When we are in pain we feel that the most important thing in the world is to stop our pain as quickly as possible, but we are far more patient when someone else is in pain. We are so familiar with self-cherishing that we find it difficult to imagine life without it—for us it is almost as natural as breathing. However, if we check with our wisdom we will see that self-cherishing is a completely mistaken mind with no basis in reality. There are no valid reasons whatsoever for thinking that we are more important than others. For Buddhas, who have unmistaken minds and see things exactly as they are, all beings are equally important.

Self-cherishing is a wrong awareness because its observed object, the inherently existent self or I, does not exist. The inherently existent self or I, the self or I that we normally see, and the truly existent self or I are synonymous. If we watch our mind when self-cherishing is manifesting strongly, such as when we are afraid, embarrassed or indignant, we will notice that we have a very vivid sense of I. Due to self-grasping ignorance our I appears to us as a solid, real entity, existing from its own side, independently of our body or mind. This independent I is called the "inherently existent I," and it does not exist at all. The I that we grasp at so strongly, cherish so dearly and devote our whole life to serving and protecting is merely a fabrication of our ignorance. If we reflect deeply on this point we will realize how ridiculous it is to cherish something that does not exist. An explanation of how the inherently existent I does not exist is given in the chapter on training in ultimate bodhichitta.

Due to the imprints of self-grasping accumulated since beginningless time, whatever appears to our mind, including our I, appears to be inherently existent. Grasping at our own self as inherently existent, we grasp at the self of others as inherently existent, and then conceive self and others to be inherently different. We then generate self-cherishing, which instinctively feels, "I am supremely important and precious." In summary, our self-grasping apprehends our I to be inherently existent, and our self-cherishing then cherishes that inherently existent I above all others. For ordinary beings, self-grasping and self-cherishing are very closely related and almost mixed together. We can say that they are both types of ignorance because they both mistakenly apprehend a non-existent object, the inherently existent I. Because any action motivated by these minds is a contaminated action that causes us to be reborn in samsara, it is also correct to say that for ordinary beings both self-grasping and self-cherishing are the root of samsara.

There is a more subtle type of self-cherishing that is not conjoined with self-grasping and that is therefore not a type of ignorance. This type of self-cherishing exists in the minds of Hinayana Foe Destroyers, who have completely abandoned the ignorance of self-grasping and all other delusions. However, they still have a subtle form of self-cherishing, which arises from the imprints of self-grasping and prevents them from working for the sake of all sentient beings. An explanation of this type of self-cherishing is not within the scope of this book. Here self-cherishing refers to the self-cherishing of ordinary beings, which is a deluded mind that cherishes a non-existent self and regards it as supremely important.

THE FAULTS OF SELF-CHERISHING

It is impossible to find a single problem, misfortune or painful experience that does not arise from self-cherishing. As Shantideva says:

All the happiness there is in this world
Arises from wishing others to be happy,
And all the suffering there is in this world
Arises from wishing ourself to be happy.

How should we understand this? As mentioned earlier, all our experiences are the effects of actions we have committed in the past: pleasant experiences are the effects of positive actions, and unpleasant experiences are the effects of negative actions. Sufferings are not given to us as a punishment. They all come from our self-cherishing mind, which wishes ourself to be happy while neglecting the happiness of others. There are two ways to understand this. First, the self-cherishing mind is the creator of all our suffering and problems; and second, self-cherishing is the basis for experiencing all our suffering and problems.

We suffer because in our previous lives we performed actions that caused others to experience suffering, motivated by selfish intention—our self-cherishing. As a result of these actions, we now experience our present suffering and problems. Therefore, the real creator of all our suffering and problems is our self-cherishing mind. If we never engaged in negative actions it would be impossible for us to experience any unpleasant effects. All negative actions are motivated by delusions, which in turn arise from self-cherishing. First we develop the thought, "I am important," and because of this we feel that the fulfillment of our wishes is of paramount importance. Then we desire for ourself that which appears attractive and develop attachment, we feel aversion for that which appears unattractive and develop anger, and we feel indifference toward that which appears neutral and develop ignorance. From these three delusions all other delusions arise. Self-grasping and self-cherishing are the roots of the tree of suffering, delusions such as anger and attachment are its trunk, negative actions are its branches and the miseries and pains of samsara are its bitter fruit.

By understanding how delusions develop we can see that self-cherishing is at the very core of our negativity and suffering. Disregarding the happiness of others and selfishly pursuing our own interests, we perform many non-virtuous actions, the effects of which are only suffering. All the misery of disease, sickness, natural disasters and war can be traced back to self-cherishing. It is impossible to experience the suffering of sickness or any other misfortune if we have not at some time in the past created its cause, which is necessarily a non-virtuous action motivated by self-cherishing.

We should not take this to mean that a person's suffering is his own fault, and that it is therefore inappropriate to feel compassion for him. Motivated by their delusions living beings perform negative actions, and whenever they are under the influence of delusions they are not in control of their minds. If a mental patient were to injure his head by banging it against a wall, the doctors would not refuse to treat him by arguing that it was his own fault. In the same way, if in a previous life someone performed a negative action that has now resulted in his experiencing a serious illness, this is no reason for us not to feel compassion for him. Indeed, by understanding that living beings are not free from the delusions that are the cause of all their suffering, our compassion will become much stronger. To be able to help others effectively we need a profoundly compassionate intention that wishes to free others from their manifest suffering and its underlying causes.

The self-cherishing mind is also the basis for experiencing all our suffering and problems. For example, when people are unable to fulfill their wishes, many experience depression, discouragement, unhappiness and mental pain, and some even want to kill themselves. This is because their self-cherishing believes that their own wishes are so important. It is therefore their self-cherishing that is mainly responsible for their problems. Without self-cherishing, there would be no basis for experiencing such suffering.

It is not difficult to see how the self-cherishing we have in this life causes us suffering. All disharmony, quarrelling and fighting come from the self-cherishing of the people involved. With self-cherishing we hold our opinions and interests very strongly and are not willing to see a situation from another point of view. As a consequence we easily get angry and wish to harm others verbally or even physically. Self-cherishing makes us feel depressed whenever our wishes are not fulfilled, we fail in our ambitions or our life does not turn out the way we planned. If we examine all the times we have been miserable, we will discover that they are characterized by an excessive concern for our own welfare. If we lose our job, our home, our reputation or our friends we feel sad, but only because we are so attached to these things. We are not nearly so concerned when other people lose their jobs or are parted from their friends.

In themselves external conditions are neither good nor bad. For example, wealth is generally thought of as desirable, but if we are strongly attached to wealth it will only cause us many worries and serve to deplete our merit. On the other hand, if our mind is governed principally by cherishing others, even losing all our money can be useful, because it gives us the opportunity to understand the suffering of those in similar situations and provides fewer distractions from our spiritual practice. Even if we did fulfill all the wishes of our self-cherishing there is no guarantee that we would be happy, because every samsaric attainment brings with it new problems and invariably leads to new desires. The relentless pursuit of our selfish desires is like drinking salt water to quench our thirst. The more we indulge our desires the greater our thirst.

When people kill themselves it is usually because their wishes were not fulfilled, but this was unbearable to them only because their self-cherishing made them feel that their wishes were the most important thing in the world. It is because of self-cherishing that we take our wishes and plans so seriously and are unable to accept and learn from the difficulties that life brings us. We do not become a better person just by fulfilling our wishes for worldly success; we are as likely to develop the qualities that really matter—such as wisdom, patience and compassion—through our failures as through our successes.

We often feel that it is someone else who is making us unhappy, and we can become quite resentful. If we look at the situation carefully, however, we will find that it is always our own mental attitude that is responsible for our unhappiness. Another person's actions make us unhappy only if we allow them to stimulate a negative response in us. Criticism, for example, has no power from its own side to hurt us; we are hurt only because of our self-cherishing. With self-cherishing we are so dependent on the opinions and approval of others that we lose our freedom to respond and act in the most constructive way.

We sometimes feel that the reason we are unhappy is that someone we love is in trouble. We need to remember that at the moment our love for others is almost invariably mixed with attachment, which is a self-centered mind. The love parents generally feel for their children, for example, is deep and genuine, but it is not always pure love. Mixed with it are feelings such as the need to feel loved and appreciated in return, the belief that their children are somehow part of them, a desire to impress other people through their children and the hope that their children will in some way fulfill their parents' ambitions and dreams. It is sometimes very difficult to distinguish between our love and our attachment for others, but when we are able to do so we will see that it is invariably the attachment that is the cause of our suffering. Pure unconditional love never causes any pain or worry but only peace and joy.

All the problems of human society, such as war, crime, pollution, drug addiction, poverty, injustice and disharmony within families, are the result of self-cherishing. Thinking that human beings alone matter, and that the natural world exists to serve human desires, we have wiped out thousands of animal species and polluted the planet to such an extent that there is great danger it could soon be unfit even for human habitation.

If everyone were to practice cherishing others, many of the major problems of the world would be solved in a few years.

Self-cherishing is like an iron chain that keeps us locked in samsara. The fundamental reason for our suffering is that we are in samsara, and we are in samsara because we continually create the deluded, self-centered actions that perpetuate the cycle of uncontrolled rebirth. Samsara is the experience of a self-centered mind. The six realms of samsara, from the god realm to the hell realm, are all the dream-like projections of a mind distorted by self-cherishing and self-grasping. By causing us to see life as a constant struggle to serve and protect our own I, these two minds impel us to perform innumerable destructive actions that keep us imprisoned in the nightmare of samsara. Until we destroy these two minds we will never know true freedom or happiness, we will never really be in control of our mind, and we will never be safe from the threat of lower rebirth.

Controlling our self-cherishing is of great value, even temporarily. All worries, anxiety and sadness are based on self-cherishing. The moment we let go of our obsessive concern for our own welfare, our mind naturally relaxes and becomes lighter. Even if we receive some bad news, if we manage to overcome our normal self-centered reaction our mind will remain at peace. On the other hand, if we fail to subdue our self-cherishing, even the most petty things disturb us. If a friend criticizes us we immediately become upset, and the frustration of even our smallest wishes leaves us dejected. If a Dharma Teacher says something we do not want to hear we may become upset with him or her, or even lose our faith. Many people can get very agitated just because a mouse comes into their room. Mice do not eat people, so what reason is there to become upset? It is only the foolish mind of self-cherishing that disturbs us. If we loved the mouse as much as we loved ourself we would welcome the mouse into our room, thinking, "He has as much right to be here as I do!"

For those who aspire to become enlightened, the worst fault is self-cherishing. Self-cherishing is the main obstacle to cherishing others, failing to cherish others is the main obstacle to developing great compassion, and failing to develop great compassion is the main obstacle to developing bodhichitta and entering the Mahayana path. Since bodhichitta is the main cause of great enlightenment, we can see that self-cherishing is also the main obstacle to the attainment of Buddhahood.

Although we might agree that objectively we are no more important than anyone else, and that self-cherishing has many faults, we may still feel that it is nevertheless indispensable. If we do not cherish and look after ourself, surely no one else will. This is a mistaken way of thinking. While it is true that we need to look after ourself, we do not need to be motivated by self-cherishing. Caring for ourself is not self-cherishing. We can take care of our health, have a job and look after our house and possessions solely out of concern for others' welfare. If we view our body as an instrument with which we can benefit others, we can feed it, clothe it, wash it and rest it—all without self-cherishing. Just as an ambulance driver can take care of his vehicle without regarding it as his own, so we can take care of our body and possessions for the benefit of others. The only way we can ever truly help all living beings is by becoming a Buddha, and the human form is the best possible vehicle for accomplishing this. Therefore we need to take good care of our body. If we do this with bodhichitta motivation, all our actions of caring for our body become part of the path to enlightenment.

We may sometimes confuse self-cherishing with self-confidence and self-respect, but in reality they are completely unrelated. It is not out of self-respect that we always want the best for ourself, nor is it out of self-respect that we deceive or exploit others or fail in our responsibilities to them. If we check honestly we will see that it is our self-cherishing that causes us to act in ways that rob us of our self-respect and destroy our confidence. Some people are driven by their self-cherishing to the depths of alcoholism or drug addiction, completely losing any modicum of self-respect in the process. On the other hand, the more we cherish others and act to benefit them the greater our self-respect and confidence will become. The Bodhisattva vow, for example, in which the Bodhisattva promises to overcome all faults and limitations, attain all good qualities and work until all living beings are liberated from the sufferings of samsara, is an expression of tremendous self-confidence, far beyond that of any self-centered being.

We might also ask, "If I had no self-cherishing, would that not mean that I dislike myself? Surely it is necessary to accept and love myself, because if I cannot love myself how can I love others?" This is an important point. In *Training the Mind in Seven Points* Geshe Chekhawa explains a number of commitments of training the mind, which serve as guidelines for practitioners of training the mind. The first of these states: "Do not allow your practice of training the mind to cause inappropriate behavior." This commitment advises such practitioners to be happy with themselves. If we are excessively self-critical we will turn in upon ourself and become discouraged, and this will make it very difficult for us to turn our mind to cherishing others. Although it is necessary to be aware of our faults, we should not hate ourself for them. This commitment also advises us to take care of ourself and look after our needs. If we try to live without basic necessities such as sufficient food and shelter we will probably damage our health and undermine our capacity to benefit others. In addition, if people see us behaving in an extreme way they may conclude that we are unbalanced, and consequently will not trust us or believe what we say; and under such circumstances we will not be able to help them. Abandoning self-cherishing completely is not easy and will take a long time. If we are not happy with ourself, or foolishly neglect our own well-being, we will have neither the confidence nor the energy to effect such a radical spiritual transformation.

Once we are free from self-cherishing we do not lose our wish to be happy, but we understand that real happiness is to be found in benefiting others. We have discovered an inexhaustible fountain of happiness within our own mind—our love for others. Difficult external conditions do not depress us, and pleasant conditions do not overexcite us, because we are able to transform and enjoy both. Rather than focusing on gathering good external conditions, our desire for happiness is channeled into a determination to attain enlightenment, which we recognize as the only means of achieving pure happiness. Though we long to enjoy the ultimate bliss of full enlightenment, we do so solely for the sake of others, because attaining enlightenment is merely the means to fulfill our real wish, which is to bestow the same happiness on all living beings. When we become a Buddha our happiness radiates eternally as compassion, nourishing all living beings and gradually drawing them into the same state.

In short, self-cherishing is an utterly worthless and unnecessary mind. We may be highly intelligent, but if we are concerned only with our own welfare we can never fulfill our basic wish to find happiness. In reality self-cherishing makes us stupid. It causes us to experience unhappiness in this life, leads us to perform countless negative actions that cause suffering in future lives, binds us to samsara and blocks the path to enlightenment. Cherishing others has the opposite effects. If we cherish only others we will be happy in this life, we will perform many virtuous actions that lead to happiness in future lives, we will become free from the delusions that keep us in samsara and we will quickly develop all the qualities needed to attain full enlightenment.

HOW TO DESTROY SELF-CHERISHING

By contemplating the faults of self-cherishing and the benefits of cherishing others we will develop a strong determination to abandon our self-cherishing and always cherish all living beings without exception. We should hold this determination in meditation for as long as possible. When we arise from meditation we should try to put our determination into practice and maintain it in all our activities. It is impossible to stop self-cherishing immediately, because it is such a deeply ingrained and all-pervasive mental habit that has been with us since beginningless time. However, through understanding its disadvantages and applying great effort we can slowly reduce it. We can stop the worst excesses of self-cherishing right now, and eliminate the more subtle types of self-cherishing gradually.

Having developed the intention to overcome our self-cherishing, the next step is to recognize it the moment it arises in our mind. To do this Geshe Langri Tangpa advises us to examine our mental continuum throughout all our actions. This means that we should practice like Geshe Ben Gungyal and watch our own mind, or mental continuum, in everything we do. Usually we keep an eye on what other people are doing, but it would be far better if we kept an eye on what is going on in our own mind. Whatever actions we are doing, whether working, talking, relaxing or studying Dharma, one part of our mind should always be watching to check what thoughts are arising. As soon as a delusion is about to arise we should try to stop it. If we catch a delusion in its early stages it is quite easy to stop, but if we allow it to develop fully it becomes very difficult to control.

One of our most destructive delusions is anger. Since it is so harmful in our daily life, I give further instructions on how we can deal with the problem of anger in the book *How to Solve Our Human Problems*. The reason we get angry is that we allow our mind to remain on an object that is likely to stimulate anger. If we catch our mind as soon as it starts to focus on such an object it is quite easy to prevent anger from arising and to channel our thoughts in a more constructive direction. All we need to do is say to ourself: "This is an inappropriate way of thinking and will soon give rise to anger, which has many faults." However, if we fail to catch the anger early on, and allow it to grow, it will soon become like a raging fire that is very difficult to extinguish. The same is true of all other delusions, including self-cherishing. If we become aware of a selfish train of thought early on we can easily avert it, but if we allow it to continue it will gather momentum until it becomes almost impossible to stop.

There are three levels of abandoning delusions. The first is to recognize a particular delusion as it is about to arise, and remembering its disadvantages, to prevent it from manifesting. As long as we keep a watch over our mind this is quite straightforward, and is something we should try to practice all the time, whatever we are doing. In particular, as soon as we notice that our mind is becoming tense or unhappy we should be especially vigilant, for such a mind is a perfect breeding ground for delusions. For this reason, in *Training the Mind in Seven Points* Geshe Chekhawa says: "Always rely upon a happy mind alone."

The second level of abandoning our delusions is to subdue them by applying their specific opponents. For example, to subdue our attachment we can meditate on the faults of samsara and replace our attachment with the opposite mind of renunciation. Through meditating on the stages of the path to enlightenment, or Lamrim, and training the mind, or Lojong, in a regular, systematic way we not only prevent deluded patterns of thinking and feeling from arising, but we also replace them with strong and stable virtuous patterns, based on wisdom rather than ignorance. In this way we can prevent most delusions from arising in the first place. For instance, through deep familiarity with the view that others are more important than ourself, self-cherishing will rarely arise.

The third level of abandoning our delusions is to abandon them completely, together with their seeds, by gaining a direct realization of emptiness. In this way we destroy self-grasping, which is the root of all delusions.

As mentioned before, in the first two verses Langri Tangpa principally explains the practice of equalizing self and others, in which we learn to cherish others as much as ourself. We think, "Just as my happiness is important, so too is the happiness of everyone else," and in this way we share our feeling of cherishing. Because this appeals to our sense of fairness and does not directly challenge our self-cherishing mind it is easier to accept and practice. We can also reflect that no matter how much we may suffer we are only one single person whereas other living beings are countless, so it is obviously important for them to experience at least some peace and happiness. Although we regard each of our fingers and thumbs as precious, we would be prepared to sacrifice one to save the other nine, whereas sacrificing nine to save one would be absurd. Similarly, nine people are more important than one, so of course countless living beings are more important than one self alone. It follows that it is logical to cherish others at least as much as we cherish ourself.

Having gained some familiarity with the practice of equalizing self and others we are ready to confront the self-cherishing mind more directly, and in the third verse Langri Tangpa urges us to do just this. With the words "Whereby I or others would act inappropriately" he explains how our self-cherishing not only causes us to act inappropriately, but also causes others to act in non-virtuous ways by disturbing their minds and setting a bad example. Because self-cherishing has so many faults, Langri Tangpa encourages us to "firmly face it and avert it" the moment it arises in our mind.

Tilopa

By keeping a close watch over our mind all the time, we can train ourself to recognize self-cherishing the moment it arises and then immediately recall its disadvantages. Geshe Chekhawa advises us to "Gather all blame into one," by which he means that we should blame self-cherishing for all our problems and suffering. Normally when things go wrong we blame others, but the real cause of our problems is our self-cherishing mind. Once we have correctly identified self-cherishing we should regard it as our worst enemy and blame it for all our suffering. Although it is good to be tolerant of others and to forgive their weaknesses, we should never tolerate our self-cherishing, because the more lenient we are with it the more it will harm us. It is far better to be utterly ruthless and blame it for everything that goes wrong. If we want to be angry with something we should be angry with the "demon" of our self-cherishing. In reality, anger directed against self-cherishing is not real anger, because it is based on wisdom rather than ignorance and functions to make our mind pure and peaceful.

To practice in this way we need to be very skillful. If as a result of blaming our self-cherishing for all our problems we find ourself feeling guilty and inadequate, this indicates that we have not made a clear distinction between blaming our self-cherishing and blaming ourself. Although it is true that self-cherishing is to blame for all our problems, this does not mean that we ourself are to blame. Once again, we have to learn to distinguish between ourself and our delusions. If we are attacked it is not our fault but the fault of our self-cherishing. Why? Because it is the karmic effect of a non-virtuous action we performed in a previous life under the influence of self-cherishing. Moreover, our attacker harms us only because of his or her self-cherishing, and blaming him will not help, because it will only make us bitter. However, if we place all the blame on our self-cherishing mind and resolve to destroy it, we will not only remain undisturbed but also undermine the basis for all our future suffering.

This teaching on recognizing the faults of our self-cherishing and subsequently developing the desire to overcome it is not easy to put into practice, and so we need to be patient. A practice that is suitable for one person is not necessarily suitable for someone else, and a practice that is appropriate for one person at one time is not necessarily appropriate for that same person at another time. Buddha did not expect us to put all his teachings into practice right away; they are intended for a great variety of practitioners of different levels and dispositions. There are also some instructions that cannot be practiced while we are emphasizing other practices, just as it is not appropriate to drink tea and coffee together at the same time. Dharma instructions are like medicine and need to be administered skillfully, taking into account the nature of the individual and his or her particular needs. For example, to encourage us to develop renunciation, the wish to attain liberation from samsara, Buddha gave extensive teachings on how ordinary life is in the nature of suffering—but not everyone can apply these teachings right away. For some people, meditating on suffering only causes them to become despondent. Instead of developing a joyful mind of renunciation, they just get depressed. For these people it is better for the time being not to meditate on suffering but to come back to it later when their minds are stronger and their wisdom clearer.

If we practice advanced teachings and find that our pride or confusion increase, this indicates that we are not yet ready for such teachings and should first emphasize building a firm foundation of basic practices. If any meditation or practice is not having a good effect on our mind, is making us unhappy, or is increasing our delusions, this is a clear sign that we are practicing incorrectly. Rather than stubbornly pushing at the practice it may be better to put it to one side for the time being and seek advice from senior practitioners. We can go back to that practice once we understand where we are going wrong and what the correct way of practicing is. What we should never do, however, is reject any Dharma instruction by thinking, "I will never practice this."

When we go shopping we do not feel impelled to buy everything in the shop, but it is useful to remember what the shop stocks so that we can return later when we need something. In a similar way, when we listen to Dharma teachings we may not immediately be able to practice all that we hear, but it is still important to remember everything so that we can build up a comprehensive understanding of Dharma. Later, when we are ready, we can put the instructions we have heard into practice. One of the great advantages of Lamrim, or the stages of the path to enlightenment, is that it gives us a structure, or storehouse, within which we can keep all the Dharma we have heard.

If we remember only those teachings that we are immediately able to apply in our present situation, when our circumstances change we will have nothing to fall back on. However, if we can remember all the teachings we have received we will have at our disposal a huge range of instructions that we can apply at the appropriate time. A practice that may seem obscure and of little significance to us now may later become an essential part of our spiritual practice. What is important is to proceed carefully and at our own pace, otherwise we might feel confused or discouraged, and may even end up rejecting Dharma altogether.

There is no greater spiritual practice than recognizing self-cherishing whenever it arises and then blaming it for all our problems. It does not matter how long we spend on this; even if it takes years or our whole life, we need to continue until our self-cherishing is completely destroyed. We should not be in a hurry to see results, but instead practice patiently and sincerely. Expecting quick results is itself based on self-cherishing and is a recipe for disappointment. If we practice with joy and steadfastness, while at the same time purifying negativity, accumulating merit and receiving blessings, we will definitely succeed in reducing and finally abandoning our self-cherishing.

Even when our meditation is not going well we can practice mindfulness and alertness in our daily life and stop self-cherishing as soon as it arises. This is a simple practice but it has great results. If we train in it continuously our problems will disappear and we will naturally be happy all the time. There are people who have succeeded in completely abandoning their self-cherishing and who now cherish only others. As a result all their problems have disappeared and their minds are always filled with joy. I guarantee that the less you cherish yourself and the more you cherish others the happier you will become.

We should keep a strong determination in our heart to abandon our self-cherishing mind. If we apply armor-like effort in this determination day by day, year by year, our self-cherishing will gradually diminish and eventually cease altogether. The early

Kadampas would often say that to lead a virtuous life all we need to do is harm our delusions as much as possible and benefit others as much as possible. Understanding this, we should wage continuous warfare against our inner enemy of self-cherishing and strive to cherish and benefit others instead.

To destroy our self-cherishing completely we need to rely upon the practice of exchanging self with others, in which we no longer grasp at our own happiness but instead feel that all living beings, and their needs and wishes, are of supreme importance. Our only concern is for the well-being of others.

Although someone who has completely exchanged himself with others has no self-cherishing, this does not mean that he does not look after himself. He does look after himself, but for the sake of others. He regards himself as a servant of all living beings and as belonging to them; but even servants need to eat and rest if they are to be effective. It would generally be very foolish, for example, if we were to give away all we owned, leaving ourself with nothing to live on or to sustain our spiritual practice. Since our real wish is to benefit all living beings, and the only way we can do this is by becoming a Buddha, we need to protect our spiritual practice by organizing our life so that we are able to practice in the most effective way. In addition, when we help others we should also make sure that in helping one person we are not undermining our capacity to help many people. Although in our hearts we would gladly give away everything we have to help one person, practically we need to manage our time and resources so that we can be of the greatest benefit to all living beings.

The practice of exchanging self with others belongs to the special wisdom lineage that came from Buddha

Shakyamuni through Manjushri and Shantideva to Atisha and the Kadampa Geshes. The bodhichitta that is developed through this method is more profound and powerful than the bodhichitta developed through other methods. Although everyone with an interest in spiritual development can reduce their self-cherishing and learn to cherish others, a complete realization of exchanging self with others is a very profound attainment. To transform our mind in such a radical way we need deep faith in this practice, an abundance of merit and powerful blessings from a Spiritual Guide who has personal experience of these teachings. With all these conducive conditions the practice of exchanging self with others is not difficult.

We may wonder why it is necessary to cherish others more than ourself. Rather than aiming for such high spiritual realizations, would it not be better just to emphasize helping people in a practical way right now? The reason why we need to train our mind in exchanging self with others is because our self-cherishing interferes with both our intention and our ability to benefit others. With self-cherishing we do not have unbiased, universal love for all living beings, and for as long as our desire to help them is mixed with self-cherishing we can never be sure that our actions will actually benefit them. Although we may genuinely want to help some people, such as our family, our friends or those in need, we usually expect something back in return and are hurt and disappointed if we do not receive it. Since our wish to benefit is mixed with selfish concerns, our help nearly always comes with the strings of expectation or personal reward. Because our intention is impure, our ability to help lacks power and remains limited.

If while making no effort to eliminate our self-cherishing we claim to be working for the benefit of all, our claim is coming from our mouth and not from our heart. Of course we should help others practically whenever we can, but we should always remember that our main intention is to develop our mind. By training in exchanging self with others we will finally experience the ultimate happiness of Buddhahood and possess complete power to benefit all living beings. Only then will we be in a position to say, "I am a benefactor of all living beings." In this way our training in exchanging self with others accomplishes both our own and others' purpose.

Our most important task at the moment is to train our mind, and in particular to strengthen our intention to be of service to others. In his *Friendly Letter* Nagarjuna says that although we may not have the ability to help others now, if we keep the intention to do so in mind all the time, our ability to help them will gradually increase. This is because the more we cherish others, the more our merit, wisdom and capacity to actually benefit them will increase, and opportunities to help in practical ways will naturally present themselves.

HOW IS IT POSSIBLE TO EXCHANGE SELF WITH OTHERS?

Exchanging self with others does not mean that we become the other person—it means that we exchange the object of our cherishing from ourself to others. To understand how this is possible we should understand that the object of our self-cherishing mind is always changing. When we are young the object of our self-cherishing is a young girl or boy, but later it changes to a teenager, then to a middle-aged person and finally to an old person. At the moment we may cherish ourself as a particular human being called Maria or John, but after we die the object of our cherishing will completely change. In this way the object of our cherishing is continually changing both during this life and from one life to the next. Since our cherishing naturally changes from one object to another, it is definitely possible through training in meditation for us to change the object of our cherishing from ourself to others.

Due to our ignorance we grasp at our body very strongly, thinking, "This is my body." Identifying with this body as "mine," we cherish and love it dearly, feeling it to be our most precious possession. In reality, however, our body belongs to others; we did not bring it with us from our previous life but received it from our parents of this life. At the moment of conception our consciousness entered into the union of our father's sperm and mother's ovum, which gradually developed into our present body. Our mind then identified with this body and we began to cherish it. As Shantideva says in *Guide to the Bodhisattva's Way of Life*, our body is not really our own but belongs to others; it was produced by others, and after our death will be disposed of by others. If we contemplate this carefully we will realize that we are already cherishing an object that in reality belongs to others, so why can we not cherish other living beings? Furthermore, while cherishing our body only leads to rebirth within samsara, cherishing others is a cause for attaining nirvana, the state beyond sorrow.

"Self" and "other" are relative terms, similar to "this mountain" and "that mountain" but not like "donkey" and "horse." When we look at a horse we cannot say that it is a donkey, and likewise we cannot say that a donkey is a horse. However, if we climb a mountain in the east we call it "this mountain" and we call the mountain to the west "that mountain"; but if we climb down the eastern mountain and up the western mountain, we then refer to the western mountain as "this mountain" and to the eastern mountain as "that mountain." "This" and "that" therefore depend upon our point of reference. This is also true of self and other. By climbing down the mountain of self it is possible to ascend the mountain of other, and thereby cherish others as much as we presently cherish ourself. We can do this by recognizing that from another person's point of view, it is he or she who is self whereas it is we who are other.

Those who are skilled in Secret Mantra, or Tantra, have a profound experience of exchanging self with others. In the Tantric practice of self-generation we exchange our present self with that of a Tantric Buddha. Suppose there is a Vajrayogini practitioner called Sarah. Whenever she is not engaged in Tantric practice her ordinary body appears to her and she identifies with it and cherishes it. When she concentrates deeply on self-generation meditation, however, the sense of being Sarah and having Sarah's body completely disappears. Instead of identifying with Sarah's body, the practitioner identifies with the divine body of Buddha Vajrayogini and develops the thought, "I am Vajrayogini." The practitioner has now entirely changed the object of cherishing from the impure body of an ordinary being to the uncontaminated body of an enlightened being, Buddha Vajrayogini. Through training in meditation the practitioner develops deep familiarity with the body of the Deity and comes to identify with it completely. Because Vajrayogini's body is a pure body, identifying with it and cherishing it is a cause of enlightenment. From this we can see that it is possible to change our basis of identification—it just depends upon our motivation and our familiarity.

THE ACTUAL PRACTICE OF
EXCHANGING SELF WITH OTHERS

When we meditate on exchanging self with others we can begin by reflecting on the following verse from *Offering to the Spiritual Guide*:

Since cherishing myself is the door to all faults
And cherishing mother beings is the foundation of all
     good qualities,
I seek your blessings to take as my essential practice
The yoga of exchanging self with others.

We can also contemplate Shantideva's advice where he asks us to compare our situation with that of the Buddhas:

The childish work only for themselves,
Whereas the Buddhas work only for others—
Just look at the difference between them!

The "childish" are ordinary beings who, motivated by self-cherishing, work for their own welfare and experience only suffering in return. By contrast, Buddhas have abandoned self-cherishing and work solely for the benefit of others, and consequently enjoy the bliss of full enlightenment. We think:

I have worked for my own purpose since beginningless time,
trying to find happiness for myself and avoid suffering, but
what do I have to show for all my efforts? I am still suffering.
I still have an uncontrolled mind. I still experience

disappointment after disappointment. I am still in samsara. This is the fault of my self-cherishing. It is my worst enemy and a terrible poison that harms both myself and others.

Cherishing others, however, is the basis of all happiness and goodness. Those who are now Buddhas saw the futility of working for their own purpose and decided to work for others instead. As a result they became pure beings, free from all the problems of samsara, and they attained the lasting happiness of full enlightenment. I must reverse my ordinary childish attitude—from now on I will stop cherishing myself and cherish only others.

With an understanding of the great disadvantages of cherishing ourself and the great advantages of cherishing all living beings, as explained above, and remembering that we have made the determination to abandon our self-cherishing and always cherish all living beings without exception, we think from the depths of our heart:

I must give up cherishing myself and instead cherish all other living beings without exception.

We then meditate on this determination. We should continually practice this meditation until we spontaneously believe that the happiness and freedom of each and every other living being are far more important than our own. This belief is the realization of exchanging self with others, and will give rise to a deep feeling of cherishing love for all living beings. We meditate on this feeling for as long as we can.

We try to carry this feeling with us during the meditation break. Whoever we meet, we think, "This person is important.

Their happiness and freedom are important." Whenever self-cherishing begins to arise in our mind, we think, "Self-cherishing is poison; I will not allow it in my mind." In this way we can change our object of cherishing from ourself to all living beings. When we have developed a love for all living beings that does not have even the slightest trace of self-concern, we have gained the realization of exchanging self with others.

If our wishes are not fulfilled and we begin to feel unhappy, we should immediately remember that the fault lies not with the other person or the situation but with our own self-cherishing mind, which instinctively feels, "My wishes are of paramount importance." Remaining continually mindful of the dangers of our self-cherishing will strengthen our resolve to abandon it, and instead of feeling sorry for ourself when we have problems, we can use our own suffering to remind us of the suffering of countless mother beings and develop love and compassion for them.

In *Guide to the Bodhisattva's Way of Life,* Shantideva explains a special method to enhance our experience of exchanging self with others. In meditation we imagine that we exchange places with another person, and we try to see the world from his or her point of view. Normally we develop the thought "I" on the basis of our own body and mind, but now we try to think "I" observing the body and mind of another person. This practice helps us to develop a profound empathy with other people, and shows us that they have a self that is also an I, and that is just as important as our own self or I. Because of her ability to identify with the feelings of her baby, a mother is able to understand her child's needs and wishes far better than other people. Similarly, as we become familiar with this meditation our understanding of and empathy with other people will increase.

This technique is particularly powerful when we apply it to someone with whom we have a difficult relationship, such as someone we dislike or see as our rival. By imagining we are that person, and seeing the situation from his or her point of view, we will find it difficult to hold onto our deluded attitudes. Understanding the relativity of self and other from our own experience, and learning to see our "self" as "other," we will become far more objective and impartial toward ourself, and our sense that we are the center of the universe will be shaken. We will become more open to others' point of view, more tolerant and more understanding; and we will naturally treat others with greater respect and consideration. More details on this practice are given in the book *Meaningful to Behold*.

In summary, through practicing the instructions on training the mind Bodhisattva Langri Tangpa and countless other practitioners of the past have attained profound spiritual realizations, including the complete realization of exchanging self with others. At the beginning these practitioners were self-centered people just like us, but through constant perseverance they managed to eliminate their self-cherishing completely. If we practice these instructions wholeheartedly and patiently there is no reason why we too should not attain similar realizations. We should not expect to destroy our self-cherishing immediately, but through patient practice it will gradually become weaker and weaker until it eventually ceases altogether. The complete eradication of self-cherishing is an uncommon Mahayana realization that can only be accomplished through the practice of exchanging self with others.

Naropa

Great Compassion

Whenever I see unfortunate beings
Oppressed by evil and violent suffering,
May I cherish them as if I had found
A rare and precious treasure.

Having gained some experience of cherishing all living beings we can now extend and deepen our compassion, and the method for doing so is revealed in this verse. In general, everyone already has some compassion. We all feel compassion when we see our family or friends in distress, and even animals feel compassion when they see their offspring in pain. Our compassion is our Buddha seed or Buddha nature, our potential to become a Buddha. It is because all living beings possess this seed that they will all eventually become Buddhas.

When a dog sees her puppies in pain she develops the wish to protect them and free them from pain, and this compassionate wish is her Buddha seed. Unfortunately, however, animals have no ability to train in compassion, and so their Buddha seed cannot ripen. Human beings, though, have a great opportunity to develop their Buddha nature. Through meditation we can extend and deepen our compassion until it transforms into the mind of universal, or great, compassion—the sincere wish to liberate all living beings from suffering permanently. Through improving this mind of universal compassion it will eventually transform into the compassion of a Buddha, which actually has the power to liberate all living beings. Therefore the way to become a Buddha is to awaken our compassionate Buddha nature and complete the training in universal compassion. Only human beings can do this.

Compassion is the very essence of Buddhadharma, and the main practice of a Mahayana Buddhist. It is the root of the Three Supreme Jewels—Buddha, Dharma and Sangha. It is the root of Buddha because all Buddhas are born from compassion. It is the root of Dharma because Buddhas give Dharma teachings motivated solely by compassion for others. It is the root of Sangha because it is by listening to and practicing Dharma teachings given out of compassion that we become Sangha, or Superior beings.

WHAT IS COMPASSION?

What exactly is compassion? Compassion is a mind that is motivated by cherishing other living beings and wishes to release them from their suffering. Sometimes out of selfish intention we can wish for another person to be free from their suffering; this is quite common in relationships that are based principally on attachment. If our friend is ill or depressed, for example, we may wish for him to recover quickly so that we can enjoy his company again; but this wish is basically self-centered and is not true compassion. True compassion is necessarily based on cherishing others.

Although we already have some degree of compassion, at present it is very biased and limited. When our family and friends are suffering we easily develop compassion for them, but we find it far more difficult to feel sympathy for people we find unpleasant or for strangers. Furthermore, we feel compassion for those who are experiencing manifest pain, but not for those who are enjoying good conditions, and especially not for those who are engaging in harmful actions. If we genuinely want to realize our potential by attaining full enlightenment we need to increase the scope of our compassion until it embraces all living beings without exception, just as a loving mother feels compassion for all her children regardless of whether they are behaving well or badly. This universal compassion is the heart of Mahayana Buddhism. Unlike our present limited compassion, which already arises naturally from time to time, universal compassion must be cultivated deliberately in meditation over a long period of time.

HOW TO DEVELOP COMPASSION

There are two essential stages to cultivating universal compassion. First we need to love all living beings, and then, on the basis of cherishing others, we need to contemplate their suffering. If we do not love someone we cannot develop real compassion for him even if he is in pain, but if we contemplate the suffering of someone we love, compassion will arise spontaneously. This is why we feel compassion for our friends or relatives but not for people we do not like. It is because cherishing others is the foundation for developing compassion that Bodhisattva Langri Tangpa says, "May I cherish them," rather than, "May I develop compassion for them." The way to develop and enhance our mind of cherishing love has already been explained. Now we must consider how each and every samsaric being is experiencing suffering.

To begin with we can think about those who are suffering intense manifest pain right now. There are so many people experiencing terrible mental and physical suffering from illnesses such as cancer, AIDS and Parkinson's disease. How many people have lost a beloved child or friend through the scourge of cancer, watching him become weaker and weaker, knowing that it is difficult to cure? Every day thousands of people experience the agony of dying from illnesses or in accidents. Without choice they are separated forever from everyone they love, and those they leave behind often experience inconsolable grief and loneliness. Imagine an old woman losing her husband and lifelong partner, sadly returning home after the funeral to an empty house to live out the rest of her days alone.

Throughout the world we can see how millions of people are suffering through the horrors of war and ethnic cleansing, from bombing, landmines and massacres. Suppose it was your child who went out to play in the fields and lost a limb, or even his very life, by stepping on a landmine. Hundreds of thousands of refugees throughout the world live in squalid camps, hoping someday to return to their ruined homes, many of them waiting to be reunited with their loved ones, every day not knowing if they are alive or dead.

Every year natural disasters such as floods, earthquakes and hurricanes devastate whole communities and leave people homeless and hungry. A few short seconds of an earthquake can kill thousands of people, destroy their homes and bury everything under tons of rubble. Think how we would feel if this were to happen to us. Famine and drought are endemic in many countries throughout the world. So many people live on a subsistence diet, barely scraping together one meager meal a day, while others who are less fortunate succumb and die of starvation. Imagine the torment of watching your loved ones slowly waste away, knowing that there is nothing you can do. Whenever we read a newspaper or watch the news on television we see living beings who are in terrible pain, and we all personally know people who are experiencing immense mental or physical suffering.

We can also consider the plight of countless animals who experience extremes of heat and cold, and suffer great hunger and thirst. Every day, all around us, we can see the suffering of animals. Animals in the wild are in almost constant fear of being prey to others, and in fact many of them are eaten alive by predators. Just think of the terror and pain a field mouse experiences when caught and ripped to shreds by a hawk! Countless animals are kept by humans for labor, food or entertainment and often live in disgusting conditions until they are slaughtered, butchered and packaged for human consumption. Hungry spirits and hell beings have to experience far worse sufferings for inconceivably long periods of time.

We also need to remember that even those who are not presently experiencing manifest pain still experience other forms of suffering. Everyone in samsara experiences the suffering of not fulfilling their wishes. So many people find it difficult to satisfy even modest desires for adequate shelter, food or companionship; and even if those desires are fulfilled we have more to take their place. The more we get what we want the stronger our attachment becomes, and the stronger our attachment the more difficult it is to find satisfaction. The desires of samsaric beings are endless. There is no such thing as an ordinary person who has fulfilled all his or her wishes; only those who have transcended selfish minds can do this.

All suffering is the result of negative karma. If we develop compassion for those who are experiencing the effects of their previous negative actions, why can we not also develop compassion for those who are creating the cause to experience suffering in the future? In the long term a torturer is in a worse position than his victim, for his suffering is just beginning. If the victim can accept his or her pain without developing hatred, he will exhaust that particular negative karma and not create any more; and so his suffering has an end in sight. The torturer, on the other hand, will first have to endure many eons in hell, and then, when he is again reborn as a human being, will have to experience pain similar to that which he inflicted on the victim. For this reason it is entirely appropriate to develop strong compassion for such people.

If a child burns himself by putting his hand in a fire, this will not stop his mother from feeling compassion, even if the child has been previously warned about the dangers of fire. No one wants to suffer, yet out of ignorance living beings create the causes of suffering—non-virtuous actions—because they are controlled by their delusions. We should therefore feel equal compassion for all living beings—for those who are creating the causes of suffering, as much as for those who are already suffering the consequences of their unskillful actions. There is not a single living being who is not a suitable object of our compassion.

We may also find it difficult to feel compassion for the rich, healthy and well respected, who do not appear to be experiencing any manifest pain. In reality, however, they too experience a great deal of mental suffering and find it hard to maintain a peaceful mind. They worry about their money, their bodies and their reputation. Like all other samsaric beings they suffer from anger, attachment and ignorance, and have no choice but to undergo the sufferings of birth, aging, sickness and death unceasingly and relentlessly, life after life. In addition, their wealth and good conditions are utterly meaningless if through their ignorance they use them only to create the cause for future suffering.

If, on the basis of cherishing all living beings, we contemplate the fact that they experience the cycle of physical suffering and mental pain in life after life without end, their inability to liberate themselves from suffering, their lack of freedom and how, by engaging in negative actions, they create the causes of future suffering, we will develop deep compassion for them. We need to empathize with them and feel their pain as keenly as we feel our own.

All living beings suffer because they take contaminated rebirths. Human beings have no choice but to experience immense human sufferings because they have taken human rebirth, which is contaminated by the inner poison of delusions. Similarly, animals have to experience animal suffering, and hungry spirits and hell beings have to experience all the sufferings of their respective realms. If living beings were to experience all this suffering for just one single life it would not be so bad, but the cycle of suffering continues life after life, endlessly.

To begin with we can contemplate the suffering of our family and close friends, and then we can extend our mind of compassion until it embraces all living beings. When this feeling of universal compassion arises we mix our mind with it and try to hold it for as long as we can. In this way we can familiarize our mind with great compassion. At first we will probably only be able to hold this feeling for a few minutes, but gradually through training we will be able to maintain it for longer and longer periods until it arises spontaneously day and night and permeates all our thoughts. From that point on everything we do will bring us closer to enlightenment, and our whole life will become meaningful.

In summary, we should think:

I cannot bear the suffering of these countless mother beings. Drowning in the vast and deep ocean of samsara, the cycle of contaminated rebirth, they have to experience unbearable physical suffering and mental pain in this life and in countless future lives. I must permanently liberate all these living beings from their suffering.

We should meditate continually on this determination, which is universal compassion, and apply great effort to fulfilling its aim.

THE INNER WEALTH OF COMPASSION

When we arise from meditation we try to carry our feeling of compassion into the meditation break. Whenever we encounter anyone we should recall how they are suffering and develop compassion for them. Then just seeing a living being will be, in Langri Tangpa's words, like finding "a rare and precious treasure." This is because the compassion we experience upon meeting others is a supreme inner wealth that is an inexhaustible source of benefit for us in both this and future lives.

As mentioned earlier, external wealth cannot help us in our future lives, and even in this life it is not certain that it will bring us happiness for it is often the cause of much anxiety and can even endanger our life. Rich people have particular worries that poor people never have. For example, they often worry about thieves, about investments and interest rates and about losing their money and social status. This is a heavy burden for them. While most people can go out freely whenever they choose, many wealthy and famous people need bodyguards and may even worry about being kidnapped. Rich people have little freedom or independence and can never fully relax. The higher up we are in the world the further we have to fall; it is safer to be nearer the bottom.

No matter how much we succeed in improving our external conditions, they can never bring us pure happiness nor provide real protection from suffering. True happiness cannot be found in this impure world. Instead of striving to obtain external wealth it would be far better if we sought the internal wealth of virtue, because unlike external wealth, this can never deceive us and will definitely bring us the peace and happiness we desire.

If we are skillful, friends can be like treasure chests, from whom we can obtain the precious wealth of love, compassion, patience and so forth. For our friends to function in this way, however, our love for them must be free from attachment. If our love for our friends is mixed with strong attachment it will be conditional upon their behaving in ways that please us, and as soon as they do something we disapprove of, our fondness for them may turn to anger. In fact, the most common objects of our anger are often our friends, not our enemies or strangers!

If we often get angry with our friends we are transforming them into maras. A mara, or obstructing demon, is someone or something that interferes with our spiritual practice. No one is a mara from his or her own side, but if we allow people to stimulate deluded minds in us, such as anger, strong attachment or self-cherishing, we transform them into maras for us. A mara does not need to have horns and a terrifying expression; someone who appears to be a good friend, who flatters us and leads us into meaningless activities, can be a greater obstacle to our spiritual practice. Whether our friends are precious treasures or maras depends entirely upon us; if we practice Dharma in a skillful way they can be like priceless jewels, but if our practice is mixed with the eight worldly concerns they can become maras.

We would be delighted to find a treasure chest buried beneath the ground or to win a large sum of money, and would consider ourself very fortunate. However, if we consider the deceptiveness of external wealth and the superiority of the inner wealth of virtue, how much more fortunate should we feel whenever we meet another living being, the potential source of limitless inner wealth? For sincere Mahayana practitioners, just seeing other living beings, speaking with them or merely thinking about them is like finding buried treasure. All their encounters with other people serve to enhance their compassion, and even everyday activities such as shopping or chatting with friends become causes of enlightenment.

Of all virtuous minds, compassion is supreme. Compassion purifies our mind, and when our mind is pure its objects also become pure. There are many accounts of spiritual practitioners who by developing strong compassion purified their minds of the negativity that had long been obstructing their spiritual progress. For example, Asanga, a great Buddhist Master who lived in India in the fifth century AD, meditated in an isolated mountain cave in order to gain a vision of Buddha Maitreya. After twelve years he still had not succeeded, and feeling discouraged, abandoned his retreat. On his way down the mountain he came across an old dog lying in the middle of the path. Its body was covered in maggot-infested sores, and it seemed close to death. This sight induced within Asanga an overwhelming feeling of compassion for all living beings trapped within samsara. As he was painstakingly removing the maggots from the dying dog, it suddenly transformed into Buddha Maitreya himself. Maitreya explained that he had been with Asanga since the beginning of his retreat, but due to the impurities in Asanga's mind, Asanga had not been able to see him. It was Asanga's extraordinary compassion that had finally purified the karmic obstructions preventing him from seeing Maitreya. In reality the dog had been an emanation of Buddha Maitreya all along—Maitreya emanated as a suffering dog for the purpose of arousing Asanga's compassion. We can see from this how Buddhas manifest in many different ways to help living beings.

Anyone who dies with a mind of pure compassion will definitely be reborn in a Pure Land, where he or she will never again have to experience the sufferings of samsara. The Bodhisattva Geshe Chekhawa's main wish was to be reborn in hell so that he could help the beings suffering there. However, as he lay on his deathbed he perceived a vision of the Pure Land and realized that his wish would not be fulfilled. Instead of being reborn in hell he had no choice but to go to the Pure Land! This was because his compassion had purified his mind to such an extent that from the point of view of his own experience impure objects such as hell realms no longer existed—for him everything was pure. However, although Geshe Chekhawa took rebirth in a Pure Land, he was able to help hell beings through his emanations.

We may find these stories difficult to believe, but this is because we do not understand the relationship between our mind and its objects. We feel that the world exists "out there," independent of the mind that perceives it; but in reality objects are totally dependent on the minds that perceive them. This impure world that we presently experience exists only in relation to our impure mind. Once we have completely purified our mind through training in exchanging self with others, compassion and so forth, this impure world will disappear and we will perceive a new, pure world. Our sense that things exist separately from our mind, with their own fixed, inherent natures, comes from our self-grasping ignorance. When we understand the true nature of things we will see that our world is like a dream, in that everything exists as a mere appearance to mind. We will realize that we can change our world simply by changing our mind, and that if we wish to be free from suffering all we need to do is purify our mind. Having purified our own mind we will then be in a position to fulfill our compassionate wish by showing others how to do the same.

Considering all these benefits of compassion we should resolve to make use of every opportunity to develop it. The most important thing is to put the teachings on compassion into practice, otherwise for us they will remain just empty words.

Pure compassion is a mind that finds the suffering of others unbearable, but it does not make us depressed. In fact it gives us tremendous energy to work for others and to complete the spiritual path for their sake. It shatters our complacency and makes it impossible to rest content with the superficial happiness of satisfying our worldly desires, yet in its place we will come to know a deep inner peace that cannot be disturbed by changing conditions. It is impossible for strong delusions to arise in a mind filled with compassion. If we do not develop delusions, external circumstances alone have no power to disturb us; so when our mind is governed by compassion it is always at peace. This is the experience of all those who have developed their compassion beyond the limited compassion normally felt for a close karmic circle into a selfless compassion for all living beings.

Developing compassion and wisdom, and helping those in need whenever possible, is the true meaning of life. By increasing our compassion we come closer to enlightenment and to the fulfillment of our deepest wishes. How kind living beings are to act as the objects of our compassion. How precious they are! If there were no suffering beings left for us to help, Buddhas would have to emanate them for us! Indeed, if we consider the story of Maitreya and Asanga we will see that we have no way of knowing for sure whether those we are presently trying to help are not in fact emanations of Buddha, manifested for our benefit. The indication that we have mastered the meditations on cherishing others and compassion is that whenever we meet another person, even someone who is harming us, we genuinely feel as if we have found a rare and precious treasure.

Atisha

Wishing Love

Even if someone I have helped
And of whom I had great hopes
Nevertheless harms me intentionally,
May I see him or her as my holy Spiritual Guide.

The main purpose of this verse is to teach us how to develop and improve our experience of wishing love. In general, there are three types of love: affectionate love, cherishing love and wishing love. Affectionate love is a mind unmixed with desirous attachment that sees another person as pleasant, likeable or beautiful. For example, when a mother looks at her children she feels great affection for them and perceives them to be beautiful, no matter how they appear to other people. Because of her affectionate love she naturally feels them to be precious and important; this feeling is cherishing love. Because she cherishes her children she sincerely wishes for them to be happy; this wish is wishing love. Wishing love arises from cherishing love, which in turn arises from affectionate love. We need to develop these three types of love toward all living beings without exception.

HOW TO DEVELOP WISHING LOVE

The way to develop and enhance our cherishing love has already been explained. Now we need to develop wishing love by contemplating how these living beings whom we cherish so dearly lack true happiness. Everyone wants to be happy, but no one in samsara experiences true happiness. In comparison with the amount of suffering they endure, the happiness of living beings is rare and fleeting, and even this is only a contaminated happiness that is in reality the nature of suffering. Buddha called the pleasurable feelings that result from worldly enjoyments "changing suffering" because they are simply the experience of a temporary reduction of manifest suffering. In other words, we experience pleasure due to the relief of our previous pain. For example, the pleasure we derive from eating is really just a temporary reduction of our hunger, the pleasure we derive from drinking is merely a temporary reduction of our thirst, and the pleasure we derive from ordinary relationships is for the most part merely a temporary reduction of our underlying loneliness.

In *Four Hundred Verses,* the Buddhist Master Aryadeva says:

> The experience of suffering will never be changed by
>   the same cause,
> But we can see the experience of happiness will be
>   changed by the same cause.

This means that, for example, the suffering caused by fire will never be changed into happiness by that fire, but we can see that the happiness caused, for example, by eating will change into suffering just through eating. How can we understand this? If we increase the cause of our worldly happiness, our happiness will gradually change into suffering. When we eat our favorite food it tastes wonderful, but if we were to continue eating plateful after plateful our enjoyment would soon change into discomfort, disgust and eventually pain. The reverse, however, does not happen with painful experiences. For instance, hitting our finger with a hammer again and again can never become pleasurable, because it is a true cause of suffering. Just as a true cause of suffering can never give rise to happiness, so a true cause of happiness can never give rise to pain. Since the pleasurable feelings resulting from worldly enjoyments do turn into pain, it follows that they cannot be real happiness. Prolonged indulgence in eating, sports, sex or any other ordinary enjoyment invariably leads to suffering. No matter how hard we try to find happiness in worldly pleasures we will never succeed. As mentioned before, indulging in samsaric pleasures is like drinking salt water; rather than satiating our thirst, the more we drink the thirstier we become. In samsara we never reach a point when we can say, "Now I am completely satisfied. I need nothing more."

Not only is worldly pleasure not true happiness, but it also does not last. People devote their lives to acquiring possessions and social standing, and building up a home, a family and a circle of friends; but when they die they lose everything. All they have worked for suddenly disappears, and they enter their next life alone and empty-handed. They long to form deep and lasting friendships with others, but in samsara this is impossible. The dearest lovers will eventually be torn apart, and when they meet again in a future life they will not recognize each other. We may feel that those who have good relationships and have fulfilled their ambitions in life are truly happy, but in reality their happiness is as fragile as a water bubble. Impermanence spares nothing and no one; in samsara all our dreams are broken in the end. As Buddha says in the *Vinaya Sutras*:

The end of collection is dispersion.
The end of rising is falling.
The end of meeting is parting.
The end of birth is death.

The nature of samsara is suffering, so for as long as living beings are reborn in samsara they can never experience true happiness. Buddha compared living in samsara to sitting on top of a pin—no matter how much we try to adjust our position it is always painful. Similarly, no matter how hard we try to adjust and improve our samsaric situation it will always irritate us and give rise to pain. True happiness can only be found by attaining liberation from samsara. Through contemplating this we will develop a heartfelt desire for all living beings to experience pure happiness by attaining liberation.

We should begin our meditation by focusing on our family and friends, reflecting that for as long as they remain in samsara they will never know true happiness, and that even the limited happiness they presently experience will soon be taken away from them. Then we extend this feeling of wishing love to include all living beings, and with the understanding and belief that the happiness and freedom of each and every living being are far more important than our own, we think:

How wonderful it would be if all living beings attained the pure and everlasting happiness of enlightenment! May they attain this happiness. I myself will work for this aim.

We remain single-pointedly on this precious mind of wishing love for all living beings for as long as possible. We repeat this meditation again and again until we spontaneously wish that each and every living being may experience the happiness of enlightenment. This spontaneous wish is the actual realization of wishing love.

We mix our mind with this feeling of wishing love for as long as possible. Out of meditation, whenever we see or remember any living being, human or animal, we mentally pray: "May they be happy all the time. May they attain the happiness of enlightenment." By constantly thinking in this way, we can maintain wishing love day and night, even during sleep.

Meditation on love is very powerful. Wishing love is also called "immeasurable love" because merely through meditating on wishing love we will receive immeasurable benefits in this life and in countless future lives, even if our concentration is not very strong. Based on Buddha's teachings, the great scholar Nagarjuna listed eight benefits of affectionate love and wishing love: (1) By meditating on affectionate love and wishing love for just one moment we accumulate greater merit than we would by giving food three times every day to all those who are hungry in the world.

When we give food to those who are hungry we are not giving real happiness. This is because the happiness that comes from eating food is not real happiness, but just a temporary reduction in the suffering of hunger. However, meditation on affectionate love and wishing love leads us and all living beings to the pure and everlasting happiness of enlightenment.

The remaining seven benefits of meditating on affectionate love and wishing love are that in the future: (2) we will receive great loving kindness from humans and non-humans; (3) we will be protected in various ways by humans and non-humans; (4) we will be mentally happy all the time; (5) we will be physically healthy all the time; (6) we will not be harmed by weapons, poison and other harmful conditions; (7) we will obtain all necessary conditions without effort; and (8) we will be born in the superior heaven of a Buddha Land.

Having contemplated these benefits we should apply effort in meditating on wishing love many times every day.

Love is the great protector, protecting us from anger and jealousy, and from harm inflicted by spirits. When Buddha Shakyamuni was meditating under the Bodhi Tree he was attacked by all the terrifying demons of this world, but his love transformed their weapons into a rain of flowers. Ultimately our love will become the universal love of a Buddha, which actually has the power to bestow happiness on all living beings.

Most relationships between people are based on a mixture of love and attachment. This is not pure love because it is based on a desire for our own happiness—we value the other person because they make us feel good. Pure love is unmixed with attachment and stems entirely from a concern for others' happiness. It never gives rise to problems but only to peace and happiness for both ourself and others. We need to remove attachment from our minds, but this does not mean that we have to abandon our relationships. Instead, we should learn to distinguish attachment from love, and gradually try to remove all traces of attachment from our relationships and to improve our love until it becomes pure.

TRANSFORMING ADVERSE CONDITIONS

When things are going well, and people are kind and treating us with respect, it is not so difficult to wish for them to be happy. However, if our love for others diminishes as soon as they cause us problems or fail to appreciate us, this indicates that our love is not pure. For as long as our good feelings for others are conditional upon their treating us well, our love will be weak and unstable and we will not be able to transform it into universal love. It is inevitable that people will sometimes respond to our kindness in ungrateful and negative ways, and so it is essential that we find a way of transforming this experience into the spiritual path.

When someone we have helped repays our kindness by harming us, instead of getting angry we should try to see that person as a Spiritual Teacher and generate a mind of gratitude toward him or her. Explicitly this verse mentions only those whom we have benefited in the hope that our help would bring wholesome results, both for them and for others, but implicitly it includes anyone who harms us. There are various lines of reasoning we can use to develop this special recognition. We can think:

The only reason people harm me is because I have created the cause for them to do so through my previous negative actions. These people are teaching me about the law of karma. By deceiving me and repaying my help with harm they are reminding me that in the past I deceived and harmed others. They are betraying me only because I betrayed them or others in previous lives. They are encouraging me to purify my negative karma and to refrain from harmful actions in the future. How kind they are! They must be my Spiritual Guide, emanated by Buddha Amitabha.

By thinking in this way, we transform a situation that would normally give rise to anger or self-pity into a powerful lesson in the need for purification and moral discipline.

Alternatively we can think:

This experience shows me that there is no certainty in samsara. Everything changes. Friends become enemies and enemies become friends. Why is this? It is because in samsara everyone is controlled by their delusions and no one has any freedom. This situation is encouraging me to abandon samsaric rebirth, so instead of getting angry or discouraged I must abandon samsaric rebirth and generate the joyful mind of renunciation—a sincere wish to attain the permanent inner peace of liberation. I pray that I may attain liberation from samsara, and that all living beings may attain the same state.

By following this line of reasoning we view the person who is treating us unkindly as a Spiritual Teacher who is encouraging us to leave samsara and experience pure happiness. This skillful way of viewing our difficulty transforms it into an opportunity to progress on the spiritual path. Since this person is teaching us a profound lesson about the nature of samsara, and having such a beneficial effect on our mind, he or she is supremely kind.

We can also think:

This person who is harming or disturbing me is in reality encouraging me to practice patience; and since it is impossible to make progress on the spiritual path without developing the strong mind of patience, he or she is of great benefit to me.

Patience is a mind motivated by a virtuous intention that happily accepts difficulties and harm from others. A person with no patience has no stability of mind, and is upset by the slightest obstacle or criticism. In contrast, when we develop real patience our mind will be as stable as a mountain and as calm as the depths of an ocean. With such a calm, strong mind it will not be difficult to perfect the spiritual realizations of universal love, great compassion and bodhichitta.

By thinking skillfully in these ways, we can regard even those who harm or deceive us as our Spiritual Teachers. This is a very important point because it means that everyone can be our Teacher. Whether someone is our Spiritual Teacher or an obstacle to our spiritual progress depends entirely upon our mind. In many ways, those who harm us are the kindest of all because they shatter our complacent view that sees samsara as a pleasure garden, and, like a powerful Spiritual Guide, they inspire us to engage more strongly in spiritual practice. By thinking in this way we can transform the harm we receive into the spiritual path, and instead of being discouraged we can learn to cherish even those who harm us. It is especially important to have this attitude toward our close friends and family. Since we spend so much time with them, it would be very beneficial if we were to regard them as pure Spiritual Teachers!

We have great expectations of our friends, hoping that they will be a source of true happiness, but in samsara we can never find such friends. Even if they do not deliberately try to harm us they will inevitably cause us problems from time to time. We think that if we search for long enough we will find the right friend or perfect partner who will never disappoint us, but in samsara there are no perfect friends. Samsaric relationships are by their very nature deceptive. We hope to find a permanently harmonious and satisfying relationship, but somehow it never works out. There is no need to blame the other person for failing to live up to our expectations—it is the fault of samsaric rebirth. Having taken rebirth in samsara we have to experience unsatisfactory relationships—it is impossible to find pure friends in this impure world. If we really want to enjoy pure, harmonious relationships we must abandon samsara. Therefore, when our friends let us down we should not get angry with them, but instead regard them as Spiritual Teachers who are showing us the faults of samsara.

Samsaric places are also by nature deceptive. We think that by moving to a new house, moving away from the city or moving to a different country we will find a place where we can be really comfortable and happy, but for as long as we remain in samsara we will never find such a place. We have moved so often, but still we are not satisfied. When we visit a new area it seems so beautiful, and we feel that if we lived there all our problems would be solved; but, once we have actually moved, new problems soon begin to surface. There are no places in this world where we will not experience any problems. If we wish to live in a pure environment, or to find a place where we will always feel at home, we need to purify our mind by developing universal love and compassion.

Although we spend our lives searching for happiness in samsara, moving from friend to friend and from place to place, we will never find true happiness. We are like the thief who entered Milarepa's cave one night, looking for something valuable to steal. Hearing him, Milarepa laughed and said, "How do you expect to find anything valuable here at night, when I cannot find anything valuable here during the day?" How can we expect to find happiness in the empty cave of samsara while obscured by the darkness of our delusions, when all the Buddhas with their omniscient wisdom have been unable to find it? Samsara is a prison from which we must escape, instead of wasting our time in a fruitless search for happiness within it.

By thinking in these ways we can transform seemingly adverse conditions into opportunities for spiritual growth. There are two ways of transforming adverse conditions into the path: by means of method and by means of wisdom. We have within us the seeds of Buddhahood, but to transform these seeds into the perfect body and mind of a Buddha we need both to nurture them and to free them from any obstructions to their growth. Practices that nurture the growth of Buddha seeds, such as renunciation, compassion and bodhichitta, are known as "method practices"; and practices that free Buddha seeds from obstructions are known as "wisdom practices." When we use our adversities to strengthen our experience of renunciation, cherishing others and so forth, we are transforming adverse conditions into the path by means of method. When we use our adversities to deepen our realization of emptiness, we are transforming adverse conditions into the path by means of wisdom. More details can be found in the book *Universal Compassion*.

Transforming adverse conditions into the path is vital in these degenerate times because we are constantly surrounded by difficulties, like a candle flame exposed to the wind, blown first from this direction, then from that. There is no way of avoiding difficult situations, but if we can change our attitude toward them they will no longer be problems for us. Instead of allowing adversities to make us unhappy and discouraged we can use them to enhance our experience of the stages of the spiritual path, and thereby maintain a pure and peaceful mind all the time.

In *Wheel of Sharp Weapons,* Dharmarakshita explains that all the difficulties we experience in this life are the result of the negative actions we committed in previous lives or earlier in this life. If we find it difficult to fulfill our wishes, it is because in the past we prevented others from fulfilling theirs. If we are separated from our friends whom we love very much, it is because we interfered with other people's relationships. If we cannot find trustworthy friends, it is because we deceived people. If our body is racked with sickness, it is because we inflicted physical pain on others. If people find us unattractive, it is because we were frequently angry with others. If we are poor, it is because we stole others' possessions. If we have a short lifespan, it is because we killed others. Dharmarakshita lists many such examples of actions and their effects that are explained by Buddha in Sutras such as the *Hundred Actions Sutra* and the *Vinaya Sutras*. If we read these Sutras, we will be able to recognize all the difficulties we experience in our daily lives as a wheel of sharp weapons that returns full circle upon us for the harm we have caused.

It is important to understand the relationship between actions and their effects. Our normal reaction when faced with a problem is to try and find someone to blame, but if we look at the situation with wisdom we will realize that we created the cause of that problem through our negative actions. The main cause of all our problems is necessarily a negative bodily, verbal or mental action that we ourself created in the past; other people's actions are only secondary conditions that enable our negative karma to ripen. If they do not provide the conditions for our negative karma to ripen, someone or something else definitely will; for once the main cause has been established, unless we purify it through purification practice, nothing can stop the effect from occurring sooner or later. Instead of blaming others for our problems, we should use our misfortunes to deepen our understanding of karma.

By training our mind to recognize the spiritual lessons in all our experiences, we can come to view everyone and everything as our Spiritual Teacher, and we can turn any and every situation to our advantage. This is a very important understanding because it means that no experience is ever wasted. The time we spend listening to Dharma teachings or reading Dharma books is usually quite limited, but if we can recognize the Dharma lessons in everyday life we will always be in the presence of our Spiritual Guide. As Milarepa said:

> I don't need to read books; everything that appears to my mind is a Dharma book. All things confirm the truth of Buddha's teachings and increase my spiritual experience.

It was because Milarepa saw everything as his Spiritual Teacher that he progressed very swiftly along the spiritual path and attained full enlightenment in that one lifetime.

The Lamrim teachings explain that the function of a Buddha is to reveal holy Dharma and to bestow blessings. Because our Spiritual Guide performs these functions, from our point of view he or she is a Buddha. In a similar way, for a qualified practitioner of training the mind all living beings are Spiritual Teachers and all situations are Dharma lessons. If we can hold this special recognition with mindfulness, there will no longer be any obstacles to our spiritual practice, because all our daily experiences will become meaningful and will serve to increase our good qualities.

If we are skillful, whoever we see can teach us about the law of karma. When we see or hear about poor people we can reflect that the experience of poverty is the result of not having practiced giving in the past. This will encourage us to practice giving. When we see animals we can think that they have taken lower rebirth because they did not practice moral discipline, and are thus teaching me that I must observe pure moral discipline now. In a similar way, those suffering from anger are teaching me how important it is to practice patience; and all those trapped in the prison of samsara are teaching me that I must abandon laziness and apply great effort to attain a permanent cessation of samsaric rebirth and to help everyone else do the same. By thinking in this way, we will gradually gain a deep experience that all living beings are giving us the priceless gift of Dharma teachings. Instead of looking down on those who are experiencing suffering, we will come to respect and value them as our incomparably precious Spiritual Guides.

Accepting Defeat and Offering the Victory

When others out of jealousy or anger
Harm me or insult me,
May I take defeat upon myself
And offer them the victory.

The sixth verse reveals that having gained some experience of love and compassion for all living beings we now need to put this good heart into practice in our daily life. For instance, when someone out of anger or jealousy harms or insults us, with our mind abiding in love and compassion we should happily accept the harm and not retaliate—this is the meaning of accepting defeat and offering the victory to others. This practice directly protects us from discouragement and unhappiness. Bodhisattva Langri Tangpa's main intention in this verse is to encourage us to practice patience. The sincere practice of patience is the basis for the realization of taking and giving that is explained in the next chapter.

When inanimate objects or other people cause us problems and we have done everything we can to improve the situation, there is nothing to do but bear our suffering patiently, without

Dromtonpa

getting angry or upset. Once the effects of our negative actions have already ripened it is impossible to avoid them, and not even a Buddha can prevent our suffering. The only thing we can do is practice patience and happily accept our difficulties. In this way we keep our mind in a balanced and positive state, no matter how bad our external circumstances may be. For example, if we practice patience when we are sick we will be able to remain calm and peaceful, and if we practice patience when someone harms us we will have the clarity and calmness of mind to respond in a constructive way, without anger or self-pity. Whenever we find ourself in an unpleasant or painful situation we should think:

This situation is the result of my negative karma. As the effect has already ripened it is too late to purify it. There is nothing to do but accept the situation patiently, with a happy mind. I myself created the cause for this problem and so it is my responsibility to accept the result. If I do not experience the results of my negative actions, who else will?

Although the patience of voluntarily enduring our suffering is not in itself the actual practice of taking, if we are able to bear our own suffering courageously we will not find it difficult to take on the suffering of others. Those who are able to practice this patience have very strong minds. They are like heroes or heroines, undaunted by the sufferings of samsara, and nothing has the power to disturb their minds. As Dharmarakshita says:

A person who accepts samsaric enjoyments but
    cannot accept suffering
Will experience many problems;
But a Bodhisattva who accepts suffering courageously
Will always be happy.

Those who expect only happiness within samsara and find it difficult to bear its sufferings will only heap more misery upon themselves. We are suffering because we are in samsara. Samsara is the creation of our impure mind of self-cherishing and self-grasping and therefore its very nature is suffering. For as long as we have the cause in our mind—self-cherishing and self-grasping ignorance—we will continue to experience the effect—samsara and all its miseries. Hoping to escape from suffering without purifying our mind of self-cherishing and self-grasping reveals a fundamental lack of wisdom. Lacking wisdom, in life after life we have sought freedom from suffering through manipulating our samsaric world while neglecting to purify our mind. Rather than continuing in this way, we should now emulate the wise and courageous attitude of a Bodhisattva and view our suffering and problems as incentives to spur us on in our spiritual practice.

The reason we find it so difficult to accept suffering is that our self-cherishing mind grossly exaggerates the importance of our own happiness. In reality, when we are happy only one person is happy, and when we are suffering only one person is suffering; compared with the suffering of countless living beings, our own suffering is insignificant. Of course even one living being is important, but if someone were to ask who is more important, one person or ten people, we would have to answer that ten people are more important. This reasoning is very useful and can help us in our practice of accepting defeat.

However, we need to use our wisdom when engaged in this practice. If our accepting defeat and offering the victory presents a serious obstacle to the fulfillment of our bodhichitta wishes, this will indirectly harm countless living beings, including the person to whom we are offering the victory. Without wisdom we might allow someone to destroy our great opportunity to progress toward enlightenment and benefit many living beings. Such compassion would be unskillful and lead to incorrect practice. Suppose there is a practitioner of training the mind called Maria who has dedicated all her activities to benefiting others. If someone out of jealousy tries to kill her, and in order to fulfill her assailant's wishes Maria allows herself to be killed, this would be crazy compassion. Compassion alone is not enough; we need to balance it with wisdom, because otherwise we will make many mistakes.

A compassionate man once found a large fish still alive on the road, which had fallen from a fisherman's cart. Wanting to save its life he carefully picked it up and took it to a nearby pond. It was not long, however, before the local people noticed that all the small fish in the pond had disappeared and that only one large fish remained. When they realized that it was the large fish that had eaten all the other fish in the pond, they were very upset and killed it. The man's compassionate action therefore led to the deaths not only of all the fish in the pond but also of the large fish that he had tried to save. This story illustrates that if we truly wish to help others, we need more than just a compassionate desire to help. We also need to develop our wisdom, for without wisdom our efforts to help can often backfire. In Buddhism, compassion and wisdom are seen as complementary and equally necessary for helping others effectively.

Suppose we have abandoned self-cherishing and someone demands that we give up our life. From our side we may have the ability to lay down our life without any sense of loss, but before we do so we must ask ourself whether it will really help others. In certain cases it may be the most beneficial thing to do. The Tibetan King Yeshe Ö sacrificed his life to invite the great Indian scholar Dhipamkara Shrijana to teach Dharma in Tibet, and as a result of Yeshe Ö's selfless act of giving, Dhipamkara Shrijana was so profoundly moved that he accepted the invitation. He was able to teach the rough and unruly Tibetans the precious Kadam Dharma, and they responded with love and gratitude. Out of respect he was given the name "Atisha," meaning "peace," and the pure Buddhadharma he taught flourished throughout Tibet and other countries. Since that time countless beings have received, and continue to receive, profound benefit from Yeshe Ö's skillful action of voluntarily giving up his life. This story is explained in more detail in the books *Joyful Path of Good Fortune* and *Modern Buddhism*.

On the other hand, there are times when giving up our life may please one person but also destroy our opportunity to help many others. If we realize that we can benefit more people by staying alive, we should not give up our life. If one person gets angry and threatens to kill us, we can even fight to protect our life for the sake of the many. Buddha said that it would be a grave mistake to give up our body for an insignificant reason, or to endanger our health unnecessarily, as this would be a great obstacle to our spiritual practice.

Usually we should try to please others by going along with their wishes and accepting any criticism or problems they give us, but there are times when it would be very unskillful to do this, such as when a person's wishes are harmful and will lead to unnecessary suffering. For example, if someone were to ask us to help him rob a bank or if our child were to ask us to buy him a fishing rod or a gun to shoot birds, we should of course refuse. We need to use our wisdom and not just blindly agree to whatever we are asked.

It can also happen that if we spend most of our time complying with others' wishes, we are left with no time for Dharma study, contemplation and meditation. Also, many people have incorrect wishes, and may misuse us. Unless we make some time every day to meditate, we will find it very difficult to maintain peaceful and positive minds in our daily life, and our spiritual practice as a whole will suffer. Since the real purpose of meditation is to increase our capacity to help others, taking time each day to meditate is not selfish. We have to manage our time and energy in such a way that we can be of maximum benefit to others, and to do this effectively we need time alone to recover our strength, collect our thoughts and see things in perspective.

Once they have been harmed, practitioners of training the mind accept their suffering patiently, but this does not mean that they do not try to prevent themselves from being hurt in the first place. It is a mistake to think that because we are trying to practice patience and destroy our self-cherishing mind we can allow others to harm us. In fact it is our duty to protect ourself from harm because if others succeed in harming us they will have created the cause to experience great suffering in the future. Bodhisattvas employ whatever peaceful and wrathful means they have at their disposal to prevent others from harming them, but their motivation for doing so is solely to protect others from creating negative karma and to safeguard their own opportunity to benefit others.

Although outwardly it may appear as if they are acting out of self-concern, in reality they are protecting their body and life out of compassion for all living beings.

A pure Dharma practitioner once went to see his Teacher with a question about his Lamrim practice, taking with him his precious Lamrim text. On the way back to his cave a dog savagely attacked him. The practitioner usually treated his Dharma books with great care and respect, but to stop the dog from biting him he hit it with the text. Was he wrong to use a Dharma text in this way? Generally, of course, we should treat Dharma texts as if they were actual Dharma Jewels. However, had he not defended himself the dog would have bitten and possibly even killed him, thus severely interrupting his Dharma practice and indirectly harming many sentient beings. Because his motivation was pure, the practitioner did not incur any negative karma. Similarly, in certain extreme circumstances, Bodhisattvas can even fight others in order to protect many sentient beings. It is very difficult to judge from someone's outward actions alone whether or not he or she is practicing Dharma purely. Perhaps if we were to live with someone for many years we would gradually come to understand his or her real motivation, but otherwise we cannot know a person's motivation from his external behavior alone.

There is also no point in our enduring suffering needlessly, such as by refusing to accept medical help when we are seriously ill. We may think, "As a practitioner of training the mind I can solve all my problems through my inner strength alone;" but in fact by refusing help we are breaking the commitment of training the mind to "Remain natural while changing your aspiration." According to the Kadampa

Tradition of Je Tsongkhapa, even if we have high realizations we should observe the conventions of ordinary society. Since it is customary to accept medical treatment when we are sick, we should not attract undue attention to ourself by refusing it if it can help us, even if we are mentally strong enough to bear the pain unaided. Je Tsongkhapa's tradition of outwardly remaining like an ordinary person while inwardly cultivating special minds is very practical and beautiful.

We may think that if we patiently practice accepting defeat all the time, our suffering and problems will multiply and completely overwhelm us; but in fact the practice of patience always lessens our suffering because we do not add mental pain to the difficulties we are having. Because suffering, worry, depression and pain are feelings, they are types of mind, so it follows that they exist inside and not outside our mind. If while experiencing adverse conditions our mind remains calm and happy through the practice of patience, we do not have a problem. We may have a challenging situation, and may even be sick or injured, but we are free from pain. By controlling our mind in this way we experience a cessation of our pain, worry and depression and find true inner peace. Furthermore, by keeping a peaceful mind in difficult situations we are far more likely to find solutions and respond constructively. Buddhist practice is very gentle. It does not require physical deprivation and hardship but is mainly concerned with the internal task of controlling and transforming the mind. Once we have learned how to do this we will understand the real meaning of Buddha's teachings.

In Tibet I met a number of humble practitioners who, although they were not famous, always practiced accepting defeat and offering the victory in their daily lives. One of these was a monk called Kachen Sangye, whom people came to recognize as a Bodhisattva. Whenever anyone said anything unpleasant to him he would accept it without retaliating, and whenever anyone asked him for something he would give it immediately without even a hint of miserliness. If he was overcharged while shopping he would pay without comment, and if the shopkeeper was poor he would give him even more. Kachen Sangye's most expensive possession was a copper pot for holding water. One day while he was out a thief entered his room and stole the pot, but as the thief was making his way down the street he met Kachen Sangye returning to his room. Since the monk knew him, the thief was so ashamed that he dropped the pot and ran off. Kachen Sangye, however, developed the strong desire to give away his copper pot, so he took it to the thief's house and said to him, "You didn't need to run away. You can take anything you want from my room at anytime!" People used to say that even if he had been asked to give up his life he would have done so happily. There are many examples in the past of such practitioners, and there is no reason why there should not be practitioners like this now and in the future. Those who are able to think and behave like this do not meet with any problems in life, because they can happily accept whatever situations they find themselves in.

In summary, if we wish to help others effectively we definitely need to be able to accept our problems without getting angry or discouraged. Helping others is not always easy—it often involves considerable hardship and inconvenience, and going against the wishes of our self-cherishing mind. Unless we are able to accept this, our commitment to benefiting others will be half-hearted and unstable. However, once we develop the ability to accept our own problems patiently we will have the strength of mind to practice taking on the suffering of others and giving them happiness. Gradually we will develop the inner realization of accepting defeat and offering the victory, and nothing will have the power to discourage us from our beneficial activities.

Geshe Potowa

Taking and Giving

In short, may I directly and indirectly
Offer help and happiness to all my mothers,
And secretly take upon myself
All their harm and suffering.

In the seventh verse Bodhisattva Langri Tangpa explains the practices of taking by means of compassion and giving by means of love as a conclusion to the preceding verses. "In short" here therefore means "in conclusion."

Bodhisattva Langri Tangpa's presentation is very beautiful. In the first verse he explains how to cherish others, in the second how to enhance the mind of cherishing others and in the third how to eliminate self-cherishing and other obstacles to cherishing love. The first two verses reveal the practice of equalizing self and others, and the third reveals the practice of exchanging self with others. In the fourth verse Langri Tangpa explains how to extend and deepen our compassion, and in the fifth how to extend and deepen our love. As our love and compassion grow and our self-cherishing diminishes, it becomes increasingly easy to accept suffering and to engage in the practices of taking and giving. In the sixth verse Langri Tangpa explains how to practice the patience of voluntarily enduring suffering, a prerequisite for the actual practice of taking. Now in the seventh verse he explains the practice of taking and giving, through which we can further improve our love and compassion. In dependence upon this practice we can develop a very special bodhichitta, and then engage successfully in the six perfections, which is the actual path to Buddhahood.

When we first meditate on taking and giving we cannot actually take on the suffering of others nor give them our happiness, but by imagining that we are doing so now, we are training our mind to be able to do so in the future. At the moment we are unable to benefit all living beings but we have the potential for this ability, which is part of our Buddha nature. Through practicing the meditations on taking and giving with strong compassion for all living beings, the potential to be able to benefit all living beings will ripen, and when this happens we will become an enlightened being, a Buddha.

"Taking" in this context means taking others' sufferings upon ourself through meditation. The word "directly" refers to actually taking on the suffering of others through the power of our concentration, and "indirectly" refers to taking on the suffering of others through our imagination. When we start our practice of taking and giving we do not need to think too much about how it is possible to relieve others' suffering through the power of mind alone. Instead we should simply practice taking and giving with a good motivation, understanding it to be a supreme method for increasing our merit and concentration. This practice also purifies our non-virtues and delusions, especially our self-cherishing, and makes our love and compassion very strong. Through gradual training, our meditation on taking and giving will become so powerful that we will develop the ability to directly take on the suffering of others and give them happiness.

There are many examples of accomplished Yogis using their concentration to take on the suffering of other beings with whom they have a karmic connection. There is a story of an Indian Buddhist Master called Maitriyogi who took on the pain of a dog that was being beaten, so that the wounds appeared on his body instead of the dog's. The great Tibetan Yogi Milarepa had completely mastered the meditation on taking and giving. On one occasion he took on the suffering of a sick man, but the man refused to believe that it was due to Milarepa that he was free from pain. To prove it, Milarepa returned the pain to him, and when the pain became too much Milarepa then transferred the pain to a door, which started to shake! Faithful Buddhist practitioners believe that when their Spiritual Guide is ill, in reality he or she is taking on the suffering of others. Many Christians also believe that by allowing himself to be crucified Jesus was taking on the sufferings of human beings. It is quite possible that Jesus was practicing taking while he was on the cross.

If Buddhas and high Bodhisattvas have the power to directly take on the suffering of others and bestow happiness upon them, we may wonder why living beings are still suffering. Because Buddhas have this power, they are continuously bestowing blessings on all living beings. As a direct result of receiving these blessings, each and every living being, including animals and hell beings, occasionally experiences peace of mind, and at these times they are happy and free from manifest suffering. However, the only way living beings can achieve permanent liberation from suffering is if they actually put Buddha's teachings into practice. Just as a doctor cannot cure a disease unless the sick person actually takes the medicine that the doctor has prescribed, so Buddhas cannot cure our inner disease of delusions unless we actually take the medicine of Dharma. In the Sutras it says:

> Buddhas cannot remove sentient beings' suffering
>   with their hands,
> Wash the evil from their minds with water
> Nor give them their realizations like a present;
> But they can lead them to liberation by revealing
>   ultimate truth.

Even when the sun is shining, if our house is shuttered only a little light can enter and our house will remain cold and dark; but if we open the shutters the warm rays of the sun will come pouring in. Similarly, even though the sun of Buddha's blessings is always shining, if our mind is shuttered by our lack of faith, few blessings can enter and our mind will remain cold and dark; but by developing strong faith our mind will open and the full sun of Buddha's blessings will come pouring in. Faith is the life force of spiritual practice. We need to have unshakeable faith in Buddha's teachings, or we will never find the energy to put these teachings into practice.

TAKING BY MEANS OF COMPASSION

For non-humans, such as animals or even gods, suffering only causes them distress and unhappiness, and they cannot learn anything from their pain. By contrast, humans who have met Buddhadharma can learn a great deal from their suffering. For us, suffering can be a great incentive to develop renunciation, compassion and bodhichitta, and can encourage us to engage in sincere purification practice.

When the Buddhist Master Je Gampopa was a young lay man he was happily married to a beautiful young woman, but before long she fell ill and died. Because of his deep attachment to his wife Gampopa was grief-stricken, but his loss made him realize that death and impermanence are the very nature of samsara, and this encouraged him to seek permanent liberation from samsara through practicing Dharma purely. First he relied upon a number of Kadampa Geshes and practiced Kadam Lamrim, and later he met Milarepa and received the Mahamudra instructions. Finally, by sincerely practicing all the teachings he had heard, he became a great Master who led many beings along spiritual paths. Thus we can see that for the qualified Dharma practitioner suffering has many good qualities. For these practitioners, samsara's sufferings are like a Spiritual Guide who leads them along the path to enlightenment.

Shantideva says:

Moreover, suffering has many good qualities.
Through experiencing it, we can dispel pride,
Develop compassion for those trapped in samsara,
Abandon non-virtue and delight in virtue.

Understanding the good qualities of suffering, we should develop joy at our opportunity to practice taking by means of compassion.

167

Taking on our own future suffering

To prepare ourself for the actual meditation on taking on others' suffering we can begin by taking on our own future suffering. This meditation is a powerful method for purifying the negative karma that is the main cause of our future suffering. If we remove the cause of our future suffering there will be no basis to experience the effect. Freedom from future suffering is more important than freedom from present suffering because our future suffering is endless whereas our present suffering is just the suffering of one short life. Therefore, while we still have the opportunity to purify the causes of our future suffering we should train in taking on this suffering. This practice also serves to reduce our self-cherishing, which is the main reason why we find our suffering so difficult to bear, and it also strengthens our patience. When through the practice of patiently accepting our own suffering we can happily endure our adversities, it will not be difficult to take on the suffering of others. In this way we gain the ability to prevent our own suffering and to benefit others. Understanding this, we make a determination to purify our non-virtues by taking on their effects now.

We imagine that all the sufferings we will experience in the future as a human, god, demi-god, animal, hungry spirit or hell being gather together in the aspect of black smoke and dissolve into our ignorance of self-grasping and self-cherishing at our heart. We strongly believe that our ignorance of self-grasping and self-cherishing is completely destroyed, and that we have purified the negative potentialities in our mind, the cause of all our future suffering. We then meditate on this belief for as long as possible. We should repeat this meditation on taking on our future suffering many times, until we receive signs that our negative karma has been purified. From engaging in this meditation we will experience a joy that will encourage us to develop a sincere wish to take on the suffering of others by means of compassion.

We can also prepare for the actual meditation on taking others' suffering by making prayers. It is very easy to say prayers, and if we say them with a good heart and strong concentration they are very powerful. While concentrating on the meaning, we pray:

Therefore, O Compassionate Venerable Guru, I seek your blessings
So that all the suffering, negativities and obstructions of mother sentient beings
Will ripen upon me right now.

We feel joy at the thought of taking on the suffering of all living beings, and we hold this special feeling for as long as possible. By repeating this prayer day and night we continually strengthen our sincere wish to take on the suffering of others. We then engage in the actual meditation on taking on others' suffering.

The benefits of taking on others' suffering

The words in this verse of the root text, "all my mothers," refer to all living beings. Through his omniscient wisdom Buddha realized that there is not a single living being who has not been our mother in the past, and each of these mothers has shown us infinite kindness. Because we cannot recall our previous lives, and because the aspect of our mothers changes from life to life, we do not recognize them or remember their kindness; but this does not alter the fact that all living beings are in essence our kind mothers. If we regard all living beings in this way it will be easy to develop pure love and compassion for them. This will prevent us from getting angry or jealous, and will encourage us to help them as much as we can. Since this recognition is based on the wisdom of all the Buddhas and leads us in the direction of enlightenment, we should adopt it without hesitation. There is no point in dwelling on others' faults—it is of far greater benefit to focus on their kindness.

Even though we may find it difficult to prove for ourself the truth of the view that all living beings are our mother, we would nevertheless be wise to accept it because there are enormous benefits in doing so. We should understand that ultimately nothing is true except emptiness. Conventional objects such as people, trees, atoms and planets have a relative degree of reality that distinguishes them from non-existents such as square circles and unicorns; but only the ultimate nature, or emptiness, of phenomena is true, because it is only emptiness that exists in the way that it appears. Objects exist only in relation to the minds that cognize them. Since an object's nature and characteristics depend upon the mind that beholds it, we can change the objects we see by changing the way we see them. We can choose to view ourself, other people and our world in whatever way is most beneficial. By steadfastly maintaining a positive view we gradually come to inhabit a positive world, and eventually a Pure Land.

There are four main benefits of the meditations on taking and giving: they are powerful methods (1) to purify the potentialities of non-virtuous actions that cause us to experience serious diseases such as cancer; (2) to accumulate a great collection of merit; (3) to ripen our potentiality to be able to benefit all living beings; and (4) to purify our mind.

When we purify our mind through the practices of taking and giving, every spiritual realization will grow easily in our mind. Through contemplating the four main benefits of meditating on taking and giving, we should encourage ourself to practice these meditations sincerely.

Through meditating on taking the sufferings of all beings our compassion becomes stronger and will eventually transform into the universal compassion of a Buddha. We will also develop a very strong mind that can bear adversity with courage. At present our mind is like an open wound—at the slightest hint of hardship we recoil in dismay. With such a weak mind even minor difficulties interfere with our Dharma practice. By training in taking, however, we can strengthen our mind until it becomes unshakeable. The Kadampa Geshes used to pray to develop a mind that is as strong and stable as a blacksmith's anvil, which does not break no matter how hard it is struck. We need a strong and stable mind, one that is undisturbed by any hardship that life throws at us. With such a mind we are like a hero or heroine, and nothing can interfere with our progress toward enlightenment.

Those with deep experience of the practice of taking can easily fulfill their own and others' wishes. Why is this? It is because they have so much merit and because their wishes are always pure and motivated by compassion. They can even fulfill their wishes by means of prayer or simply by declaring the truth. During the time when Je Monlam Palwa was the throneholder of Je Tsongkhapa at Ganden Monastery, there was a terrible flood which had already swamped the surrounding fields and destroyed many houses, and which was threatening the nearby town. When the local people asked Je Monlam Palwa to help them, he responded simply by writing on a piece of paper, "If it is true that I have bodhichitta, you must go immediately," and told the people to show this to the flood waters. They followed his instructions and the flood receded.

There are many stories of Bodhisattvas performing miraculous feats through the power of their declaration of truth. These declarations are very powerful because they are motivated by bodhichitta, and bodhichitta derives its power from great compassion. When I was a young monk at Jampaling Monastery in Western Tibet, I was seriously ill for a few months. When the pain got so bad that I could hardly bear it, my Teacher Geshe Palden came to see me. He had a blessed mala and would often tell us how special it was, but we used to think he was joking. However, on this occasion he stood by my bedside and said to me, "If it is true that my mala is blessed by the Wisdom Buddha Manjushri, may you soon be cured," and then blessed me by touching my crown with the mala. After this, I recovered completely.

Geshe Palden was the reincarnation of a practitioner called Lama Gelong, who had lived at a small monastery called Deshar Rito near Jampaling. Lama Gelong frequently engaged in Nyungnay fasting retreats and emphasized the practice of the Compassion Buddha, Avalokiteshvara. He was able to cure people of certain diseases caused by naga spirits that could not be cured by ordinary medicine. On his shrine he had a beautiful statue of Avalokiteshvara that kept increasing in size, which meant that he had to keep increasing the size of his shrine cabinet! This was an indication of his ever-increasing realizations, and it caused many people to develop strong faith in him.

The actual meditation on taking

There are two ways of training in taking by means of compassion. The first is to focus on all living beings in general and imagine taking on their suffering, and the second is to focus on particular living beings and imagine taking on their sufferings.

To practice the first method, we visualize ourself surrounded by the assembly of all mother living beings without exception. For auspiciousness, and to help us relate to them more easily, we can visualize them all in human aspect, but we should remember that each of them is experiencing the suffering of their own particular realm. It is not necessary to picture them clearly—a rough mental image will suffice.

We then develop compassion for all these living beings by thinking about their suffering. Human beings experience the sufferings of birth, sickness, aging and death, of poverty, hunger and thirst, of meeting adverse conditions and not fulfilling their wishes and of being separated from their loved ones, as well as countless other sorrows. Animals experience the same sufferings, only far worse. In addition they suffer from great ignorance, exploitation by humans and living in constant fear of being killed by other animals. Hungry spirits experience the sufferings of intense hunger and thirst, and hell beings experience unimaginable sufferings of heat and cold. Demi-gods experience the sufferings of jealousy and conflict for long periods of time. Even the gods, who spend most of their lives enjoying the pleasures of samsara, are not free from suffering. Their enjoyments, environments and bodies are contaminated and in the nature of suffering, and they experience great anguish at the time of death. Because they too are under the control of their delusions, they have no freedom from samsaric rebirth and have to experience samsara's sufferings endlessly, life after life.

Focusing on all living beings of the six realms and contemplating their suffering, we think from the depths of our heart:

In their countless future lives, these living beings will continually experience without choice the sufferings of humans, animals, hungry spirits, hell beings, demi-gods and gods. How wonderful it would be if all these living beings were permanently freed from the suffering and fears in this life and countless future lives! May they achieve this. I myself will work for them to achieve this. I must do this.

Thinking in this way, we imagine that the sufferings of all living beings gather together in the aspect of black smoke. This dissolves into our ignorance of self-grasping and self-cherishing at our heart. We then strongly believe that all living beings are permanently freed from suffering, and that our ignorance of self-grasping and self-cherishing is completely destroyed. We meditate on this belief single-pointedly for as long as possible.

With compassion for all living beings we should continually practice this meditation until we experience signs that indicate our mind has been purified. These signs can include the curing of any sickness we may have had, the reducing of our delusions, our having a more peaceful and happy mind, the increasing of our faith, correct intention and correct view and especially the strengthening of our experience of universal compassion.

We may think our belief that living beings have attained permanent liberation from suffering through our meditation is incorrect, because living beings have not actually attained this. Although it is true that living beings have not actually attained permanent liberation, our belief is still correct because it arises from our compassion and wisdom. Meditating on this belief will cause our potentiality of being able to liberate all living beings permanently from suffering to ripen quickly, so that we will attain enlightenment quickly. Therefore we should never abandon such a beneficial belief, which is the nature of wisdom.

It is true that at first we do not have the power to take on others' suffering directly, but through repeatedly meditating on the conviction that we have taken on their suffering we will gradually develop the actual power to do so. Meditation on taking is the quick path to enlightenment, and is similar to the Tantric practice of bringing the result into the path, in which through strongly imagining that we are already a Buddha we gradually become a Buddha. The fact is that if we cannot even imagine attaining enlightenment we will never be able to attain it! The words "secretly take upon myself" indicate that this practice is similar to the practice of Secret Mantra, or Tantra. It is said that Tantric realizations can be achieved simply through relying upon correct belief and imagination. This practice is very simple; all we need to do is to become deeply familiar with meditation on correct belief and imagination as presented in Tantra, by applying continual effort.

How is it possible for something that exists only in our imagination to become a reality? It is a remarkable quality of the mind that we first create objects with our imagination and then bring them into our everyday reality. In fact everything starts in the imagination. For example, the house we are presently living in was first created in the imagination of the architect. He or she then made a design on paper, which acted as the blueprint for the actual building. If no one had first imagined our house it would never have been built. In reality, our mind is the creator of all we experience. All external creations such as money, cars and computers were developed in dependence upon someone's imagination; if no one had imagined them, they would never have been invented. In the same way, all inner creations and all Dharma realizations, even liberation and enlightenment, are developed in dependence upon the imagination. Therefore for both worldly and spiritual attainments the imagination is of primary importance.

If we imagine something that could in theory exist and then familiarize our mind with it for long enough, eventually it will appear directly to our mind, first to our mental awareness and then even to our sense awarenesses. For as long as the object is still just an imagined object, the mind that apprehends it is simply a belief. If the object is a beneficial one it is a correct belief, and if the object stimulates delusions it is an incorrect belief. A belief is a conceptual mind that apprehends its object by means of a generic, or mental, image of that object. If we meditate on a correct belief for long enough, the generic image will become progressively more transparent until eventually it disappears entirely and we perceive the object directly. The imagined object will then have become a real object. By meditating on the beneficial belief that we have liberated all sentient beings and destroyed our self-cherishing mind, eventually we will actually accomplish this. Our correct belief will have transformed into a valid cognizer, a completely reliable mind.

In the second way of training in taking by means of compassion, we take on the sufferings of particular individuals or groups of living beings throughout infinite worlds. For example, we focus on the assembly of living beings who experience the suffering of sickness, and develop compassion. We then think:

> *These living beings experience the suffering of sickness in this life and in their countless future lives without end. How wonderful it would be if these living beings were permanently freed from sickness! May they achieve this. I myself will work for them to achieve this. I must do this.*

Thinking in this way, we imagine that the suffering of sickness of all living beings gathers together in the aspect of black smoke. This dissolves into our ignorance of self-grasping and self-cherishing at our heart. We then strongly believe that all these living beings are permanently freed from sickness, and that our ignorance of self-grasping and self-cherishing is completely destroyed. We meditate on this belief single-pointedly for as long as possible.

In the same way, we can practice the meditation on taking while focusing on a particular individual or group of living beings who are experiencing other sufferings such as poverty, fighting and famine.

Whenever we are experiencing a particular problem, whether from sickness, lack of resources or our delusions, we can think about the countless sentient beings who are experiencing similar problems, and then with a compassionate motivation we imagine taking on their suffering. This will help us deal with our own problem, and by purifying the negative karma that prolongs the problem, may even rid us of it. If we are suffering from strong attachment, for example, we can consider all those who are also suffering from attachment, develop compassion for them and imagine that we take on all their attachment together with the suffering it causes. This is a powerful method for destroying our own attachment.

Taking motivated by compassion is an extremely pure mind, unstained by self-cherishing. When our mind is pure, this in turn makes all our actions pure so that we become a pure being. If we die with strong compassion for all living beings we will definitely be born in the Pure Land of a Buddha. This is because our compassion that manifests when we are dying will directly cause our potential for taking rebirth in the Pure Land of a Buddha to ripen. This is the good result of a good heart. The result of maintaining the good heart of sincerely wishing to liberate permanently all living beings from suffering is that we ourself will experience permanent liberation from suffering by taking rebirth in the Pure Land of a Buddha.

To conclude our meditation sessions on taking we dedicate our merit to freeing all sentient beings from their suffering and problems, and to lasting peace in this world.

GIVING BY MEANS OF LOVE

"Giving" in this context means, with a pure mind of wishing love, giving our own happiness to others through meditation.

In general, in the cycle of impure life, samsara, there is no real happiness at all. As mentioned previously, the happiness that we normally experience through eating, drinking, sex and so forth is not real happiness, but merely a reduction of a previous problem or dissatisfaction.

How do we meditate on giving? In *Guide to the Bodhisattva's Way of Life*, Shantideva says:

> ... to accomplish the welfare of all living beings
> I will transform my body into an enlightened wish-
>   fulfilling jewel.

We should regard our continuously residing body, our very subtle body, as the real wishfulfilling jewel; this is our Buddha nature through which the wishes of ourself and all other living beings will be fulfilled. We then think:

> *All living beings wish to be happy all the time, but they do not know how to do this. They never experience real happiness, because out of ignorance they destroy their own happiness by developing delusions such as anger and performing non-virtuous actions. How wonderful it would be if all these living beings experienced the pure and everlasting happiness of enlightenment! May they experience this happiness. I will now give my own future happiness of enlightenment to each and every living being.*

Thinking in this way we imagine that from our continuously residing body at our heart we emanate infinite rays of light, which are in nature our future happiness of enlightenment. These reach all living beings of the six realms, and we strongly believe that each and every living being experiences the pure and everlasting happiness of enlightenment. We meditate on this belief single-pointedly for as long as possible. We should continually practice this meditation until we spontaneously believe that all living beings have actually received our future happiness of enlightenment now.

If we wish to meditate on giving more extensively we can imagine that the rays of light we emanate fulfill all the individual needs and wishes of each and every living being. Human beings receive close friends, comfortable houses, good jobs, delicious food, beautiful clothes and anything else they need or desire. Animals receive food, secure and warm homes and freedom from fear; hungry spirits receive food and drink; beings in the hot hells receive cooling breezes; and beings in the cold hells receive warm sunshine. The demi-gods receive peace and satisfaction, and the gods receive uncontaminated happiness and a meaningful life. Through enjoying these objects of desire all living beings are completely satisfied and experience the uncontaminated bliss of enlightenment.

Although we are principally training in the thought of giving, we can also engage in taking and giving in practical ways whenever we have the opportunity. At our stage we cannot take on the suffering of others through the power of our concentration, but we can often be of practical benefit to them. We can ease the pain of sick people by taking good care of them, and we can help others when they are busy or by doing some of the jobs they dislike. Accepting hardship while engaged in helping others is also a form of giving. We can also give material help, our labor, our skills, Dharma teachings or good advice. When we meet people who are depressed and need cheering up we can give our time and love.

We can also give to animals. Saving insects from drowning or gently picking worms up from the road is an example of giving fearlessness, or protection. Even allowing a mouse to rummage through our wastepaper basket without getting irritated can be a form of giving. Animals want to be happy just as much as we do, and they need our help even more than humans. Most humans have some power to help themselves, but animals are so deeply enveloped in ignorance that they have no freedom whatsoever to improve their situation. Animals have taken rebirth in a lower state of existence than humans but we should never regard them as less important. Buddhas and Bodhisattvas have complete equanimity and cherish animals and human beings equally.

At the end of our meditation on giving we dedicate our merit so that all living beings may find true happiness. We can also make specific dedications, praying that the sick be restored to health, the poor obtain wealth, the unemployed find good jobs, the unsuccessful meet with success, the anxious find peace of mind and so forth. Through the strength of our pure motivation and the power and blessings of Buddhadharma, our dedications can certainly help, especially if we have a strong karmic link with the people for whom we are praying. Dedicating our merit to others is itself a form of giving. We can also mentally practice giving in daily life. Whenever we see or read about people who are poor, unhealthy, fearful, unsuccessful or unhappy, we can increase our wishing love for them and dedicate our merit toward their happiness and freedom from suffering.

MOUNTING TAKING AND GIVING UPON THE BREATH

Once we have become familiar with the meditations on taking and giving we can combine the two and practice them in conjunction with our breathing. We begin by meditating on compassion and love for all living beings, and developing a strong determination to take on their suffering and give them pure happiness. With this determination we imagine that we inhale through our nostrils the suffering, delusions and non-virtues of all living beings in the form of black smoke, which dissolves into our heart and completely destroys our self-cherishing. As we exhale we imagine that our breath in the aspect of wisdom light, its nature pure uncontaminated happiness, pervades the entire universe. Each and every living being receives whatever they need and desire, and in particular the supreme happiness of permanent inner peace. We practice this cycle of breathing day and night, with each breath taking on the suffering of all living beings and giving them pure happiness, until we gain a deep experience of this practice.

Once we are proficient at this meditation on mounting taking and giving upon the breath, it is very powerful because there is a close relationship between the breath and the mind. The breath is related to the inner energy winds that flow through the channels of our body, and that act as the vehicles, or mounts, for different types of awareness. By harnessing our breath for virtuous purposes we purify our inner winds, and when pure winds are flowing through our channels pure minds arise naturally.

Many people practice breathing meditation, but the most widely practiced type consists simply of concentrating on the sensation of the breath entering and leaving the nostrils. This serves to calm the mind temporarily and reduces distracting thoughts, but it does not have the power to effect a deep and lasting transformation of our mind. Combining breathing meditation with the practice of taking and giving, however, has the power to transform our mind from its present miserable and self-centered state into the blissful and altruistic mind of a Bodhisattva. It improves our concentration, makes our love and compassion very strong, and accumulates vast merit. In this way the simple act of breathing is transformed into a powerful spiritual practice. At first we do this practice only in meditation, but with familiarity we can do it at any time. Through deep familiarity with this practice our mind will eventually transform into the compassion of a Buddha.

Meditating on taking and giving can also be very effective in curing disease. By taking on the sickness and suffering of others with a mind of compassion we can purify the negative karma that causes the continuation of our disease. Although we should always seek medical advice when we are ill, there may be times when doctors are unable to help us. There are many stories in Tibet of people curing themselves of otherwise incurable diseases through sincerely meditating on taking and giving. There was a meditator called Kharak Gomchen who contracted a disease that doctors were unable to cure. Thinking that he was going to die, he gave away all his possessions as offerings to Avalokiteshvara and retired to a cemetery, where he intended to make the last few weeks of his life meaningful by meditating on taking and giving. However, through his practice of taking and giving he purified the karma that was perpetuating his illness, and much to everyone's surprise, returned home completely cured. This shows us how powerful the practice of taking and giving can be.

If we purify our negative karma it is easy to cure even the heaviest disease. My mother told me about a monk she met who had contracted leprosy. Hoping to purify his sickness he made a pilgrimage to Mount Kailash in western Tibet, which Tibetans believe to be Buddha Heruka's Pure Land. He was extremely poor and so my mother helped him on his way by giving him food and shelter, which was very kind as most people avoided lepers out of fear of catching leprosy. He stayed around Mount Kailash for about six months, prostrating and circumambulating the holy mountain as his purification practice. Afterward, while he was sleeping near a lake, he dreamed that many worms crawled out of his body and into the water. When he awoke he felt extremely comfortable, and later discovered that he was completely cured. On his way home he stopped to see my mother and told her what had happened.

We can reflect that since beginningless time we have had countless lives and countless bodies, but that we have wasted them all in meaningless activities. Now we have the opportunity to derive the greatest meaning from our present body by using it to engage in the path of compassion and wisdom. How wonderful would it be for our world if many modern-day practitioners emulated the training the mind practitioners of ancient times and became actual Bodhisattvas!

The Precious Mind
of Bodhichitta

The main purpose of training in the practices explained in the first seven verses, from developing the mind of cherishing others up to the practice of taking and giving, is to generate a special realization of bodhichitta. Bodhichitta is born from great compassion, which itself depends upon cherishing love. Cherishing love can be likened to a field, compassion to the seeds, taking and giving to the supreme methods for making the seeds grow and bodhichitta to the harvest. The cherishing love that is developed through the practice of exchanging self with others is more profound than that developed through other methods, and so the resultant compassion and bodhichitta are also more profound.

"Bodhi" is the Sanskrit word for "enlightenment," and "chitta" is the word for "mind"; therefore "bodhichitta" literally means "mind of enlightenment." It is defined as a mind, motivated by great compassion, that spontaneously seeks enlightenment to benefit each and every living being directly. Through training in the first seven verses we will develop universal or great compassion, the spontaneous wish to protect all living beings from suffering. Without great compassion,

Je Tsongkhapa

bodhichitta cannot arise in our mind, but if we have great compassion, especially the great compassion generated through exchanging self with others, bodhichitta will arise naturally. This is why in *Eight Verses* Bodhisattva Langri Tangpa explains how to develop great compassion but does not explicitly mention bodhichitta. In fact, the strength of our bodhichitta depends entirely upon the strength of our great compassion.

Of all Dharma realizations, bodhichitta is supreme. This profoundly compassionate mind is the very essence of Buddhadharma. Developing the good heart of bodhichitta enables us to perfect all our virtues, solve all our problems, fulfill all our wishes and develop the power to help others in the most appropriate and beneficial ways. Bodhichitta is the best friend we can have and the highest quality we can develop. We generally consider someone who is kind to his or her friends, takes care of his parents and gives freely to worthwhile causes to be a good person; but how much more praiseworthy is a person who has dedicated his or her whole life to relieving the suffering of each and every sentient being? Atisha had many Teachers, but the one he revered above all was Guru Serlingpa. Whenever he heard Serlingpa's name, he would prostrate. When Atisha's disciples asked him why he respected Serlingpa more than his other Teachers, he replied, "It is due to the kindness of Guru Serlingpa that I have been able to develop the good heart of bodhichitta." Through the power of his bodhichitta Atisha was able to bring great joy and happiness to everyone he met, and whatever he did was of benefit to others.

How does bodhichitta solve all our problems and fulfill all our wishes? As already explained, problems do not exist outside of the mind—it is our mental attitude that transforms a situation into either a problem or an opportunity. If we have bodhichitta, negative states of mind such as attachment, anger and jealousy have no power over us. If we cannot find a well-paid job, a comfortable home or good friends we will not be upset. Instead we will think, "My main wish is to attain enlightenment. It does not matter if I cannot obtain these worldly enjoyments, which in any case serve only to bind me to samsara." With such a pure mind there will be no basis for self-pity or blaming others, and nothing will be able to obstruct our progress toward enlightenment. Furthermore, with the supremely altruistic mind of bodhichitta we will create a vast amount of merit because we engage in all our actions for the benefit of others. With such an accumulation of merit our wishes will easily be fulfilled, we will develop a tremendous capacity to benefit others, and all our Dharma activities will be successful.

We need to contemplate the benefits of bodhichitta until we are deeply inspired to develop this rare and precious mind. An extensive presentation of these benefits can be found in the books *Meaningful to Behold* and *Joyful Path of Good Fortune*. In addition to a strong wish to generate bodhichitta that arises from contemplating its immeasurable benefits, to gain a deep realization we need four conditions: a great accumulation of merit, great wisdom, our Spiritual Guide's blessings and continual effort in our practice.

At the moment we have a very special opportunity to develop bodhichitta. However, we do not know how long our good fortune will last, and if we waste this opportunity it will not arise again. If we wasted an opportunity to make a lot of money, or to obtain a good job or an attractive partner, we would probably feel strong regret, but in reality we have not lost a great deal. These things are not so difficult to find, and even when found they do not bring us real happiness. Not taking advantage of this unique opportunity to develop bodhichitta, however, is an irretrievable loss. Humans have the greatest opportunity for spiritual development, and of all the possible types of rebirth we could have taken we have been born human. Nowadays most humans have no interest in spiritual development, and of those who do, only a few have met Buddhadharma. If we contemplate this carefully we will realize how very fortunate we are to have this precious opportunity to attain the supreme happiness of Buddhahood.

DEVELOPING BODHICHITTA

Although we have developed superior great compassion—the spontaneous wish to take the sufferings of all living beings upon ourself—we understand that despite our strong desire to protect all living beings we do not have the power to do so at present. Just as one drowning person cannot save another, no matter how fervently he or she may wish to do so, likewise it is only when we have freed ourself from suffering and mental limitations that we are able to free others. If we ask ourself who has the actual power to protect all living beings, we will realize that it is only a Buddha. Only a Buddha is free from all faults and limitations and has both the omniscient wisdom and the skill to help each and every living being in accordance with his or her individual needs and dispositions. Only a Buddha has reached the shore of enlightenment and is in a position to release all mother beings from the cruel ocean of samsara.

Enlightenment is the inner light of wisdom that is permanently free from all mistaken appearance, and whose function is to bestow mental peace upon each and every living being every day. When we attain a Buddha's enlightenment we will be able to benefit each and every living being directly through bestowing blessings and through our countless emanations. If we consider this deeply, bodhichitta will arise naturally in our mind. We contemplate:

I want to protect all living beings from suffering, but in my present, limited state I have no power to do this. Because it is only a Buddha who has such power, I must become a Buddha as quickly as possible.

We meditate on this determination single-pointedly again and again until we develop the spontaneous wish to attain enlightenment to benefit each and every living being directly.

We need to have this precious mind of bodhichitta in our heart. It is our inner Spiritual Guide, who leads us directly to the state of supreme happiness of enlightenment; and it is the real wishfulfilling jewel through which we can fulfill our own and others' wishes. There is no greater beneficial intention than this.

When we want a cup of tea our main wish is to drink tea, but to fulfill this wish we naturally develop the secondary wish to find a cup. In a similar way, the main wish of those who have great compassion is to protect all living beings from their suffering, but to fulfill this wish they know that they must first attain Buddhahood themselves and so they naturally develop the secondary wish to attain enlightenment.

Just as finding a cup is the means to accomplish our goal of drinking tea, so attaining enlightenment is the means to accomplish our ultimate goal of benefiting all living beings.

At first our bodhichitta will be artificial, or fabricated, bodhichitta, arising only when we make a specific effort to generate it. The best way to transform this into spontaneous bodhichitta is to gain deep familiarity with it through continual practice. As most of our time is spent out of meditation, it is vital that we make use of every opportunity to improve our virtuous minds during our daily life. We need to make our meditation sessions and meditation breaks mutually supportive. During our meditation session we may experience a peaceful state of mind and develop many virtuous intentions, but if we forget them all as soon as we arise from meditation we will not be able to solve our daily problems of anger, attachment and ignorance, nor make progress in our spiritual practice. We must learn to integrate our spiritual practice into our daily activities so that day and night we can maintain the peaceful states of mind and pure intentions that we developed in meditation.

At the moment we may find that our meditations and our daily life are pulling in different directions. In meditation we try to generate virtuous minds, but because we cannot stop thinking about our other activities our concentration is very poor. The virtuous feelings we do manage to develop are then quickly dissipated in the busyness of daily life, and we return to our meditation seat tired, tense and filled with distracting thoughts. We can overcome this problem by transforming all our daily activities and experiences into the spiritual path by developing special ways of thinking. Activities such as cooking, working, talking and relaxing are not intrinsically mundane; they are mundane only if done with a mundane mind. By doing exactly the same actions with a spiritual motivation they become pure spiritual practices. For example, when we talk to our friends our motivation is usually mixed with self-cherishing and we say whatever comes into our head, regardless of whether or not it is beneficial. We can however talk to others with the sole purpose of benefiting them, encouraging them to develop positive states of mind and taking care not to say anything that will upset them. Instead of thinking about how we can impress people, we should think about how we can help them, recalling how they are trapped in samsara and lack pure happiness. In this way, talking with our friends can become a means of improving our love, compassion and other Mahayana realizations. If we can skillfully transform all our daily activities in this way, instead of feeling drained and tired when we sit down to meditate we will feel joyful and inspired, and it will be easy to develop pure concentration.

Developing great compassion is the main, or substantial, cause of generating bodhichitta—it is like the seed of bodhichitta. To enable this seed to grow we also need the cooperative conditions of accumulating merit, purifying negativity and receiving the blessings of the Buddhas and Bodhisattvas. If we gather all these causes and conditions together, it is not difficult to develop bodhichitta.

ENHANCING BODHICHITTA

Once we have the sincere wish to release all living beings from the prison of samsara, it is not difficult to develop the wish to become enlightened for their sake. To maintain and enhance this wish until it transforms into spontaneous bodhichitta, however, is much more difficult. This is because as soon as we finish our meditation session we usually become distracted by our daily affairs and forget the virtuous intentions we developed during those meditations. One way to sustain our bodhichitta experience in our daily life is to keep the precepts of aspiring bodhichitta. To take these precepts we first generate the mind of bodhichitta, and then in the presence of our Spiritual Guide, an image of Buddha, or a visualized assembly of Buddhas we repeat after them the following prayer:

> O Gurus, Buddhas and Bodhisattvas
> Please listen to what I now say.
> From this time forth until I become a Buddha,
> I shall keep even at the cost of my life
> A mind wishing to attain complete enlightenment
> To free all living beings from the fears of samsara and
>   solitary peace.

Having made this promise we should always be mindful not to break it, and we should refrain from any actions that cause our bodhichitta to degenerate. The eight precepts of aspiring bodhichitta, which are the supreme method to maintain and enhance our bodhichitta, are:

1. To remember the benefits of bodhichitta six times a day
2. To generate bodhichitta six times a day
3. Not to abandon any living being
4. To accumulate merit and wisdom

5. Not to cheat or deceive our Preceptors or Spiritual Guides
6. Not to criticize those who have entered the Mahayana
7. Not to cause others to regret their virtuous actions
8. Not to pretend to have good qualities or hide our faults without a special, pure intention

To keep the first two precepts we can divide the day into six periods of four hours, three in the daytime and three at night. At the beginning of each period we should stop to remember our precepts, go for refuge and generate bodhichitta. If we find it difficult to wake in the middle of the night, instead of dividing twenty-four hours into six periods we can divide the daytime into six parts. For example, if we normally sleep six hours a night we can divide our day into six periods of three hours each. Our fabricated bodhichitta is like a clock that needs regular winding to keep it working. If we remember the benefits of bodhichitta and generate it every three or four hours, it will never be far from our mind. This practice is an excellent method for gaining deep familiarity with bodhichitta.

We need to be skillful in our approach to Dharma practice. It is almost inevitable that there will be times when our meditation does not go well, and it is easy then to become discouraged, thinking that we cannot practice Dharma at all. However, Dharma practice is not just meditation. There are many practices that we can and should do in our everyday life, during the meditation break. Once we know what to do, we can then try to put our understanding into practice. For example, whenever we see any living being suffering we can remember that the only way we can ever remove our own and others' suffering is by attaining Buddhahood, and that the main road to Buddhahood is bodhichitta. Remembering the inconceivable benefits of bodhichitta, we should generate it over and over again throughout the day.

The third precept, not to abandon any living being, means that we should always be happy to help any person or group of people, even if they have harmed us. Having generated the thought, "May I become a Buddha for the benefit of all," if we then exclude those who have harmed us or who dislike us, this way of thinking is the opposite of bodhichitta and will cause our bodhichitta to degenerate.

The fourth precept advises us that we need to apply effort in accumulating merit and wisdom. A simple and effective way of increasing our merit is to make offerings to the holy beings. Every day we can make water offerings, even offering a hundred bowls a day if we wish, regarding the water as pure nectar. We can also make imagined offerings, filling the whole of space with beautiful objccts of enjoyment that delight the holy beings. A profound method of increasing our merit is to make mandala offerings, in which we mentally transform all worlds, beings and enjoyments into Pure Lands, pure beings and pure enjoyments and offer them to the holy beings. It is also very important to try and make prostrations every day with a mind of deep faith. Dedicating all our activities toward the flourishing of holy Dharma is a powerful method of increasing our merit or good fortune. These and many other methods for increasing our merit are explained in detail in the book *Joyful Path of Good Fortune*. The principal way to improve our wisdom is by listening to, reading and contemplating Dharma teachings.

The first four precepts are methods to prevent our bodhichitta from degenerating in this life, and the remaining four are methods to prevent it from degenerating in future lives.

The fifth precept is not to cheat or deceive our Preceptors or Spiritual Guides. Deceiving our Spiritual Guide is such a negative action that, even if we have generated bodhichitta in this life and try to keep the first four precepts, we create such heavy karmic obscurations that we will not be able to carry our bodhichitta with us into our next life.

The sixth precept is not to criticize those who have entered the Mahayana. If out of dislike for the Mahayana we criticize Mahayana teachings, Teachers, communities or practitioners, we create the non-virtuous action of abandoning Dharma. This will make it almost impossible in future lives to meet with Mahayana Teachers and teachings, or to engage in Mahayana practice.

The seventh precept is not to cause others to regret their virtuous actions. Since Bodhisattvas wish for the happiness of all beings they are especially delighted when they see people creating virtue, the cause of future happiness. If we cause someone to regret a virtuous action he has performed by telling him that the action was negative or unnecessary, this is contrary to the Bodhisattva attitude and will cause our bodhichitta to degenerate.

The eighth precept is to avoid dishonesty and deceit. If with the motivation of deceiving others for our own gain we pretend to have good qualities, realizations or knowledge that we lack, we are not acting out of love or compassion. If we really loved living beings, how could we deceive them? The reason a mother never deceives her children is because she loves them. If we are dishonest with others our love and compassion will become weaker, our bodhichitta will degenerate, and it will be very difficult for us to carry our experience of bodhichitta with us into our next life. In addition, by deceiving other people we destroy their trust in us, making it very difficult for us to give advice or teach Dharma. For this reason, Bodhisattvas consider deceiving others to be one of their main objects of abandonment.

Although we should never conceal our faults out of pride or the wish to cheat others, it is generally unskillful to declare them in public. Even though we may be sincerely trying to control our mind and live a virtuous life we will probably not always be successful, but if without good reason we tell everyone about our failings this may discourage those who look up to us as a good example. In this respect we should generally follow the customs of the society in which we live, maintaining a humble, unpretentious manner but not drawing unnecessary attention to ourself with public confessions of our faults. If someone points out a fault in us and there is some benefit in confessing it, we should of course do so honestly; but generally we do not need to go out of our way to draw attention to either our virtues or our faults. Instead of declaring our faults in public, we can confess them privately to the Buddhas and Bodhisattvas.

By keeping these eight precepts purely, we prevent our wish to attain enlightenment for the sake of others from degenerating in this and future lives. Our fabricated bodhichitta will grow steadily stronger and more stable, and eventually it will transform into spontaneous bodhichitta. With such a precious mind all our actions will bring us closer to enlightenment.

To fulfill our bodhichitta wish we need to take the Bodhisattva vows and engage in the Bodhisattva's way of life, which is principally the practice of the six perfections. The six perfections—the perfections of giving, moral discipline, patience, effort, concentration and wisdom—are called "perfections" because they are motivated by bodhichitta. The bodhichitta that is associated with the practice of the six perfections is the actual method for becoming a Buddha, and the main highway along which we need to travel to reach enlightenment.

Whenever we practice the instructions given in *Eight Verses* we are also practicing giving, moral discipline, patience and the other perfections. Whenever we practice cherishing love we are giving love to others; whenever we try to abandon our self-cherishing, other delusions and non-virtues we are practicing moral discipline; whenever we practice accepting defeat and offering the victory to others we are practicing patience; whenever we strive to make progress in our meditations, contemplations and so forth we are practicing effort; whenever we emphasize single-pointed meditation we are practicing concentration; and whenever we contemplate and meditate on emptiness we are practicing wisdom. If any of these practices is motivated by bodhichitta it becomes a "perfection." Further explanation on taking the Bodhisattva vows and practicing the six perfections can be found in the books *Modern Buddhism*, *The Bodhisattva Vow* and *Meaningful to Behold*.

All the practices of the six perfections, including the Tantric practices of generation stage and completion stage, are in reality parts of bodhichitta practice because they are all methods for fulfilling the wishes of bodhichitta. Bodhichitta is like the main body of the Bodhisattva's path, and the other realizations of the Bodhisattva are like its limbs. The attainment of enlightenment depends upon making progress in and completing the practice of bodhichitta. This is described in the *Perfection of Wisdom Sutras*, in which Buddha explains the twenty-two types of bodhichitta.

The twenty-two types of bodhichitta are:
1. Earth-like bodhichitta
2. Gold-like bodhichitta
3. New-moon-like bodhichitta
4. Fire-like bodhichitta
5. Treasure-like bodhichitta
6. Jewel-mine-like bodhichitta
7. Ocean-like bodhichitta
8. Vajra-like bodhichitta
9. Mountain-like bodhichitta
10. Medicine-like bodhichitta
11. Spiritual-Guide-like bodhichitta
12. Wish-granting-jewel-like bodhichitta
13. Sun-like bodhichitta
14. Song-of-Dharma-like bodhichitta
15. King-like bodhichitta
16. Treasury-like bodhichitta
17. Highway-like bodhichitta
18. Vehicle-like bodhichitta
19. Spring-like bodhichitta
20. Melodious-sound-like bodhichitta
21. River-like bodhichitta
22. Cloud-like bodhichitta

1. Earth-like bodhichitta

The first bodhichitta to develop is simply the aspiration to become a Buddha for the benefit of all sentient beings. This aspiring bodhichitta is called "earth-like bodhichitta" because just as the earth is the basis for the growth of all plants, trees, crops and so forth, so this bodhichitta is the foundation for all subsequent Mahayana realizations. It is like a sprout that has grown from the seed of great compassion. We must cherish and nurture this sprout, recognizing it to be a precious Dharma Jewel, for it is fragile and will easily die if we neglect it.

2. Gold-like bodhichitta

Having generated earth-like bodhichitta, the Bodhisattva stabilizes his or her bodhichitta by taking the Bodhisattva vows and engaging in the Bodhisattva's way of life. This engaging bodhichitta is called "gold-like bodhichitta" because just as gold does not tarnish, so from now on his or her bodhichitta will never degenerate. Aspiring bodhichitta is like making the decision to go to a particular destination, whereas engaging bodhichitta is like actually embarking upon the journey.

3. New-moon-like bodhichitta

Having generated gold-like bodhichitta, the Bodhisattva now emphasizes the practice of the six perfections, and in particular the perfection of concentration. Through this he or she attains the concentration of the Dharma continuum, a realization whereby he is able to remember any Dharma instruction he has ever received and to see Buddhas directly. The bodhichitta associated with the concentration of the Dharma continuum is called "new-moon-like bodhichitta" because just as the new moon waxes with every passing night until it is full, so does this bodhichitta increase with every passing moment.

4. Fire-like bodhichitta

Having generated new-moon-like bodhichitta, the Bodhisattva now emphasizes the practice of the perfection of wisdom, and through this attains the wisdom of superior seeing observing emptiness. The bodhichitta associated with this wisdom is called "fire-like bodhichitta" because it burns up manifest self-grasping as well as the delusions and non-virtuous actions that cause lower rebirth. An explanation of the wisdom of superior seeing observing emptiness can be found in the books *Modern Buddhism*, *The New Heart of Wisdom* and *Joyful Path of Good Fortune*.

5. Treasure-like bodhichitta

When the Bodhisattva realizes emptiness directly, he or she attains the first of the ten Bodhisattva grounds and a surpassing realization of the perfection of giving. The bodhichitta associated with this perfection of giving is called "treasure-like bodhichitta" because it fulfills the wishes of many living beings.

6. Jewel-mine-like bodhichitta

Through continually engaging in the practice of the perfection of wisdom, the Bodhisattva advances to the second

Bodhisattva ground, and attains a surpassing realization of the perfection of moral discipline. The bodhichitta associated with this perfection of moral discipline is called "jewel-mine-like bodhichitta" because it is the source of jewel-like virtuous qualities for many living beings.

7. Ocean-like bodhichitta

The bodhichitta of the Bodhisattva on the third ground is held by a surpassing realization of the perfection of patience. With such patience the Bodhisattva's mind cannot be disturbed by any conditions, good or bad, and so this bodhichitta is said to resemble the depths of an ocean, which remain undisturbed at all times.

8. Vajra-like bodhichitta

The bodhichitta of the Bodhisattva on the fourth ground is held by a surpassing realization of the perfection of effort. With such effort the Bodhisattva's realizations cannot be destroyed under any circumstances; and so, because it is indestructible, this bodhichitta is called "vajra-like bodhichitta."

9. Mountain-like bodhichitta

The bodhichitta of the Bodhisattva on the fifth ground is held by a surpassing realization of the perfection of concentration. This concentration is stable like a mountain, and so this bodhichitta is called "mountain-like bodhichitta."

10. Medicine-like bodhichitta

The bodhichitta of the Bodhisattva on the sixth ground is held by a surpassing realization of the perfection of wisdom.

Because this bodhichitta is especially powerful in curing the disease of the delusions, it is called "medicine-like bodhichitta."

11. Spiritual-Guide-like bodhichitta

The bodhichitta of the Bodhisattva on the seventh ground is held by a surpassing realization of the perfection of skillful means. Because this bodhichitta enables the Bodhisattva to lead living beings along spiritual paths very effectively, it is compared to a Spiritual Guide.

12. Wish-granting-jewel-like bodhichitta

The bodhichitta of the Bodhisattva on the eighth ground is held by a surpassing realization of the perfection of prayer. At this stage the Bodhisattva's prayers will definitely be fulfilled, and he is able to benefit living beings extensively through the power of his prayers alone. His or her bodhichitta therefore resembles a wish-granting jewel, which is able to grant the wishes of countless living beings.

13. Sun-like bodhichitta

The bodhichitta of the Bodhisattva on the ninth ground is held by a surpassing realization of the perfection of force. This perfection is a Mahayana realization that is able to overcome all unfavorable conditions—nothing can obstruct the virtuous activities of a Bodhisattva at this level. Just as the sun has the power to ripen many crops, so sun-like bodhichitta has the power to ripen the mental continuums of many sentient beings.

14. Song-of-Dharma-like bodhichitta

The bodhichitta of the Bodhisattva on the tenth ground is held by a surpassing realization of the perfection of exalted wisdom. Whereas the sixth perfection principally observes ultimate truth, the tenth perfection principally observes conventional truth. Because this perfection gives the Bodhisattva immense ability to help others by proclaiming the melodious sound of Dharma, the bodhichitta of the tenth ground Bodhisattva is called "Song-of-Dharma-like bodhichitta."

> *15. King-like bodhichitta*
> *16. Treasury-like bodhichitta*
> *17. Highway-like bodhichitta*
> *18. Vehicle-like bodhichitta*
> *19. Spring-like bodhichitta*
> *20. Melodious-sound-like bodhichitta*
> *21. River-like bodhichitta*

These seven types of bodhichitta should not be considered as separate from the bodhichitta of the Bodhisattva on the tenth ground. The bodhichitta of the tenth ground is like the body and these seven bodhichittas are like the limbs.

The first limb is called "king-like bodhichitta" because it is the highest path of the Bodhisattva. The second limb is called "treasury-like bodhichitta" because it has a superior collection of merit and wisdom with the power to bestow a great wealth of virtue on countless living beings. The third is called "highway-like bodhichitta" because it has great power to lead countless living beings along the highway to Buddhahood. "Vehicle-like bodhichitta" is the superior vehicle that carries the Bodhisattva directly to the Buddha grounds. "Spring-like bodhichitta" enables the Bodhisattva to give teachings without ever running out of things to say, like a spring that never runs dry. With "melodious-sound-like bodhichitta" the Bodhisattva actually benefits countless living beings by proclaiming the melodious sound of Dharma. "River-like bodhichitta" is like a river flowing into the sea because in the next stage the bodhichitta of the Bodhisattva on the tenth ground will flow into the ocean of Buddha's compassion.

22. Cloud-like bodhichitta

When a Bodhisattva on the tenth ground has progressed through and completed these seven stages of bodhichitta, he or she becomes a Buddha. At the same time his or her bodhichitta transforms into the compassion of a Buddha, which has the actual power to benefit all living beings without exception. Just as rain falls from clouds and waters crops throughout the world, so from the clouds of Buddha's compassion the rain of holy Dharma falls upon countless fortunate beings, enabling the crops of virtue and peace to grow within their minds. Therefore Buddha's compassion is called "cloud-like bodhichitta."

There is some debate as to whether a Buddha has actual bodhichitta or not. Some scholars assert that a Buddha does not have bodhichitta, because bodhichitta is a wish to attain enlightenment and Buddhas have already attained enlightenment. For these scholars, cloud-like bodhichitta refers to the bodhichitta of the tenth ground. Other scholars say that a Buddha's compassion is both compassion and bodhichitta, both compassion and wisdom and both conventional bodhichitta and ultimate bodhichitta. These are the uncommon qualities of a Buddha.

Jampel Gyatso

Training in Ultimate Bodhichitta

Furthermore, through all the above practices,
Together with a mind undefiled by stains of conceptions
  of the eight extremes
And that sees all phenomena as illusory,
May I and all living beings be released from the bondage of
  mistaken appearance and conception.

The main practices of training the mind are the two bodhi-chittas, conventional bodhichitta and ultimate bodhichitta. The first seven verses teach us how to develop conventional bodhichitta, and the eighth and last verse reveals how to de-velop ultimate bodhichitta.

As explained in the previous chapter, conventional bod-hichitta is the wish to attain enlightenment for the sake of all living beings. Ultimate bodhichitta is a wisdom that directly realizes ultimate truth, or emptiness, motivated by conventional bodhichitta. When we meditate on emptiness to develop or increase ultimate bodhichitta we are training in ultimate bodhichitta. It is called "ultimate bodhichitta" because its object is ultimate truth, emptiness, and it is one of the main paths to enlightenment.

The bodhichitta that has been explained so far is conventional bodhichitta, and this is the nature of compassion, whereas ultimate bodhichitta is the nature of wisdom. These two bodhichittas are like the two wings of a bird with which we can fly to the enlightened world.

If we do not know the meaning of emptiness there is no basis for training in ultimate bodhichitta, because emptiness is the object of ultimate bodhichitta. What is the difference between empty and emptiness? In Buddhism, emptiness has great meaning. It is the real nature of things, and is a very profound and meaningful object. If we realize emptiness directly we will attain permanent liberation from all the sufferings of this life and countless future lives; there is no greater meaning than this. So emptiness is a very meaningful object, but an empty is just empty – it has no special meaning. There is an empty of inherent existence, but there is no emptiness of inherent existence because inherent existence itself does not exist.

Je Tsongkhapa said:

The knowledge of emptiness is superior to any other
    knowledge,
The Teacher who teaches emptiness unmistakenly is
    superior to any other teacher,
And the realization of emptiness is the very essence of
    Buddhadharma.

Emptiness is a difficult subject, and so we will need to read the following explanation carefully and think about it deeply.

The first line of the eighth verse indicates that all the practices explained in the previous seven verses should be practiced in conjunction with an understanding of emptiness, the true nature of all phenomena. The second line describes the practice of ultimate bodhichitta during the meditation session, the third line describes the practice of ultimate bodhichitta during the meditation break, and the fourth line explains the purpose of meditating on ultimate bodhichitta.

The first line, "Furthermore, through all the above practices," also indicates that ultimate bodhichitta is not an isolated realization but depends upon all the realizations explained in the first seven verses. For a realization of emptiness to be ultimate bodhichitta it must be motivated by conventional bodhichitta, and to develop conventional bodhichitta we need the realizations of cherishing others, great compassion and so forth. Moreover, for our study and meditation on emptiness to have a deep impact on our mind it must be motivated at least by renunciation, the wish to attain liberation from samsara by abandoning our delusions. If we are motivated only by philosophical curiosity the best we can hope to achieve is a superficial, intellectual understanding of emptiness; we will never achieve a deep and liberating experience.

WHAT IS EMPTINESS?

Emptiness is the way things really are. It is the way things exist as opposed to the way they appear. We naturally believe that the things we see around us, such as tables, chairs and houses, are truly existent, because we believe that they exist in exactly the way that they appear. However, the way things appear to our senses is deceptive and completely contradictory to the way in which they actually exist. Things appear to exist from their own side, without depending upon our mind. This book that appears to our mind, for example, seems to have its own independent, objective existence. It seems to be "outside" whereas our mind seems to be "inside." We feel that the book can exist without our mind; we do not feel that our mind is in any way involved in bringing the book into existence. This way of existing independent of our mind is variously called "true existence," "inherent existence," "existence from its own side" and "existence from the side of the object."

Although things appear directly to our senses to be truly, or inherently, existent, in reality all phenomena lack, or are empty of, true existence. This book, our body, our friends, we ourself and the entire universe are in reality just appearances to mind, like things seen in a dream. If we dream of an elephant, the elephant appears vividly in all its detail—we can see it, hear it, smell it and touch it—but when we wake up we realize that it was just an appearance to mind. We do not wonder, "Where is the elephant now?" because we understand that it was simply a projection of our mind and had no existence outside our mind. When the dream awareness that apprehended the elephant ceased, the elephant did not go anywhere—it simply disappeared, for it was just an appearance to the mind and did not exist separately from the mind. Buddha said that the same is true for all phenomena; they are mere appearances to mind, totally dependent upon the minds that perceive them.

The world we experience when we are awake and the world we experience when we are dreaming are both mere appearances to mind that arise from our mistaken conceptions. If we want to say that the dream world is false, we also have to say that the waking world is false; and if we want to say that the waking world is true, we also have to say that the dream world is true. The only difference between them is that the dream world is an appearance to our subtle dreaming mind whereas the waking world is an appearance to our gross waking mind. The dream world exists only for as long as the dream awareness to which it appears exists, and the waking world exists only for as long as the waking awareness to which it appears exists. Buddha said: "You should know that all phenomena are like dreams." When we die, our gross waking minds dissolve into our very subtle mind and the world we experienced when we were alive simply disappears. The world as others perceive it will continue, but our personal world will disappear as completely and irrevocably as the world of last night's dream.

Buddha also said that all phenomena are like illusions. There are many different types of illusion, such as mirages, rainbows or drug-induced hallucinations. In ancient times there used to be magicians who would cast a spell over their audience, causing them to see objects, such as a piece of wood, as something else, such as a tiger. Those deceived by the spell would see what appeared to be a real tiger and develop fear, but those who arrived after the spell had been cast would simply see a piece of wood. What all illusions have in common is that the way they appear does not coincide with the way they exist. Buddha likened all phenomena to illusions because through the force of the imprints of self-grasping ignorance accumulated since beginningless time, whatever appears to our mind naturally appears to be truly existent and we instinctively assent to this appearance, but in reality everything is totally empty of true existence. Like a mirage that appears to be water but is not in fact water, things appear in a deceptive way. Not understanding their real nature we are fooled by appearances, and grasp at books and tables, bodies and worlds as truly existent. The result of grasping at phenomena in this way is that we develop self-cherishing, attachment, hatred, jealousy and other delusions, our mind becomes agitated and unbalanced, and our peace of mind is destroyed. We are like travelers in a desert who exhaust themselves running after mirages, or like someone walking down a road at night mistaking the shadows of the trees for criminals or wild animals waiting to attack.

THE EMPTINESS OF OUR BODY

To understand how phenomena are empty of true, or inherent, existence we should consider our own body. Once we have understood how our body lacks true existence we can easily apply the same reasoning to other objects.

In *Guide to the Bodhisattva's Way of Life,* Shantideva says:

Therefore, there is no body,
But, because of ignorance, we see a body within the
   hands and so forth,
Just like a mind mistakenly apprehending a person
When observing the shape of a pile of stones at dusk.

On one level we know our body very well—we know whether it is healthy or unhealthy, beautiful or ugly and so forth. However, we never examine it more deeply, asking ourself,

"What precisely is my body? Where is my body? What is its real nature?" If we did examine our body in this way we would not be able to find it—instead of finding our body the result of this examination would be that our body disappears. The meaning of the first part of Shantideva's verse, "Therefore, there is no body," is that if we search for our "real" body, there is no body; our body exists only if we do not search for a real body behind its mere appearance.

There are two ways of searching for an object. An example of the first way, which we can call a "conventional search," is searching for our car in a parking lot. The conclusion of this type of search is that we find the car, in the sense that we see the thing that everyone agrees is our car. However, having located our car in the parking lot, suppose we are still not satisfied with the mere appearance of the car and we want to determine exactly what the car is. We might then engage in what we can call an "ultimate search" for the car, in which we look within the object itself to find something that is the object. To do this we ask ourself, "Are any of the individual parts of the car, the car? Are the wheels the car? Is the engine the car? Is the chassis the car?" and so forth. When conducting an ultimate search for our car we are not satisfied with just pointing to the hood, wheels and so forth and then saying "car"; we want to know what the car really is. Instead of just using the word "car" as ordinary people do, we want to know what the word really refers to. We want to mentally separate the car from all that is not car, so that we can say, "This is what the car really is." We want to find a car, but in truth there is no car; we can find nothing. In *Condensed Perfection of Wisdom Sutra*, Buddha says, "If you search for your body with wisdom you cannot find it." This also applies to our car, our house and all other phenomena.

In *Guide to the Bodhisattva's Way of Life*, Shantideva says:

When examined in this way,
Who is living and who is it who will die?
What is the future and what is the past?
Who are our friends and who are our relatives?

I beseech you who are just like me,
Please know that all things are empty, like space.

The essential meaning of these words is that when we search for things with wisdom, there is no person who is living or dying, there is no past or future and there is no present, including our friends and relatives. We should know that all phenomena are empty, like space, which means we should know that all phenomena are not other than emptiness.

To understand Shantideva's claim that in reality there is no body, we need to conduct an ultimate search for our body. If we are ordinary beings, all objects, including our body, appear to exist inherently. As mentioned above, objects seem to be independent of our mind and independent of other phenomena. The universe appears to consist of discrete objects that have an existence from their own side. These objects appear to exist in themselves as stars, planets, mountains, people and so forth, "waiting" to be experienced by conscious beings. Normally it does not occur to us that we are involved in any way in the existence of these phenomena. For example, we feel that our body exists from its own side and does not depend upon our mind, or anyone else's, to bring it into existence. However, if our body did exist in the way that we instinctively grasp it—as an external object rather than just a projection of mind—we should be able to point to our body without pointing to any phenomenon that is not our body. We should be able to find it among its parts or outside its parts. Since there is no third possibility, if our body cannot be found either among its parts or outside its parts we must conclude that our body that we normally see does not exist.

It is not difficult to understand that the individual parts of our body are not our body—it is absurd to say that our back, our legs or our head are our body. If one of the parts, say our back, is our body, then the other parts are equally our body, and it would follow that we have many bodies. Furthermore, our back, legs and so forth cannot be our body because they are parts of our body. The body is the part-possessor, and the back, legs and so forth are the possessed parts; and possessor and possessed cannot be one and the same.

Some people believe that although none of the individual parts of the body is the body, the collection of all the parts assembled together is the body. According to them, it is possible to find our body when we search for it analytically because the collection of all the parts of our body is our body. However, this assertion can be refuted with many valid reasons. The force of these reasons may not be immediately obvious to us, but if we contemplate them carefully with a calm and positive mind we will come to appreciate their validity.

Since none of the individual parts of our body is our body, how can the collection of all the parts be our body? For example, a collection of dogs cannot be a human being, because none of the individual dogs is human. As each individual member is "non-human," how can this collection of non-humans magically transform into a human? Similarly, since the collection of the parts of our body is a collection of things that are not our body, it cannot be our body. Just as the collection of dogs remains simply dogs, so the collection of all the parts of our body remains simply parts of our body—it does not magically transform into the part-possessor, our body.

We may find this point difficult to understand, but if we think about it for a long time with a calm and positive mind, and discuss it with more experienced practitioners, it will gradually become clearer. We can also consult authentic books on the subject, such as *The New Heart of Wisdom* and *Ocean of Nectar*.

There is another way in which we can know that the collection of the parts of our body is not our body. If we can point to the collection of the parts of our body and say that this is, in itself, our body, then the collection of the parts of our body must exist independently of all phenomena that are not our body. Thus it would follow that the collection of the parts of our body exists independently of the parts themselves. This is clearly absurd—if it were true, we could remove all the parts of our body and the collection of the parts would remain. We can therefore conclude that the collection of the parts of our body is not our body.

Since the body cannot be found within its parts, either as an individual part or as the collection, the only possibility that remains is that it exists separately from its parts. If this is the case, it should be possible mentally or physically to remove all the parts of our body and still be left with the body. However, if we remove our arms, our legs, our head, our trunk and all the other parts of our body, no body is left. This proves that there is no body separate from its parts. It is because of ignorance that whenever we point to our body we are pointing only to a part of our body, which is not our body.

We have now searched in every possible place and have been unable to find our body either among its parts or anywhere else. We can find nothing that corresponds to the vividly appearing body that we normally grasp at. We are forced to agree with Shantideva that when we search for our body, there is no body to be found. This clearly proves that our body that we normally see does not exist. It is almost as if our body does not exist at all. Indeed, the only sense in which we can say that our body does exist is if we are satisfied with the mere name "body" and do not expect to find a real body behind the name. If we try to find, or point to, a real body to which the name "body" refers, we will not find anything at all. Instead of finding a truly existent body, we will perceive the mere absence of our body that we normally see. This mere absence of our body that we normally see is the way our body actually exists. We will realize that the body we normally perceive, grasp at and cherish does not exist at all. This non-existence of the body we normally grasp at is the emptiness of our body, the true nature of our body.

The term "true nature" is very meaningful. Not being satisfied with the mere appearance and name "body," we examined our body to discover its true nature. The result of this examination was a definite non-finding of our body. Where we expected to find a truly existent body, we discovered the utter non-existence of that truly existent body. This non-existence, or emptiness, is the true nature of our body. Apart from the mere absence of a truly existent body, there is no other true nature of our body—every other attribute of the body is just part of its deceptive nature. Since this is the case, why do we spend so much time focusing on the deceptive nature of our body? At present we ignore the true nature of our body and other phenomena, and concentrate only on their deceptive nature; yet the result of concentrating on deceptive objects all the time is that our mind becomes disturbed and we remain in the miserable life of samsara. If we wish to experience pure happiness, we must acquaint our mind with the truth. Instead of wasting our energy focusing only on meaningless, deceptive objects, we should focus on the true nature of things.

Although it is impossible to find our body when we search for it analytically, when we do not engage in analysis our body appears very clearly. Why is this? Shantideva says that because of ignorance we see our body within the hands and other parts of our body. In reality, our body does not exist within its parts. Just as at dusk we might see a pile of stones as a man even though there is no man within the stones, so in the same way our ignorant mind sees a body within the collection of arms, legs and so forth, even though no body exists there. The body we see within the collection of arms and legs is simply a hallucination of our ignorant mind. Not recognizing it as such, however, we grasp at it very strongly, cherish it and exhaust ourself in trying to protect it from any discomfort.

The way to familiarize our mind with the true nature of the body is to use the above reasoning to search for our body, and then when we have searched in every possible place and not found it, to concentrate on the space-like emptiness that is the mere absence of the body that we normally see. This space-like emptiness is the true nature of our body. Although it resembles empty space, it is a meaningful emptiness. Its meaning is the utter non-existence of the body that we normally see, the body that we grasp at so strongly and have cherished all our life.

Through becoming familiar with the experience of the space-like ultimate nature of the body, our grasping at our body will be reduced. As a result we will experience far less suffering, anxiety and frustration in relation to our body. Our physical tension will diminish and our health will improve, and even when we do become sick our physical discomfort will not disturb our mind. Those who have a direct experience of emptiness do not feel any pain even if they are beaten or shot. Knowing that the real nature of their body is like space, for them being beaten is like space being beaten and being shot is like space being shot. In addition, good and bad external conditions no longer have the power to disturb their mind, because they realize these to be like a magician's illusion, with no existence separate from the mind. Instead of being pulled about by changing conditions like a puppet on a string, their minds remain free and tranquil in the knowledge of the equal and unchanging ultimate nature of all things. In this way, a person who directly realizes emptiness, the true nature of phenomena, experiences peace and happiness day and night, life after life.

We need to distinguish between the conventionally existent body that does exist and the inherently existent body that does not exist; but we must take care not to be misled by the words into thinking that the conventionally existent body is anything more than a mere appearance to mind. It is perhaps less confusing simply to say that for a mind that directly sees the truth, or emptiness, there is no body. A body exists only for an ordinary mind to which a body appears.

Shantideva advises us that unless we wish to understand emptiness we should not examine conventional truths such as our body, possessions, places and friends, but instead be satisfied with their mere names, as worldly people are. Once a worldly person knows an object's name and purpose, he is satisfied that he knows the object and does not investigate further. We must do the same, unless we want to meditate on emptiness. However, we should remember that if we did examine objects more closely we would not find them, because they would simply disappear, just as a mirage disappears if we try to look for it.

The same reasoning that we have used to prove the lack of true existence of our body can be applied to all other phenomena. This book, for example, seems to exist from its own side, somewhere within its parts; but when we examine the book more precisely we discover that none of the individual pages nor the collection of the pages is the book, yet without them there is no book. Instead of finding a truly existent book we are left beholding an emptiness that is the non-existence of the book we previously held to exist. Because of our ignorance the book appears to exist separately from our mind, as if our mind were inside and the book outside, but through analyzing the book we discover that this appearance is completely false. There is no book outside the mind. There is no book "out there," within the pages. The only way the book exists is as a mere appearance to mind, a mere projection of the mind.

All phenomena exist by way of convention; nothing is inherently existent. This applies to mind, to Buddha and even to emptiness itself. Everything is merely imputed by mind. All phenomena have parts—physical phenomena have physical parts, and non-physical phenomena have various parts, or attributes, that can be distinguished by thought. Using the same type of reasoning as above, we can realize that any phenomenon is not one of its parts, not the collection of its parts and not separate from its parts. In this way we can realize the emptiness of all phenomena, the mere absence of all phenomena that we normally see or perceive.

It is particularly helpful to meditate on the emptiness of objects that arouse strong delusions in us like attachment or anger. By analyzing correctly we will realize that the object we desire, or the object we dislike, does not exist from its own side. Its beauty or ugliness, and even its very existence, are imputed by mind. By thinking in this way we will discover that there is no basis for attachment or anger.

THE EMPTINESS OF OUR MIND

In *Training the Mind in Seven Points*, after outlining how to engage in analytical meditation on the emptiness of inherent existence of outer phenomena such as our body, Geshe Chekhawa continues by saying that we should then analyze our own mind to understand how it lacks inherent existence.

Our mind is not an independent entity, but an ever-changing continuum that depends upon many factors, such as its previous moments, its objects and the inner energy winds upon which our minds are mounted. Like everything else, our mind is imputed upon a collection of many factors and therefore lacks inherent existence. A primary mind, or consciousness, for example, has five parts or "mental factors": feeling, discrimination, intention, contact and attention. Neither the individual mental factors nor the collection of these mental factors is the primary mind itself, because they are mental factors and therefore parts of the primary mind. However, there is no primary mind that is separate from these mental factors. A primary mind is merely imputed upon the mental factors that are its basis of imputation, and therefore it does not exist from its own side.

Having identified the nature of our primary mind, which is an empty-like space that perceives or understands objects, we then search for it within its parts—feeling, discrimination, intention, contact and attention—until finally we realize its unfindability. This unfindability is its ultimate nature or emptiness. We then think:

All phenomena that appear to my mind are the nature of my mind. My mind is the nature of emptiness.

In this way we feel that everything dissolves into emptiness. We perceive only the emptiness of all phenomena and we meditate on this emptiness. This way of meditating on emptiness is more profound than the meditation on the emptiness of our body. Gradually our experience of emptiness will become clearer and clearer until finally we gain an undefiled wisdom that directly realizes the emptiness of all phenomena.

THE EMPTINESS OF OUR I

The object we grasp at most strongly is our self or I. Due to the imprints of self-grasping ignorance accumulated over time without beginning, our I appears to us as inherently existent, and our self-grasping mind automatically grasps at it in this way. Although we grasp at an inherently existent I all the time, even during sleep, it is not easy to identify how it appears to our mind. To identify it clearly, we must begin by allowing it to manifest strongly by contemplating situations in which we have an exaggerated sense of I, such as when we are embarrassed, ashamed, afraid or indignant. We recall or imagine such a situation and then, without any comment or analysis, try to gain a clear mental image of how the I naturally appears at such times. We have to be patient at this stage because it may take many sessions before we gain a clear image. Eventually we will see that the I appears to be completely solid and real, existing from its own side without depending upon the body or the mind. This vividly appearing I is the inherently existent I that we cherish so strongly. It is the I that we defend when we are criticized and that we are so proud of when we are praised.

Once we have an image of how the I appears in these extreme circumstances, we should try to identify how it appears normally, in less extreme situations. For example, we can observe the I that is presently reading this book and try to discover how it appears to our mind. Eventually we will see that although in this case there is not such an inflated sense of I, nevertheless the I still appears to be inherently existent, existing from its own side without depending

Khedrubje

upon the body or the mind. Once we have an image of the inherently existent I, we focus on it for a while with single-pointed concentration. Then in meditation we proceed to the next stage, which is to contemplate valid reasons to prove that the inherently existent I we are grasping at does not in fact exist. The inherently existent I and our self that we normally see are the same; we should know that neither exists, both are objects negated by emptiness.

If the I exists in the way that it appears, it must exist in one of four ways: as the body, as the mind, as the collection of the body and mind or as something separate from the body and mind; there is no other possibility. We contemplate this carefully until we become convinced that this is the case and then we proceed to examine each of the four possibilities:

1. If our I is our body, there is no sense in saying "my body," because the possessor and the possessed are identical.

   If our I is our body, there is no future rebirth because the I ceases when the body dies.

   If our I and our body are identical, then since we are capable of developing faith, dreaming, solving mathematical puzzles and so on, it follows that flesh, blood and bones can do the same.

   Since none of this is true, it follows that our I is not our body.

2. If our I is our mind, there is no sense in saying "my mind," because the possessor and the possessed are identical; but usually when we focus on our mind

we say "my mind." This clearly indicates that our I is not our mind.

If our I is our mind, then since we have many types of mind, such as the six consciousnesses, conceptual minds and non-conceptual minds, it follows that we have just as many I's. Since this is absurd, our I cannot be our mind.

3. Since our body is not our I and our mind is not our I, the collection of our body and mind cannot be our I. The collection of our body and mind is a collection of things that are not our I, so how can the collection itself be our I? For example, in a herd of cows none of the animals is a sheep, therefore the herd itself is not sheep. In the same way, in the collection of our body and mind, neither our body nor our mind is our I, therefore the collection itself is not our I.

4. If our I is not our body, not our mind and not the collection of our body and mind, the only possibility that remains is that it is something separate from our body and mind. If this is the case, we must be able to apprehend our I without either our body or our mind appearing, but if we imagine that our body and our mind were completely to disappear there would be nothing remaining that could be called our I. Therefore it follows that our I is not separate from our body and mind.

We should imagine that our body gradually dissolves into thin air, and then our mind dissolves, our thoughts scatter with the wind, our feelings,

wishes and awareness melt into nothingness. Is
there anything left that is our I? There is nothing.
Clearly our I is not something separate from our
body and mind.

We have now examined all four possibilities and have failed
to find our I or self. Since we have already decided that there
is no fifth possibility, we must conclude that our I that we
normally grasp at and cherish does not exist at all. Where there
previously appeared an inherently existent I, there now appears
an absence of that I. This absence of an inherently existent I is
emptiness, ultimate truth.

We contemplate in this way until there appears to us a
generic, or mental, image of the absence of our self that we
normally see. This image is our object of placement meditation.
We try to become completely familiar with it by continually
meditating on it single-pointedly for as long as possible.

Because we have grasped at our inherently existent I since
beginningless time, and have cherished it more dearly than anything else, the experience of failing to find our self in meditation
can be quite shocking at first. Some people develop fear, thinking, "I have become completely non-existent." Others feel great
joy, as if the source of all their problems were vanishing. Both
reactions are good signs and indicate correct meditation. After a
while, these initial reactions will subside and our mind will settle
into a more balanced state. Then we will be able to meditate on
the emptiness of our self in a calm, controlled manner.

We should allow our mind to become absorbed in space-
like emptiness for as long as possible. It is important to
remember that our object is emptiness, the mere absence

of our self that we normally see, not mere nothingness. Occasionally we should check our meditation with alertness. If our mind has wandered to another object, or if we have lost the meaning of emptiness and are focusing on mere nothingness, we should return to the contemplations to bring the emptiness of our self clearly to mind once again.

We may wonder, "If my self that I normally see does not exist, then who is meditating? Who will get up from meditation, speak to others and reply when my name is called?" Although our self that we normally see does not exist, this does not mean that our self does not exist at all. We exist as a mere imputation. As long as we are satisfied with the mere imputation of our "self," there is no problem. We can think, "I exist," "I am going to town" and so on. The problem arises only when we look for our self other than the mere conceptual imputation "I," or "self." Our mind grasps at an I that ultimately exists, independently of conceptual imputation, as if there were a "real" I existing behind the label. If such an I existed, we would be able to find it, but we have seen that our I cannot be found upon investigation. The conclusion of our search was a definite non-finding of our self. This unfindability of our self is the emptiness of our self, the ultimate nature of our self. Our self that exists as mere imputation is our existent self. In the same way, phenomena that exist as mere imputation are existent phenomena. There are no self and other phenomena that exist other than mere imputation. In truth, our self and other phenomena that exist as mere imputation are the ultimate nature of our self and other phenomena, not the conventional nature. At first these explanations are difficult to understand, but please be patient. We should apply effort to receive the powerful blessings of Wisdom Buddha Je Tsongkhapa through sincerely engaging in the practice of *Heart Jewel*.

THE EMPTINESS THAT IS EMPTY OF EIGHT EXTREMES

The second line of the eighth verse, "Together with a mind undefiled by stains of conceptions of the eight extremes," refers to the wisdom of meditative equipoise that directly realizes emptiness. When we first realize emptiness we do so conceptually, by means of a generic image. By continuing to meditate on emptiness over and over again, the generic image gradually becomes more and more transparent until it disappears entirely and we see emptiness directly. This direct realization of emptiness will be our first completely non-mistaken awareness, or "undefiled" mind. Until we realize emptiness directly, all our minds are mistaken awarenesses, because due to the imprints of self-grasping or true-grasping ignorance, their objects appear as inherently existent.

Langri Tangpa calls these imprints "stains of conceptions of the eight extremes." The eight extremes refer to the extremes of the eight phenomena. These are:

1. The extreme of produced phenomena
2. The extreme of disintegration
3. The extreme of impermanent phenomena
4. The extreme of permanent phenomena
5. The extreme of going
6. The extreme of coming
7. The extreme of singularity
8. The extreme of plurality

The extreme of produced phenomena refers to inherently

existent produced phenomena, the extreme of disintegration refers to inherently existent disintegration and so forth.

In general, there are two extremes—the extreme of existence and the extreme of non-existence. Everything that exists is free from these two extremes. This book, for example, is free from the extreme of existence because it does not exist inherently, and it is free from the extreme of non-existence because it does exist conventionally. By understanding the two truths we will realize the middle way that is free from the two extremes.

Most people veer toward the extreme of existence, thinking that if something exists it must exist inherently, thus exaggerating the way in which things exist without being satisfied with them as mere name. Others may veer toward the extreme of non-existence, thinking that if phenomena do not exist inherently they do not exist at all, thus exaggerating their lack of inherent existence. We need to realize that although phenomena lack any trace of existence from their own side, they do exist conventionally as mere appearances to a valid mind.

Regarding the second line of the eighth verse, some people believe that the eight phenomena refer to the eight worldly concerns, but if this were Langri Tangpa's intended meaning he would have explained them earlier when explaining the previous practices. There is no relationship between this topic and the explanation of the eight worldly concerns. At this point in his commentary to *Eight Verses*, *Training the Mind in Seven Points*, Geshe Chekhawa specifically explains the practice of wisdom, that is, the wisdom realizing the lack of the extremes of the eight phenomena. Je Tsongkhapa is also very clear on this point. In accordance with Je Tsongkhapa's and Geshe Chekhawa's intention, the great scholar Changkya

Ngawang Chogden wrote a commentary to Langri Tangpa's *Eight Verses* in which he explains that these eight phenomena refer to the extremes of the eight phenomena. This wisdom topic originally came from the *Perfection of Wisdom Sutras* and Nagarjuna's *Fundamental Wisdom*.

The conceptual minds grasping at our I and other phenomena as being truly existent are wrong awarenesses and should therefore be abandoned, but Bodhisattva Langri Tangpa is not saying that all conceptual thoughts are wrong awarenesses and should therefore be abandoned. There are many correct conceptual minds that are useful in our day-to-day lives, such as the conceptual mind remembering what we did yesterday or the conceptual mind understanding what we will do tomorrow. There are also many conceptual minds that need to be cultivated on the spiritual path. For example, conventional bodhichitta in the mental continuum of a Bodhisattva is a conceptual mind because it apprehends its object, great enlightenment, by means of a generic image. In addition, before we can realize emptiness directly with a non-conceptual mind, we need to realize it by means of a subsequent valid cognizer, which is a conceptual mind. Through contemplating the reasons that refute inherent existence, there appears to our mind a generic image of the absence, or empty, of inherent existence. This is the only way that emptiness can initially appear to our mind. We then meditate on this image with stronger and stronger concentration until finally we perceive emptiness directly.

There are some people who say that the way to meditate on emptiness is simply to empty our mind of all conceptual thoughts, arguing that just as white clouds obscure the sun as much as black clouds, so positive conceptual thoughts obscure our mind as much as negative conceptual thoughts. This view is completely mistaken, because if we make no effort to gain a conceptual understanding of emptiness, but try instead to suppress all conceptual thoughts, actual emptiness will never appear to our mind. We may achieve a vivid experience of a space-like vacuity, but this is just the absence of conceptual thought—it is not emptiness, the true nature of phenomena. Meditation on this vacuity may temporarily calm our mind, but it will never destroy our delusions nor liberate us from samsara and its sufferings.

If all the necessary atmospheric causes and conditions come together, clouds will appear. If these are absent, clouds cannot form. The clouds are completely dependent upon causes and conditions for their development; without these they have no power to develop. The same is true for mountains, planets, bodies, minds and all other produced phenomena. Because they depend upon factors outside themselves for their existence, they are empty of inherent, or independent, existence and are mere imputations of the mind.

Contemplating the teachings on karma—actions and their effects—can help us to understand this. Where do all our good and bad experiences come from? According to Buddhism they are the result of the positive and negative karma we created in the past. As a result of positive karma, attractive and agreeable people appear in our life, pleasant material conditions arise and we live in a beautiful environment; but as a result of negative karma, unpleasant people and things appear. This world is the effect of the collective karma created by the beings who inhabit it. Because karma originates in the mind—specifically in our mental intentions—we can see that all worlds arise from the mind. This is similar to the way in which appearances arise in a dream. Everything we perceive when we are dreaming is the result of the ripening of karmic potentials in our mind and has no existence outside of our mind. When our mind is calm and pure, positive karmic imprints ripen and pleasant dream appearances arise; but when our mind is agitated and impure, negative karmic imprints ripen and unpleasant, nightmarish appearances arise. In a similar way, all the appearances of our waking world are simply the ripening of positive, negative or neutral karmic imprints in our mind.

Once we understand how things arise from their inner and outer causes and conditions and have no independent existence, then just seeing or thinking about the production of phenomena will remind us of their emptiness. Instead of reinforcing our sense of the solidity and objectivity of things, we will begin to see things as manifestations of their emptiness, with no more concrete existence than a rainbow arising out of an empty sky.

Just as the production of things depends upon causes and conditions, so too does the disintegration of things. Therefore, neither production nor disintegration can be truly existent. For example, if our new car were destroyed we would feel unhappy because we grasp at both the car and the disintegration of the car as truly existent; but if we understood that our car is merely an appearance to our mind, like a car in a dream, its destruction would not disturb us. This is true for all objects of our attachment; if we realize that both objects and their cessations lack true existence, there is no basis for becoming upset if we are separated from them.

All functioning things—our environments, enjoyments, body, mind and our self—change from moment to moment.

They are impermanent in the sense that they do not last for a second moment. The book you are reading in this moment is not the same book that you were reading a moment ago, and it could only come into existence because the book of a moment ago ceased to exist. When we understand subtle impermanence—that our body, our mind, our self and so forth do not abide for a second moment—it is not difficult to understand that they are empty of inherent existence.

Even though we may agree that impermanent phenomena are empty of inherent existence, we might think that because permanent phenomena are unchanging and do not arise from causes and conditions, they must exist inherently. However, even permanent phenomena such as emptiness and unproduced space—the mere absence of physical obstruction—are dependent-related phenomena because they depend upon their parts, their bases and the minds that impute them; and therefore they are not inherently existent. Although emptiness is ultimate reality, it is not independent or inherently existent because it too depends upon its parts, its bases and the minds that impute it. Just as a gold coin does not exist separately from its gold, so the emptiness of our body does not exist separately from our body, because it is simply our body's lack of inherent existence.

Whenever we go anywhere we develop the thought, "I am going," and grasp at an inherently existent act of going. In a similar way, when someone comes to visit us we think, "They are coming," and we grasp at an inherently existent act of coming. Both these conceptions are self-grasping and wrong awarenesses. When someone goes away we feel that a truly existent person has truly left, and when they come back we feel that a truly existent person has truly returned. However, the coming and going of people is like the appearance and disappearance of a rainbow in the sky. When the causes and conditions for a rainbow to appear are assembled, a rainbow appears, and when the causes and conditions for the continued appearance of the rainbow disperse, the rainbow disappears; but the rainbow does not come from anywhere, nor does it go anywhere.

When we observe one object, such as our I, we strongly feel that it is a single, indivisible entity, and that its singularity is inherently existent. In reality, however, our I has many parts, such as the parts that look, listen, walk and think, or the parts that are, for example, a teacher, a mother, a daughter and a wife. Our I is imputed upon the collection of all these parts. As with each individual phenomenon it is a singularity, but its singularity is merely imputed, like an army that is merely imputed upon a collection of soldiers, or a forest that is imputed upon a collection of trees.

When we see more than one object, we regard the multiplicity of these objects to be inherently existent. However, just as singularity is merely imputed, likewise plurality is just an imputation by mind and does not exist from the side of the object. For example, instead of looking at a collection of soldiers or trees from the point of view of the individual soldiers or trees, we could look at them as an army or a forest, that is, as a singular collection or whole, in which case we would be looking at a singularity rather than a plurality.

In summary, singularity does not exist from its own side because it is just imputed upon a plurality—its parts. In the same way, plurality does not exist from its own side because it is just imputed upon a singularity—the collection of its parts. Therefore, singularity and plurality are mere imputations by conceptual mind and they lack true existence. If we realize this clearly, there is no basis for developing attachment and anger toward objects, either singular or plural. We tend to project the faults or qualities of the few onto the many, and then develop hatred or attachment on the basis of, for example, race, religion or country. Contemplating the emptiness of singularity and plurality can be helpful in reducing such hatred and attachment.

Although production, disintegration and so forth do exist, they do not exist inherently. It is our conceptual minds of self-grasping ignorance that grasp them as inherently existent. These conceptions grasp at the eight extremes: inherently existent production, inherently existent disintegration, inherently existent impermanence, inherently existent permanence, inherently existent going, inherently existent coming, inherently existent singularity and inherently existent plurality. Although these extremes do not exist, due to our ignorance we are always grasping them. The conceptions of these extremes lie at the root of all other delusions, and because delusions give rise to our performing contaminated actions that keep us trapped in the prison of samsara, these conceptions are the root of samsara, the cycle of impure life.

Inherently existent production is the same as the production that we normally see, and we should know that in reality neither of these exists. This is the same for the remaining seven extremes. For example, inherently existent disintegration and destruction and the disintegration and destruction that we normally see are the same, and we should know that neither of these exists. Our minds that grasp at these eight extremes are different aspects of our self-grasping ignorance.

Because it is our self-grasping ignorance that causes us to experience endless suffering and problems, when this ignorance ceases permanently through meditation on the emptiness of all phenomena, all our suffering of this life and countless future lives will cease permanently and we will accomplish the real meaning of human life.

The subject of the eight extremes is profound and requires detailed explanation and lengthy study. Buddha explains them in detail in the *Perfection of Wisdom Sutras*; and in *Fundamental Wisdom*, a commentary to the *Perfection of Wisdom Sutras*, Nagarjuna also uses many profound and powerful reasons to establish that the eight extremes do not exist by showing how all phenomena are empty of inherent existence. Through analyzing conventional truths he establishes their ultimate nature, and shows why it is necessary to understand both the conventional and ultimate natures of an object in order to understand that object fully.

CONVENTIONAL AND ULTIMATE TRUTHS

Whatever exists is either a conventional truth or an ultimate truth, and, since ultimate truth refers just to emptiness, everything except emptiness is a conventional truth. For example, things such as houses, cars and tables, are all conventional truths.

All conventional truths are false objects because the way they appear and the way they exist do not correspond. If someone appears to be friendly and kind but his real intention is to gain our confidence in order to rob us, we would say that he is false or deceptive because there is a discrepancy between the way he appears and his real nature. Similarly, objects such as forms and sounds are false or deceptive because they appear to exist inherently, but in reality are completely devoid of inherent existence. Because the way they appear does not coincide with the way they exist, conventional truths are known as "deceptive phenomena." A cup, for instance, appears to exist independently of its parts, its causes and the mind that apprehends it, but in reality it totally depends upon these things. Because the way the cup appears to our mind and the way it exists do not correspond, the cup is a false object.

Although conventional truths are false objects, nevertheless they actually exist because a mind directly perceiving a conventional truth is a valid mind, a completely reliable mind. For instance, an eye consciousness directly perceiving a cup on the table is a valid mind because it will not deceive us—if we reach out to pick up the cup we will find it where our eye consciousness sees it. In this respect, an eye consciousness perceiving a cup on the table is different from an eye consciousness mistaking a cup reflected in a mirror for a real cup, or an eye consciousness seeing a mirage as water. Even though a cup is a false object, for practical purposes the eye consciousness that directly perceives it is a valid, reliable mind. However, although it is a valid mind it is nevertheless a mistaken awareness insofar as the cup appears to that mind to be truly existent. It is valid and non-deceptive with respect to the conventional characteristics of the cup—its position, size, color and so forth—but mistaken with respect to its appearance.

To summarize, conventional objects are false because, although they appear to exist from their own side, in reality they are mere appearances to mind, like things seen in a dream. Within the context of a dream, however, dream objects have a relative validity, and this distinguishes them from things that do not exist at all. Suppose in a dream we steal a diamond and someone then asks us whether it was we who stole it. Even though the dream is merely a creation of our mind, if we answer "yes" we are telling the truth whereas if we answer "no" we are telling a lie. In the same way, even though in reality the whole universe is just an appearance to mind, within the context of the experience of ordinary beings we can distinguish between relative truths and relative falsities.

Conventional truths can be divided into gross conventional truths and subtle conventional truths. We can understand how all phenomena have these two levels of conventional truth by considering the example of a car. The car itself, the car depending on its causes and the car depending on its parts are all gross conventional truths of the car. They are called "gross" because they are relatively easy to understand. The car depending on its basis of imputation is quite subtle and is not easy to understand, but it is still a gross conventional truth. The basis of imputation of the car is the parts of the car. To apprehend car, the parts of the car must appear to our mind; without the parts appearing, there is no way to develop the thought "car." For this reason, the parts are the basis of imputation of the car. We say, "I see a car," but strictly speaking all we ever see is parts of the car. However, when we develop the thought "car" by seeing its parts, we see the car. There is no car other than its parts, there is no body other than its parts and so on. The car existing merely as an imputation by thought is the subtle conventional truth of the car. We have understood this when we realize that the car is nothing more than a mere imputation by a valid mind. We cannot understand subtle conventional truths unless we have understood emptiness. When we thoroughly realize subtle conventional truth we have realized both conventional truth and ultimate truth.

Strictly speaking, truth, ultimate truth and emptiness are synonymous because conventional truths are not real truths but false objects. They are true only for the minds of those who have not realized emptiness. Only emptiness is true because only emptiness exists in the way that it appears. When the mind of any sentient being directly perceives conventional truths, such as forms, they appear to exist from their own side. When the mind of a Superior being directly perceives emptiness, however, nothing appears other than emptiness; this mind is totally mixed with the mere absence of inherently existent phenomena. The way in which emptiness appears to the mind of a non-conceptual direct perceiver corresponds exactly to the way in which emptiness exists.

It should be noted that although emptiness is ultimate truth it is not inherently existent. Emptiness is not a separate reality existing behind conventional appearances, but is the real nature of those appearances. We cannot talk about emptiness in isolation, because emptiness is always the mere lack of inherent existence of something. For example, the emptiness of our body is the lack of inherent existence of our body, and without our body as its basis this emptiness cannot exist. Because emptiness necessarily depends upon a basis, it lacks inherent existence.

In *Guide to the Bodhisattva's Way of Life,* Shantideva defines ultimate truth as a phenomenon that is true for the uncontaminated mind of a Superior being. An uncontaminated mind is a mind that realizes emptiness directly. This mind is the only unmistaken awareness and is possessed exclusively by Superior beings. Because uncontaminated minds are completely unmistaken, anything directly perceived by them to be true is necessarily an ultimate truth. In contrast, anything that is directly perceived to be true by the mind of an ordinary being is necessarily not an ultimate truth, because all minds of ordinary beings are mistaken, and mistaken minds can never directly perceive the truth.

Bodhisattva Langri Tangpa describes the wisdom of meditative equipoise that directly realizes emptiness as undefiled by the imprints, or stains, of conceptual thoughts that grasp at the eight extremes. Because of these imprints, everything that appears to the minds of ordinary beings appears to be inherently existent. Only the wisdom of meditative equipoise that directly realizes emptiness is undefiled by the imprints of these conceptual thoughts. This is the only wisdom that has no mistaken appearance.

When a Superior Bodhisattva meditates on emptiness his or her mind mixes with emptiness completely, with no appearance of inherent existence. He develops a completely pure, uncontaminated wisdom that is ultimate bodhichitta. When he arises from meditative equipoise, however, due to the imprints of true-grasping, conventional phenomena again appear to his mind as inherently existent, and his uncontaminated wisdom temporarily becomes non-manifest. Only a Buddha can manifest uncontaminated wisdom at the same time as directly perceiving conventional truths. An uncommon quality of a Buddha is that a single moment of a Buddha's mind realizes both conventional truth and ultimate truth directly and simultaneously. There are many levels of ultimate bodhichitta. For instance, the ultimate bodhichitta attained through Tantric practice is more profound than that developed through Sutra practice alone, and the supreme ultimate bodhichitta is that of a Buddha.

If through valid reasoning we realize the emptiness that is empty of the first extreme, the extreme of production, we will easily be able to realize the emptiness that is empty of the remaining seven extremes. Once we have realized the emptiness that is empty of the eight extremes we have realized the emptiness of all phenomena. Having gained this realization, we continue to contemplate and meditate on the emptiness of produced phenomena and so forth, and as our meditations deepen we will feel all phenomena dissolving into emptiness. We will then be able to maintain a single-pointed concentration on the emptiness of all phenomena.

To meditate on the emptiness of produced phenomena we can think:

My self who was born, through causes and conditions, as a human being is unfindable when I search for it with wisdom within my body and my mind, or separate from my body and mind. This proves that my self that I normally see does not exist at all.

Having contemplated in this way we feel our self that we normally see disappears and we perceive a space-like emptiness that is the mere absence of our self that we normally see. We feel that our mind enters into this space-like emptiness and remains there single-pointedly. This meditation is called "space-like meditative equipoise on emptiness."

Just as eagles soar through the vast expanse of the sky without meeting any obstructions, needing only minimal effort to maintain their flight, so advanced meditators concentrating on emptiness can meditate on emptiness for a long time with little effort. Their minds soar through space-like emptiness, undistracted by any other phenomenon. When we meditate on emptiness we should try to emulate these meditators. Once we have found our object of meditation, the mere absence of our self that we normally see, we should refrain from further analysis and simply rest our mind in the experience of this emptiness. From time to time we should check to make sure that we have lost neither the clear appearance of emptiness nor the recognition of its meaning, but we should not check too forcefully as this will disturb our concentration. Our meditation should not be like the flight of a small bird, which never stops flapping its wings and is always changing direction, but like the flight of an eagle, which soars gently with only occasional adjustments to its wings. Through meditating in this way we will feel our mind dissolving into and becoming one with emptiness.

If we are successful in doing this, then during our meditation we are free from manifest self-grasping. If, on the other hand, we spend all our time checking and analyzing, never allowing our mind to relax into the space of emptiness, we will never gain this experience and our meditation will not serve to reduce our self-grasping.

In general we need to improve our understanding of emptiness through extensive study, approaching it from many angles and using many different lines of reasoning. It is also important to become thoroughly familiar with one complete meditation on emptiness through continuous contemplation, understanding exactly how to use the reasoning to lead to an experience of emptiness. We can then concentrate on emptiness single-pointedly and try to mix our mind with it, like water mixing with water.

THE UNION OF THE TWO TRUTHS

Strictly speaking, when we say the union of conventional truth and ultimate truth, in this context conventional truth refers only to subtle conventional truth, which is things existing as mere appearances. This subtle conventional truth and ultimate truth are in union, which means that they are non-dual, or one object. Thus, subtle conventional truth is not actual conventional truth but ultimate truth, a non-deceptive object. From the point of view of truth, conventional truths do not exist; they are false objects created by the ignorant mind of self-grasping. However, conventional truths exist for ordinary beings, who do not understand emptiness, but they do not exist for Superior beings, who realize emptiness directly. The instruction of the union of the two truths, the union of appearance and emptiness, is Buddha's ultimate view and intention. When we receive the fourth empowerment of Highest Yoga Tantra, we receive the oral instructions of this union. When, through training continually in this union, we realize directly the union of the two truths, the union of appearance and emptiness, we become an enlightened Buddha who is completely free from subtle mistaken appearance and has the ability to benefit each and every living being every day through our countless emanations.

When something such as our body appears to us, both the body and the inherently existent body appear simultaneously. This is dualistic appearance, which is subtle mistaken appearance. Only Buddhas are free from such mistaken appearances. The main purpose of understanding and meditating on the union of the two truths is to prevent dualistic appearances—appearances of inherent existence to the mind that is meditating on emptiness—and thereby enable our mind to dissolve into emptiness. Once we can do this, our meditation on emptiness will be very powerful in eliminating our delusions. If we correctly identify and negate the inherently existent body, the body that we normally see, and meditate on the mere absence of such a body with strong concentration, we will feel our normal body dissolving into emptiness. We will understand that the real nature of our body is emptiness and that our body is merely a manifestation of emptiness.

Emptiness is like the sky and our body is like the blue of the sky. Just as the blue is a manifestation of the sky itself and cannot be separated from it, so our blue-like body is simply a manifestation of the sky of its emptiness and cannot be separated from it. If we realize this, when we focus on the emptiness of our body we feel that our body itself dissolves into its ultimate nature. In this way, we can easily overcome the conventional appearance of the body in our meditations, and our mind naturally mixes with emptiness.

In the *Heart Sutra,* Avalokiteshvara says, "Form is not other than emptiness." This means that conventional phenomena, such as our body, do not exist separately from their emptiness. When we meditate on the emptiness of our body with this understanding, we know that the emptiness appearing to our mind is the very nature of our body, and that apart from this emptiness there is no body. Meditating in this way will greatly weaken our self-grasping mind. If we really believed that our body and its emptiness were the same nature, our self-grasping would definitely become weaker.

Although we can divide emptinesses from the point of view of their bases, and speak of the emptiness of the body, the emptiness of the I and so forth, in truth all emptinesses are the same nature. If we look at ten bottles, we can distinguish ten different spaces inside the bottles, but in reality these spaces are the same nature; and if we break the bottles, the spaces become indistinguishable. In the same way, although we can speak of the emptiness of the body, the mind, the I and so forth, in reality they are the same nature and indistinguishable. The only way in which they can be distinguished is by their conventional bases.

There are two principal benefits of understanding that all emptinesses are the same nature: in the meditation session our mind will mix with emptiness more easily, and in the meditation break we will be able to see all appearances as equal manifestations of their emptiness.

For as long as we feel that there is a gap between our mind and emptiness—that our mind is "here" and emptiness is "there"—our mind will not mix with emptiness. Knowing that all emptinesses are the same nature helps to close this gap. In ordinary life we experience many different objects—good, bad, attractive, unattractive—and our feelings toward them differ. Because we feel that the differences exist from the side of the objects, our mind is unbalanced and we develop attachment to attractive objects, aversion to unattractive objects and indifference to neutral objects. It is very difficult to mix such an uneven mind with emptiness. To mix our mind with emptiness we need to know that although phenomena appear in many different aspects, in essence they are all empty. The differences we see are just appearances to mistaken minds; from the point of view of ultimate truth all phenomena are equal in emptiness. For a qualified meditator single-pointedly absorbed in emptiness, there is no difference between production and disintegration, impermanence and permanence, going and coming, singularity and plurality—everything is equal in emptiness and all problems of attachment, anger and self-grasping ignorance are solved. In this experience, everything becomes very peaceful and comfortable, balanced and harmonious, joyful and wonderful. There is no heat, no cold, no lower, no higher, no here, no there, no self, no other, no samsara—everything is equal in the peace of emptiness. This realization is called the "yoga of equalizing samsara and nirvana," and is explained in detail in both the Sutras and Tantras.

Since all emptinesses are the same nature, the ultimate nature of a mind that is meditating on emptiness is the same nature as the ultimate nature of its object. When we first meditate on emptiness, our mind and emptiness appear to be two separate phenomena, but when we understand that all emptinesses are the same nature we will know that this feeling of separation is simply the experience of a mistaken mind. In reality our mind and emptiness are ultimately of one taste. If we apply this knowledge in our meditations, it will help to prevent the appearance of the conventional nature of our mind and allow our mind to dissolve into emptiness.

Having mixed our mind with emptiness, when we arise from meditation we will experience all phenomena equally as manifestations of their emptiness. Instead of feeling that the attractive, unattractive and neutral objects we see are inherently different, we will know that in essence they are the same nature. Just as both the gentlest and most violent waves in an ocean are equally water, likewise both attractive forms and repulsive forms are equally manifestations of emptiness. Realizing this, our mind will become balanced and peaceful. We will recognize all conventional appearances as the magical play of the mind, and we will not grasp strongly at their apparent differences.

When Milarepa once taught emptiness to a woman, he compared emptiness to the sky and conventional truths to clouds and told her to meditate on the sky. She followed his instructions with great success, but she had one problem—when she meditated on the sky of emptiness everything disappeared, and she could not understand how phenomena could exist conventionally. She said to Milarepa, "I find it easy to meditate on the sky but difficult to establish the clouds. Please teach me how to meditate on the clouds." Milarepa replied, "If your meditation on the sky is going well, the clouds will not be a problem. Clouds simply appear in the sky—they arise from the sky and dissolve back into the sky. As your experience of the sky improves, you will naturally come to understand the clouds."

In Tibetan, the word for both sky and space is "namkha," although space is different from sky. There are two types of space: produced space and unproduced space. Produced space is the visible space we can see inside a room or in the sky. This space may become dark at night and light during the day, and as it undergoes change in this way it is an impermanent phenomenon. The characteristic property of produced space is that it does not obstruct objects—if there is space in a room we can place objects there without obstruction. Similarly, birds are able to fly through the space of the sky because it lacks obstruction, but they cannot fly through a mountain! Therefore it is clear that produced space lacks, or is empty of, obstructive contact. This mere lack, or empty, of obstructive contact is unproduced space.

Because unproduced space is the mere absence of obstructive contact it does not undergo momentary change and is therefore a permanent phenomenon. Whereas produced space is visible and quite easy to understand, unproduced space is a mere absence of obstructive contact and is somewhat more subtle. However, once we understand unproduced space, we will find it easier to understand emptiness.

The only difference between emptiness and unproduced space is their object of negation. The object of negation of unproduced space is obstructive contact, whereas the object of negation of emptiness is inherent existence. Because unproduced space is the best analogy for understanding emptiness, it is used in the Sutras and in many scriptures. Unproduced space is a non-affirming negative phenomenon—a phenomenon that is realized by a mind that merely eliminates its negated object without realizing another positive phenomenon. Produced space is an affirmative, or positive, phenomenon—a phenomenon that is realized without the mind explicitly eliminating a negated object. More details on these two types of phenomenon can be found in the books *The New Heart of Wisdom* and *Ocean of Nectar*.

THE PRACTICE OF EMPTINESS IN
OUR DAILY ACTIVITIES

The third line of the verse, "And that sees all phenomena as illusory," teaches us how to practice emptiness in our daily activities. In our daily activities, we should believe that all appearances are illusory. Although things appear to us as inherently existent, we should remember that these appearances are deceptive and that in reality the things that we normally see do not exist. In *King of Concentration Sutra* Buddha says:

> A magician creates various things
> Such as horses, elephants and so forth.
> His creations do not actually exist;
> You should know all things in the same way.

The last two lines of this verse mean that just as we know that the horses and elephants created by the magician do not exist, in the same way we should know that all the things that we normally see do not actually exist. This chapter "Training in Ultimate Bodhichitta" has extensively explained how all the things that we normally see do not exist.

When a magician creates an illusory horse, a horse appears very clearly to his mind but he knows that it is just an illusion. Indeed, the very appearance of the horse reminds him that there is no horse in front of him. In the same way, when we are very familiar with emptiness, the very fact that things appear to be inherently existent will remind us that they are not inherently existent. We should therefore recognize that whatever appears to us in our daily life is like an illusion and lacks inherent existence. In this way our wisdom will increase day by day, and our self-grasping ignorance and other delusions will naturally diminish.

Between meditation sessions we should be like an actor. When an actor plays the part of a king he dresses, speaks and acts like a king, but he knows all the time that he is not a real king. In the same way we should live and function in the conventional world yet always remember that we ourself, our environment and the people around us that we normally see do not exist at all.

If we think like this we will be able to live in the conventional world without grasping at it. We will treat it lightly, and have the flexibility of mind to respond to every situation in a constructive way. Knowing that whatever appears to our mind is mere appearance, when attractive objects appear we will not grasp at them and develop attachment, and when unattractive objects appear we will not grasp at them and develop aversion or anger.

In *Training the Mind in Seven Points*, Geshe Chekhawa says, "Think that all phenomena are like dreams." Some of the things we see in our dreams are beautiful and some are ugly, but they are all mere appearances to our dreaming mind. They do not exist from their own side, and are empty of inherent existence. It is the same with the objects we perceive when we are awake—they too are mere appearances to mind and lack inherent existence.

All phenomena lack inherent existence. When we look at a rainbow it appears to occupy a particular location in space, and it seems that if we searched we would be able to find where the rainbow touches the ground. However, we know that no matter how hard we search we will never be able to find the end of the rainbow, for as soon as we arrive at the place where

Je Phabongkhapa

we saw the rainbow touch the ground, the rainbow will have disappeared. If we do not search for it, the rainbow appears clearly; but when we look for it, it is not there. All phenomena are like this. If we do not analyze them they appear clearly, but when we search for them analytically, trying to isolate them from everything else, they are not there.

If something did exist inherently, and we investigated it by separating it from all other phenomena, we would be able to find it. However, all phenomena are like rainbows—if we search for them we will never find them. At first we might find this idea very uncomfortable and difficult to accept, but this is quite natural. With greater familiarity we will find this reasoning more acceptable, and eventually we will realize that it is true.

It is important to understand that emptiness does not mean nothingness. Although things do not exist from their own side, independent of the mind, they do exist in the sense that they are understood by a valid mind. The world we experience when we are awake is similar to the world we experience when we are dreaming. We cannot say that dream things do not exist, but if we believe that they exist as more than mere appearances to the mind, existing "out there," then we are mistaken, as we will discover when we wake up.

THE PURPOSE OF MEDITATING ON EMPTINESS

In the last line of the verse, "May I and all living beings be released from the bondage of mistaken appearance and conception," Bodhisattva Langri Tangpa explains the purpose of meditating on emptiness. In this context, "mistaken conception" refers to the mind of self-grasping ignorance—a conceptual mind that grasps objects as inherently existent; and "mistaken appearance" refers to the appearance of inherently existent objects. The former is the obstructions to liberation and the latter the obstructions to omniscience. Only a Buddha has abandoned both obstructions. The main purpose of meditating on ultimate bodhichitta is to release our mind from these two obstructions and become a Buddha.

As mentioned before, there is no greater method for experiencing peace of mind and happiness than to understand and meditate on emptiness. Since it is our self-grasping that keeps us bound to the prison of samsara and is the source of all our suffering, meditation on emptiness is the universal solution to all problems. It is the medicine that cures all mental and physical diseases, and the nectar that bestows the everlasting happiness of nirvana and enlightenment.

A SIMPLE TRAINING IN ULTIMATE BODHICHITTA

We begin by thinking:

I must attain enlightenment to benefit directly each and every living being every day. For this purpose I will attain a direct realization of the way things really are.

With this bodhichitta motivation, we contemplate:

Normally I see my body within its parts—the hands, back and so forth—but neither the individual parts nor the collection of the parts are my body because they are the parts of my body and not the body itself. However, there is no "my body" other than its parts. Through searching with wisdom for my body in this way, I realize that my body is unfindable. This is a valid reason to prove that my body that I normally see does not exist at all.

Through contemplating this point we try to perceive the mere absence of the body that we normally see. This mere absence of the body that we normally see is the emptiness of our body, and we meditate on this emptiness single-pointedly for as long as possible.

We should continually practice this contemplation and meditation, and then move to the next stage, meditation on the emptiness of our self. We should contemplate and think:

Normally I see my self within my body and mind, but neither my body, nor my mind nor the collection of my body and mind are my self, because these are my possessions and my self is the possessor; and possessor and possessions cannot be the same. However, there is no "my self" other than my body and mind. Through searching with wisdom for my self in this way, I realize that my self is unfindable. This is a valid reason to prove that my self that I normally see does not exist at all.

Through contemplating this point we try to perceive the mere absence of our self that we normally see. This mere absence of our self that we normally see is the emptiness of our self, and we meditate on this emptiness single-pointedly for as long as possible.

We should continually practice this contemplation and meditation, and then move to the next stage, meditation on the emptiness of all phenomena. We should contemplate and think:

As with my body and my self, all other phenomena are unfindable when I search for them with wisdom. This is a valid reason to prove that all phenomena that I normally see or perceive do not exist at all.

Through contemplating this point we try to perceive the mere absence of all phenomena that we normally see or perceive. This mere absence of all phenomena that we normally see or perceive is the emptiness of all phenomena. We meditate continually on this emptiness of all phenomena with bodhichitta motivation until we are able to maintain our concentration clearly for one minute every time we meditate on it. Our concentration that has this ability is called "concentration of placing the mind."

In the second stage, with the concentration of placing the mind, we meditate continually on the emptiness of all phenomena until we are able to maintain our concentration clearly for five minutes every time we meditate on it. Our concentration that has this ability is called "concentration of continual placement." In the third stage, with the concentration of continual placement, we meditate continually on the emptiness of all phenomena until we are able to immediately remember our object of meditation—the mere absence of all phenomena that we normally see or perceive—whenever we lose it during meditation. Our concentration that has this ability is called "concentration of replacement." In the fourth stage, with the concentration of replacement, we meditate continually on the emptiness of all phenomena until we are able to maintain our concentration clearly during the entire meditation session without forgetting the object of meditation. Our concentration that has this ability is called "concentration of close placement." At this stage we have very stable and clear concentration focused on the emptiness of all phenomena.

Then, with the concentration of close placement, we meditate continually on the emptiness of all phenomena until finally we attain the concentration of tranquil abiding focused on emptiness, which causes us to experience special physical and mental suppleness and bliss. With this concentration of tranquil abiding we will develop a special wisdom that realizes the emptiness of all phenomena very clearly. This wisdom is called "superior seeing." Through continually meditating on the concentration of tranquil abiding associated with superior seeing, our wisdom of superior seeing will transform into the wisdom that directly realizes the emptiness of all phenomena. This direct realization of emptiness is the actual ultimate bodhichitta. The moment we attain the wisdom of ultimate bodhichitta we become a Superior Bodhisattva. As mentioned before, conventional bodhichitta is the nature of compassion and ultimate bodhichitta is the nature of wisdom. These two bodhichittas are like the two wings of a bird with which we can fly and very quickly reach the enlightened world.

In *Advice from Atisha's Heart*, Atisha says:

Friends, until you attain enlightenment, the Spiritual Teacher is indispensable, therefore rely upon the holy Spiritual Guide.

We need to rely upon our Spiritual Guide until we attain enlightenment. The reason for this is very simple. The ultimate goal of human life is to attain enlightenment, and this depends upon continually receiving the special blessings of Buddha through our Spiritual Guide. Buddha attained enlightenment with the sole intention of leading all living beings along the stages of the path to enlightenment through his emanations. Who is his emanation who is leading us along the stages of the path to enlightenment? It is clearly our present Spiritual Teacher who is sincerely and correctly leading us along the paths of renunciation, bodhichitta and the correct view of emptiness by giving these teachings and showing a practical example of someone who is sincerely practicing them. With this understanding we should strongly believe that our Spiritual Guide is an emanation of Buddha, and develop and maintain deep faith in him or her.

Atisha also says:

> Until you realize ultimate truth, listening is indispensable, therefore listen to the instructions of the Spiritual Guide.

Even if we were mistakenly to see two moons in the sky, this mistaken appearance would remind us that in fact there are not two moons, but only one. In a similar way, if seeing inherently existent things reminds us there are no inherently existent things, this indicates that our understanding of emptiness, ultimate truth, is correct. Until our understanding of emptiness is perfect, and to prevent ourself from falling into one of the two extremes—the extreme of existence and the extreme of non-existence—we should listen to, read and contemplate the instructions of our Spiritual Guide. A more detailed explanation of relying upon our Spiritual Guide can be found in the book *Joyful Path of Good Fortune.*

How to Integrate the Practice of These Instructions

*A*s explained in Geshe Chekhawa's *Training the Mind in Seven Points*, we need to train in the practice of *Eight Verses of Training the Mind* in conjunction with the five forces. By applying these to each specific practice we can easily make progress. We should therefore integrate our practices of training the mind into our daily life by means of the five forces. These are: the force of motivation, the force of familiarity, the force of white seed, the force of destruction and the force of aspirational prayer.

The force of motivation

In this context the force of motivation, or intention, means having a strong wish to practice these instructions on training the mind and making the firm decision: "From now on I will practice these instructions sincerely and diligently." If we have such a strong motivation we will apply powerful and consistent effort in our practice, and as a result we will definitely attain realizations. With effort anything can be accomplished, even things that previously seemed beyond our

Vajradhara Trijang Rinpoche

imagination. Since effort depends upon motivation, the force of motivation is of utmost importance.

To help us generate a strong wish to put the teachings on training the mind into practice, we should read this book carefully and precisely as many times as we can, until we understand and deeply appreciate its meaning. We should remember our wish to practice these teachings at all times. When we wake up each day we should make a special resolution: "I must try to practice training the mind throughout the day," and then, by relying upon mindfulness and alertness, we should maintain this determination. Whatever we do depends upon making the decision to do it. For example, if before falling asleep, we make a strong decision to wake early, we will do so. Similarly, if when we wake up each day we make a strong determination to practice these teachings throughout the day, we will be able to do so. This is how to apply the force of motivation to the practice of training the mind.

The force of familiarity

Applying the force of familiarity to the practice of training the mind means familiarizing our mind with this practice. Having generated the force of motivation we should practice these instructions repeatedly, both in the meditation session and during the meditation break, until we attain a deep and stable experience. To gain a realization we need to practice repeatedly the methods for training our mind so as to become well-acquainted with them. This is similar to learning to use a computer. To begin with, it is difficult to learn all the different commands and we make many mistakes, but with practice we gradually gain familiarity until eventually we can use the computer easily and efficiently. In a similar way, meditating on training the mind can be difficult at first, but with regular practice we become familiar with it and our experience develops naturally.

To gain proficiency in the practice of training the mind, as in all activities, we need both motivation and familiarity. For instance, if we have some understanding of emptiness it is important to become very familiar with this knowledge through continual and sincere contemplation and meditation. In this way we will be able to wake from the sleep of ignorance and free ourself from the dream-like problems of samsara. We should not waste this rare and precious opportunity.

The force of white seed

"White seeds" are virtues, which are the seeds of our future happiness. However, in this context "white seed" refers to our accumulated merit. Attaining a pure experience of training the mind and then increasing this experience both depend upon our accumulated merit. Of the many methods for increasing our merit, one that is especially important is the daily practice of the six preparatory practices, and in particular the practice of offering. We can also offer the first portion of whatever we eat or drink to all the Buddhas and Bodhisattvas with the following prayer:

> To the Buddha Jewel, supreme Blessed One,
> To the Dharma Jewel, supreme Protector,
> To the Sangha Jewel, supreme Guides,
> To you, most sublime Three Jewels, I make offerings.

It is also important that whenever we engage in virtuous actions we dedicate them for the benefit of all mother sentient beings. This directs the merit we have created toward the greatest of all goals and ensures that it is not wasted or destroyed. Those who have accumulated sufficient merit can fulfill all their wishes and easily attain spiritual realizations.

The force of destruction

To attain authentic realizations of *Eight Verses of Training the Mind* we must also employ the force of destruction, which means applying strong effort in eliminating inner and outer obstacles. Inner obstacles include strong self-grasping, self-cherishing, laziness and wrong views, as well as the imprints of negative actions we have committed in the past. Outer obstacles include not finding a qualified Teacher, having no opportunity to practice Dharma, having a short life and lacking the basic necessities of life. Because all these obstacles arise from the imprints of the negative karma that we have accumulated over many lifetimes, we must purify them by engaging sincerely in the practice of purification. More details on purification can be found in the book *The Bodhisattva Vow*.

The force of aspirational prayer

We should begin any practice of training the mind by making special prayers to gain the realization of that practice, and we should finish it by dedicating the merit we have created toward gaining a full realization of that practice. For example, if we are going to meditate on cherishing love we should begin by making repeated requests to all the enlightened beings to grant us their blessings so that we may attain this specific realization, and after completing the meditation we should make a prayer dedicating our merit toward attaining this realization.

Making repeated prayers and requests to the holy beings is a powerful method for receiving their blessings. Our ability to accomplish the spiritual path depends upon our receiving the blessings of the enlightened beings, because without these blessings we are powerless and can make little or no progress.

If we sincerely engage in the training the mind practices of *Eight Verses of Training the Mind*, from cherishing others up to the practice of ultimate bodhichitta, in conjunction with the five forces, we will gather all the causes and conditions for attaining the realizations of *Eight Verses*. If all the causes and conditions for deep and genuine realizations are assembled, nothing can prevent the effect.

THE COMMITMENTS AND PRECEPTS OF TRAINING THE MIND

Another way of protecting and enhancing our practice of training the mind is to observe the eighteen commitments and twenty-two precepts of training the mind. These are mentioned in Geshe Chekhawa's *Training the Mind in Seven Points* and explained in detail in the book *Universal Compassion*. We do not need to take these commitments and precepts in front of our Spiritual Guides or the visualized Buddhas and Bodhisattvas, as we do with other vows, but can simply make a determination to keep them. Some of these commitments and precepts encourage us to engage in positive actions, whereas others advise us to avoid negative actions.

Observing these commitments and precepts is a special practice of moral discipline. Moral discipline is like a precious vessel in which we keep the nectar of spiritual realizations; without moral discipline it is impossible to hold any spiritual experiences in our mind. Even if we do manage to generate some positive feelings in meditation, if we make no effort to guard ourself against committing negative actions of body, speech and mind these will quickly disappear. Maintaining pure moral discipline ensures that all our bodily, verbal and mental actions are pure and positive, thereby enabling us to integrate the insights and positive experiences we gain during our meditation sessions into our daily life. We should not regard commitments and precepts as restrictions, or as laws that will lead to punishment if we transgress them, but instead, as guidelines for a healthy mind and a happier way of life.

Although we will not be able to keep all these commitments and precepts immediately, we can certainly begin to refrain from many negative actions and overcome our bad habits. For example, if we drink too much alcohol we can start to cut down right away, if we get angry easily we can try to be less aggressive and hostile, and if we are prone to jealousy we can try to rejoice more in others' happiness and good fortune. Unless we make an effort to reduce our gross delusions and bad habits, they will prevent us from making any progress in our spiritual practice.

To put these instructions on training the mind into practice we do not need to give up our normal daily activities but we do need to change our mental attitude toward them. As Geshe Chekhawa says, "Remain natural while changing your aspiration." We are living in human society and so we should behave in ways that accord with the way other people behave. We do not need to make an outward show of our spiritual practice. Of course we need to refrain from harmful actions, but mainly we need to change our mind. If we transform our present ordinary mind into love and compassion we will naturally act in a positive way that will be a good example to others and inspire them to enter the spiritual path. Gradually, through integrating Geshe Langri Tangpa's special instructions into our lives, we will become a very special being, a Bodhisattva, and eventually we will attain full enlightenment. We will then have the power to give happiness to all living beings everywhere. How wonderful!

Dedication

*T*hrough the virtues I have collected by writing this book, may there never arise in this world the miseries of incurable disease, famine or war, or the dangers of earthquakes, fires, floods, storms and so forth. However many living beings there are experiencing suffering, may their suffering cease and may they find everlasting happiness and joy. The Buddhadharma is the supreme medicine that relieves all mental pain, so may this precious Dharma Jewel pervade all worlds throughout space.

Venerable Geshe Kelsang Gyatso Rinpoche

The Root Text:

Eight Verses of Training the Mind

by Geshe Langri Tangpa (1054–1123)

The Root Text:
Eight Verses of Training the Mind

First we visualize, contemplate and recite the following:

In the space before me is the living Buddha Shakyamuni surrounded by all the Buddhas and Bodhisattvas like the full moon surrounded by stars.

The Actual Root Text:
Eight Verses of Training the Mind

With the intention to attain
The ultimate, supreme goal
That surpasses even the wish-granting jewel,
May I constantly cherish all living beings.

> *Our mind transforms into this intention, "May I constantly cherish all living beings," and remains on it single-pointedly for as long as possible.*
> *This way of meditating can be applied to the remaining seven verses.*

Whenever I associate with others,
May I view myself as the lowest of all;
And with a pure intention,
May I cherish others as supreme.

Examining my mental continuum throughout all my
    actions,
As soon as a delusion of self-cherishing develops
Whereby I or others would act inappropriately,
May I firmly face it and avert it.

Whenever I see unfortunate beings
Oppressed by evil and violent suffering,
May I cherish them as if I had found
A rare and precious treasure.

Even if someone I have helped
And of whom I had great hopes
Nevertheless harms me intentionally,
May I see him or her as my holy Spiritual Guide.

When others out of jealousy or anger
Harm me or insult me,
May I take defeat upon myself
And offer them the victory.

In short, may I directly and indirectly
Offer help and happiness to all my mothers,
And secretly take upon myself
All their harm and suffering.

Furthermore, through all the above practices,
Together with a mind undefiled by stains of conceptions of
    the eight extremes
And that sees all phenomena as illusory,
May I and all living beings be released from the bondage of
    mistaken appearance and conception.

Colophon: This text was translated by Venerable
Geshe Kelsang Gyatso Rinpoche.

The Condensed Meaning of the Commentary

The Condensed Meaning of the Commentary

The commentary to *Eight Verses of Training the Mind* has five parts:

1. The pre-eminent qualities of the author, Bodhisattva Langri Tangpa
2. The pre-eminent qualities of these instructions
3. The preliminary practices
4. The main practice: training in the two bodhichittas
5. How to integrate the practice of these instructions

The preliminary practices has six parts:

1. Cleaning the meditation room and setting up a shrine
2. Arranging beautiful offerings
3. Sitting in the correct meditation posture, going for refuge and generating bodhichitta
4. Visualizing the Field for Accumulating Merit
5. Offering the seven limbs and the mandala
6. Requesting the holy beings to bestow their blessings

Cleaning the meditation room and setting up a shrine has two parts:

    1. Cleaning practice
    2. Setting up a shrine

Sitting in the correct meditation posture, going for refuge and generating bodhichitta has three parts:

    1. Sitting in the correct meditation posture
    2. Going for refuge
    3. Generating bodhichitta

Offering the seven limbs and the mandala has eight parts:

    1. Prostration
    2. Offering
    3. Confession
    4. Rejoicing
    5. Beseeching the holy beings to remain
    6. Requesting the turning of the Wheel of Dharma
    7. Dedication
    8. Offering the mandala

Requesting the holy beings to bestow their blessings has two parts:

    1. Requesting blessings
    2. Receiving blessings

The main practice: training in the two bodhichittas, has two parts:

    1. Training in conventional bodhichitta
    2. Training in ultimate bodhichitta

Training in conventional bodhichitta has eight parts:

    1. Learning to cherish others
    2. Enhancing cherishing love
    3. Exchanging self with others
    4. Great compassion
    5. Wishing love
    6. Accepting defeat and offering the victory
    7. Taking and giving
    8. The precious mind of bodhichitta

Learning to cherish others has two parts:

    1. The kindness of others
    2. The benefits of cherishing others

Enhancing cherishing love has four parts:

    1. Recognizing our faults in the mirror of Dharma
    2. Viewing all living beings as supreme
    3. Living beings have no faults
    4. Developing humility

Exchanging self with others has five parts:

1. What is self-cherishing?
2. The faults of self-cherishing
3. How to destroy self-cherishing
4. How is it possible to exchange self with others?
5. The actual practice of exchanging self with others

Great compassion has three parts:

1. What is compassion?
2. How to develop compassion
3. The inner wealth of compassion

Wishing love has two parts:

1. How to develop wishing love
2. Transforming adverse conditions

Taking and giving has three parts:

1. Taking by means of compassion
2. Giving by means of love
3. Mounting taking and giving upon the breath

Taking by means of compassion has three parts:

1. Taking on our own future suffering
2. The benefits of taking on others' suffering
3. The actual meditation on taking

The precious mind of bodhichitta has two parts:

    1. Developing bodhichitta
    2. Enhancing bodhichitta

Training in ultimate bodhichitta has ten parts:

    1. What is emptiness?
    2. The emptiness of our body
    3. The emptiness of our mind
    4. The emptiness of our I
    5. The emptiness that is empty of eight extremes
    6. Conventional and ultimate truths
    7. The union of the two truths
    8. The practice of emptiness in our daily activities
    9. The purpose of meditating on emptiness
    10. A simple training in ultimate bodhichitta

The emptiness that is empty of eight extremes has eight parts:

    1. The extreme of produced phenomena
    2. The extreme of disintegration
    3. The extreme of impermanent phenomena
    4. The extreme of permanent phenomena
    5. The extreme of going
    6. The extreme of coming
    7. The extreme of singularity
    8. The extreme of plurality

How to integrate the practice of these instructions has two parts:

    1. Applying the five forces
    2. The commitments and precepts of training the mind

Applying the five forces has five parts:

    1. The force of motivation
    2. The force of familiarity
    3. The force of white seed
    4. The force of destruction
    5. The force of aspirational prayer

APPENDIX III
*S*adhanas

CONTENTS

Liberating Prayer

PRAISE TO BUDDHA SHAKYAMUNI

O Blessed One, Shakyamuni Buddha,
Precious treasury of compassion,
Bestower of supreme inner peace,

You, who love all beings without exception,
Are the source of happiness and goodness;
And you guide us to the liberating path.

Your body is a wishfulfilling jewel,
Your speech is supreme, purifying nectar,
And your mind is refuge for all living beings.

With folded hands I turn to you,
Supreme unchanging friend,
I request from the depths of my heart:

Please give me the light of your wisdom
To dispel the darkness of my mind
And to heal my mental continuum.

Please nourish me with your goodness,
That I in turn may nourish all beings
With an unceasing banquet of delight.

Through your compassionate intention,
Your blessings and virtuous deeds,
And my strong wish to rely upon you,

May all suffering quickly cease
And all happiness and joy be fulfilled;
And may holy Dharma flourish for evermore.

Colophon: This prayer was composed by Venerable Geshe Kelsang Gyatso Rinpoche and is recited regularly at the beginning of teachings, meditations and prayers in Kadampa Buddhist Centers throughout the world.

Essence of Good Fortune

PRAYERS FOR THE SIX PREPARATORY
PRACTICES FOR MEDITATION ON THE STAGES
OF THE PATH TO ENLIGHTENMENT

Introduction

Developing the realizations of the stages of the path to enlightenment depends upon four things: accumulating merit, purifying negativities, receiving the blessings of the Buddhas, Bodhisattvas and Spiritual Guides, and training the mind in the actual meditation on the stages of the path. The supreme method for accomplishing the first three is the six preparatory practices. These are:

1. Cleaning the meditation room and setting up a shrine with representations of Buddha's body, speech and mind.
2. Arranging suitable offerings.
3. Sitting in the correct meditation posture, going for refuge, generating and enhancing bodhichitta.
4. Visualizing the Field for Accumulating Merit.
5. Accumulating merit and purifying negativity by offering the practice of the seven limbs and the mandala.
6. Requesting the Field for Accumulating Merit in general and the Lamrim lineage Gurus in particular to bestow their blessings.

The essence of these six preparatory practices is contained in the following prayers, which should be recited with each session of meditation.

For more information on the six preparatory practices, see *The New Meditation Handbook* or *Joyful Path of Good Fortune*.

Geshe Kelsang Gyatso, 1986

Essence of Good Fortune

Mentally purifying the environment

May the whole ground
Become completely pure,
As level as the palm of a hand,
And as smooth as lapis lazuli.

Mentally arranging pure offerings

May all of space be filled
With offerings from gods and men,
Both set out and imagined,
Like offerings of the All Good One.

Visualizing the objects of refuge

In the space in front, on a lion throne, on a cushion of
lotus, sun and moon, sits Buddha Shakyamuni, the essence
of all my kind Teachers, surrounded by the assembly of
direct and indirect Gurus, Yidams, Buddhas, Bodhisattvas,
Hearers, Solitary Conquerors, Heroes, Dakinis and
Dharma Protectors.

Generating the causes of going for refuge

I and all my kind mothers, fearing samsara's torments, turn to Buddha, Dharma and Sangha, the only sources of refuge. From now until enlightenment, to the Three Jewels we go for refuge.

Short prayer of going for refuge

I and all sentient beings, until we achieve enlightenment,
Go for refuge to Buddha, Dharma and Sangha.

(7x, 100x, etc.)

Generating bodhichitta

Through the virtues I collect by giving and other
    perfections,
May I become a Buddha for the benefit of all.   (3x)

Purifying and receiving blessings

From the hearts of all refuge objects, lights and nectars stream down and dissolve into myself and all living beings, purifying negative karma and obstructions, increasing our lives, our virtues and Dharma realizations.

Generating the four immeasurables

May everyone be happy,
May everyone be free from misery,
May no one ever be separated from their happiness,
May everyone have equanimity, free from hatred and
    attachment.

Inviting the Field for Accumulating Merit

You, Protector of all beings,
Great Destroyer of hosts of demons,
Please, O Blessed One, Knower of All,
Come to this place with your retinue.

Prayer of seven limbs

With my body, speech and mind, humbly I prostrate,
And make offerings both set out and imagined.
I confess my wrong deeds from all time,
And rejoice in the virtues of all.
Please stay until samsara ceases,
And turn the Wheel of Dharma for us.
I dedicate all virtues to great enlightenment.

Offering the mandala

The ground sprinkled with perfume and spread with
    flowers,
The Great Mountain, four lands, sun and moon,
Seen as a Buddha Land and offered thus,
May all beings enjoy such Pure Lands.

I offer without any sense of loss
The objects that give rise to my attachment, hatred and
    confusion,
My friends, enemies and strangers, our bodies and
    enjoyments;
Please accept these and bless me to be released directly from
    the three poisons.

IDAM GURU RATNA MANDALAKAM NIRYATAYAMI

Requests to the Field for Accumulating Merit and the Lamrim lineage Gurus

So now my most kind root Guru,
Please sit on the lotus and moon on my crown
And grant me out of your great kindness,
Your body, speech and mind's attainments.

Visualize that your root Guru comes to the crown of your head and makes the following requests with you:

I make requests to you, Buddha Shakyamuni,
Whose body comes from countless virtues,
Whose speech fulfills the hopes of mortals,
Whose mind sees clearly all existence.

I make requests to you, Gurus of the lineage of extensive deeds,
Venerable Maitreya, Noble Asanga, Vasubandhu
And all the other precious Teachers
Who have revealed the path of vastness.

I make requests to you, Gurus of the lineage of profound view,
Venerable Manjushri, Nagarjuna, Chandrakirti
And all the other precious Teachers
Who have revealed the most profound path.

I make requests to you, Gurus of the lineage of Secret Mantra,
Conqueror Vajradhara, Tilopa, and Naropa
And all the other precious Teachers
Who have revealed the path of Tantra.

I make requests to you, Gurus of the Old Kadam lineage,
The second Buddha Atisha, Dromtonpa, Geshe Potowa
And all the other precious Teachers
Who have revealed the union of vast and profound paths.

I make requests to you, Gurus of the New Kadam lineage,
Venerable Tsongkhapa, Jampel Gyatso, Khedrubje
And all the other precious Teachers
Who have revealed the union of Sutra and Tantra.

I make requests to you, Venerable Kelsang Gyatso,
Protector of a vast ocean of living beings,
Unequalled Teacher of the paths to liberation and
     enlightenment,
Who accomplish and explain everything that was revealed
By the Fourth Deliverer of this Fortunate Eon.

I make requests to you, my kind precious Teacher,
Who care for those with uncontrolled minds
Untamed by all the previous Buddhas,
As if they were fortunate disciples.

Requesting the three great purposes

Please pour down your inspiring blessings upon myself and
all my mothers so that we may quickly stop all perverse
minds, from disrespect for our kind Teacher to the most
subtle dual appearance.

Please pour down your inspiring blessings so that we may
quickly generate pure minds, from respect for our kind
Teacher to the supreme mind of Union.

Please pour down your inspiring blessings to pacify all outer
and inner obstructions.   (3x)

Receiving blessings and purifying

From the hearts of all the holy beings, streams of light and
nectar flow down, granting blessings and purifying.

Prayer of the Stages of the Path

The path begins with strong reliance
On my kind Teacher, source of all good;
O Bless me with this understanding
To follow him with great devotion.

This human life with all its freedoms,
Extremely rare, with so much meaning;
O Bless me with this understanding
All day and night to seize its essence.

My body, like a water bubble,
Decays and dies so very quickly;
After death come results of karma,
Just like the shadow of a body.

With this firm knowledge and remembrance
Bless me to be extremely cautious,
Always avoiding harmful actions
And gathering abundant virtue.

Samsara's pleasures are deceptive,
Give no contentment, only torment;

So please bless me to strive sincerely
To gain the bliss of perfect freedom.

O Bless me so that from this pure thought
Come mindfulness and greatest caution,
To keep as my essential practice
The doctrine's root, the Pratimoksha.

Just like myself all my kind mothers
Are drowning in samsara's ocean;
O So that I may soon release them,
Bless me to train in bodhichitta.

But I cannot become a Buddha
By this alone without three ethics;
So bless me with the strength to practice
The Bodhisattva's ordination.

By pacifying my distractions
And analyzing perfect meanings,
Bless me to quickly gain the union
Of special insight and quiescence.

When I become a pure container
Through common paths, bless me to enter
The essence practice of good fortune,
The supreme vehicle, Vajrayana.

The two attainments both depend on
My sacred vows and my commitments;
Bless me to understand this clearly
And keep them at the cost of my life.

By constant practice in four sessions,
The way explained by holy Teachers,
O Bless me to gain both the stages,
Which are the essence of the Tantras.

May those who guide me on the good path,
And my companions all have long lives;
Bless me to pacify completely
All obstacles, outer and inner.

May I always find perfect Teachers,
And take delight in holy Dharma,
Accomplish all grounds and paths swiftly,
And gain the state of Vajradhara.

You may do your meditation here or at any appropriate point within the Prayer of the Stages of the Path.

Mantra recitation

After our meditation we contemplate that from the heart of Buddha Shakyamuni, the principal Field of Merit in front of us, infinite light rays emanate, reaching all environments and all beings. These dissolve into light and gradually gather into the Field of Merit. This dissolves into the central figure, Buddha Shakyamuni, who then dissolves into our root Guru at the crown of our head, instantly transforming him into the aspect of Guru Buddha Shakyamuni. He then diminishes in size, enters through our crown and descends to our heart. His mind and our mind become one nature. We recite the mantra:

OM MUNI MUNI MAHA MUNIYE SÖHA (7x, 100x, etc.)

Dedication prayers

Through the virtues I have collected
By practicing the stages of the path,
May all living beings find the opportunity
To practice in the same way.

However many living beings there are
Experiencing mental and physical suffering,
May their suffering cease through the power of my merit,
And may they find everlasting happiness and joy.

May everyone experience
The happiness of humans and gods,
And quickly attain enlightenment,
So that samsara is finally extinguished.

For the benefit of all living beings as extensive as space,
May I attain great wisdom like that of Manjushri,
Great compassion like that of Avalokiteshvara,
Great power like that of Vajrapani.

The Buddhadharma is the supreme medicine
That relieves all mental pain,
So may this precious Dharma Jewel
Pervade all worlds throughout space.

May there arise in the minds of all living beings
Great faith in Buddha, Dharma and Sangha,
And thus may they always receive
The blessings of the Three Precious Gems.

May there never arise in this world
The miseries of incurable disease, famine or war,
Or the dangers of earthquakes, fires,
Floods, storms and so forth.

May all mother beings meet precious Teachers
Who reveal the stages of the path to enlightenment,
And through engaging in this path
May they quickly attain the ultimate peace of full
    enlightenment.

Through the blessings of the Buddhas and Bodhisattvas,
The truth of actions and their effects,
And the power of my pure superior intention,
May all my prayers be fulfilled.

Prayers for the Virtuous Tradition

So that the tradition of Je Tsongkhapa,
The King of the Dharma, may flourish,
May all obstacles be pacified
And may all favorable conditions abound.

Through the two collections of myself and others
Gathered throughout the three times,
May the doctrine of Conqueror Losang Dragpa
Flourish for evermore.

The nine-line *Migtsema* prayer

Tsongkhapa, crown ornament of the scholars of the Land of
   the Snows,
You are Buddha Shakyamuni and Vajradhara, the source of
   all attainments,
Avalokiteshvara, the treasury of unobservable compassion,
Manjushri, the supreme stainless wisdom,
And Vajrapani, the destroyer of the hosts of maras.
O Venerable Guru-Buddha, synthesis of all Three Jewels,
With my body, speech and mind, respectfully I make
   requests:
Please grant your blessings to ripen and liberate myself and
   others,
And bestow the common and supreme attainments.   (3x)

*If we are unable to recite all these prayers for the six
preparatory practices in every meditation session, we should
at least always remember Guru Buddha Shakyamuni at the
crown of our head, recalling that his mind is the synthesis
of all Buddha Jewels, his speech the synthesis of all Dharma
Jewels and his body the synthesis of all Sangha Jewels. Then
with strong faith we should go for refuge by reciting the
short prayer of going for refuge, generate bodhichitta with
the words, 'Through the virtues . . . for the benefit of all',
offer the mandala, request the three great purposes and
receive blessings and purify.*

If we perform these three practices every time we sit down to meditate—namely, accumulating merit, purifying negative karma and making requests to receive blessings and inspiration—we shall have accomplished the three purposes of engaging in preparatory practices. At the conclusion of every meditation session, we should dedicate our merit.

Colophon: These prayers were compiled from traditional sources by Venerable Geshe Kelsang Gyatso Rinpoche. The verse of request to Venerable Geshe Kelsang Gyatso Rinpoche was composed by the Dharma Protector Duldzin Dorje Shugden and included in the prayers at the request of Venerable Geshe Kelsang's faithful disciples.

Prayers for Meditation

BRIEF PREPARATORY PRAYERS FOR MEDITATION

Introduction

We all have the potential to gain realizations of all the stages of the path to enlightenment. These potentials are like seeds in the field of our mind, and our meditation practice is like cultivating these seeds. However, our meditation practice will be successful only if we make good preparations beforehand.

If we want to cultivate external crops, we begin by making careful preparations. First, we remove from the soil anything that might obstruct their growth, such as stones and weeds. Second, we enrich the soil with compost or fertilizer to give it the strength to sustain growth. Third, we provide warm, moist conditions to enable the seeds to germinate and the plants to grow. In the same way, to cultivate our inner crops of Dharma realizations we must also begin by making careful preparations.

First, we must purify our mind to eliminate the negative karma we have accumulated in the past, because if we do not purify this karma it will obstruct the growth of Dharma realizations. Second, we need to give our mind the strength to support the growth of Dharma realizations by accumulating merit. Third, we need to activate and sustain the growth of Dharma realizations by receiving the blessings of the holy beings.

The brief prayers that follow contain the essence of these three preparations. For more information on them, see the books *The New Meditation Handbook* or *Joyful Path of Good Fortune*.

Geshe Kelsang Gyatso, 1987

Prayers for Meditation

Going for refuge

I and all sentient beings, until we achieve enlightenment,
Go for refuge to Buddha, Dharma and Sangha.

(3x, 7x, 100x or more)

Generating bodhichitta

Through the virtues I collect by giving and other
  perfections,
May I become a Buddha for the benefit of all.   (3x)

Generating the four immeasurables

May everyone be happy,
May everyone be free from misery,
May no one ever be separated from their happiness,
May everyone have equanimity, free from hatred and
  attachment.

Visualizing the Field for Accumulating Merit

In the space before me is the living Buddha Shakyamuni surrounded by all the Buddhas and Bodhisattvas, like the full moon surrounded by stars.

Prayer of seven limbs

With my body, speech and mind, humbly I prostrate,
And make offerings both set out and imagined.
I confess my wrong deeds from all time,
And rejoice in the virtues of all.
Please stay until samsara ceases,
And turn the Wheel of Dharma for us.
I dedicate all virtues to great enlightenment.

Offering the mandala

The ground sprinkled with perfume and spread with
    flowers,
The Great Mountain, four lands, sun and moon,
Seen as a Buddha Land and offered thus,
May all beings enjoy such Pure Lands.

I offer without any sense of loss
The objects that give rise to my attachment, hatred and
    confusion,
My friends, enemies and strangers, our bodies and
    enjoyments;
Please accept these and bless me to be released directly from
    the three poisons.

IDAM GURU RATNA MANDALAKAM NIRYATAYAMI

Prayer of the Stages of the Path

The path begins with strong reliance
On my kind Teacher, source of all good;
O Bless me with this understanding
To follow him with great devotion.

This human life with all its freedoms,
Extremely rare, with so much meaning;
O Bless me with this understanding
All day and night to seize its essence.

My body, like a water bubble,
Decays and dies so very quickly;
After death come results of karma,
Just like the shadow of a body.

With this firm knowledge and remembrance
Bless me to be extremely cautious,
Always avoiding harmful actions
And gathering abundant virtue.

Samsara's pleasures are deceptive,
Give no contentment, only torment;
So please bless me to strive sincerely
To gain the bliss of perfect freedom.

O Bless me so that from this pure thought
Come mindfulness and greatest caution,
To keep as my essential practice
The doctrine's root, the Pratimoksha.

Just like myself all my kind mothers
Are drowning in samsara's ocean;
O So that I may soon release them,
Bless me to train in bodhichitta.

But I cannot become a Buddha
By this alone without three ethics;
So bless me with the strength to practice
The Bodhisattva's ordination.

By pacifying my distractions
And analyzing perfect meanings,
Bless me to quickly gain the union
Of special insight and quiescence.

When I become a pure container
Through common paths, bless me to enter
The essence practice of good fortune,
The supreme vehicle, Vajrayana.

The two attainments both depend on
My sacred vows and my commitments;
Bless me to understand this clearly
And keep them at the cost of my life.

By constant practice in four sessions,
The way explained by holy Teachers,
O Bless me to gain both the stages,
Which are the essence of the Tantras.

May those who guide me on the good path,
And my companions all have long lives;
Bless me to pacify completely
All obstacles, outer and inner.

May I always find perfect Teachers,
And take delight in holy Dharma,
Accomplish all grounds and paths swiftly,
And gain the state of Vajradhara.

Receiving blessings and purifying

From the hearts of all the holy beings, streams of light and
nectar flow down, granting blessings and purifying.

*At this point we begin the actual contemplation and medi-
tation. After the meditation we dedicate our merit while
reciting the following prayers:*

Dedication prayers

Through the virtues I have collected
By practicing the stages of the path,
May all living beings find the opportunity
To practice in the same way.

May everyone experience
The happiness of humans and gods,
And quickly attain enlightenment,
So that samsara is finally extinguished.

Prayers for the Virtuous Tradition

So that the tradition of Je Tsongkhapa,
The King of the Dharma, may flourish,
May all obstacles be pacified
And may all favorable conditions abound.

Through the two collections of myself and others
Gathered throughout the three times,
May the doctrine of Conqueror Losang Dragpa
Flourish for evermore.

The nine-line *Migtsema* prayer

Tsongkhapa, crown ornament of the scholars of the Land of
    the Snows,
You are Buddha Shakyamuni and Vajradhara, the source of
    all attainments,
Avalokiteshvara, the treasury of unobservable compassion,
Manjushri, the supreme stainless wisdom,
And Vajrapani, the destroyer of the hosts of maras.
O Venerable Guru-Buddha, synthesis of all Three Jewels,
With my body, speech and mind, respectfully I make
    requests:
Please grant your blessings to ripen and liberate myself and
    others,
And bestow the common and supreme attainments.   (3x)

Colophon: These prayers were compiled from traditional
    sources by Venerable Geshe Kelsang Gyatso Rinpoche.

APPENDIX IV

The Kadampa Way of Life

THE ESSENTIAL PRACTICE OF KADAM LAMRIM

Introduction

This essential practice of Kadam Lamrim, known as *The Kadampa Way of Life*, contains two texts: *Advice from Atisha's Heart* and Je Tsongkhapa's *The Three Principal Aspects of the Path*. The first encapsulates the way of life of the early Kadampa practitioners, whose example of purity and sincerity we should all try to emulate. The second is a profound guide to meditation on the stages of the path, Lamrim, which Je Tsongkhapa composed based on the instructions he received directly from the Wisdom Buddha Manjushri.

If we try our best to put Atisha's advice into practice, and to meditate on Lamrim according to Je Tsongkhapa's instructions, we will develop a pure and happy mind and gradually progress toward the ultimate peace of full enlightenment. As Bodhisattva Shantideva says:

> By depending upon this boat-like human form
> We can cross the great ocean of suffering.
> Since such a vessel will be hard to find again,
> This is no time to sleep, you fool!

Practicing in this way is the very essence of the Kadampa way of life.

Geshe Kelsang Gyatso, 1994

Advice from Atisha's Heart

When Venerable Atisha came to Tibet he first went to Ngari, where he remained for two years giving many teachings to the disciples of Jangchub Ö. After two years had passed he decided to return to India, and Jangchub Ö requested him to give one last teaching before he left. Atisha replied that he had already given them all the advice they needed, but Jangchub Ö persisted in his request and so Atisha accepted and gave the following advice.

How wonderful!

Friends, since you already have great knowledge and clear understanding, whereas I am of no importance and have little wisdom, it is not suitable for you to request advice from me. However because you dear friends, whom I cherish from my heart, have requested me, I shall give you this essential advice from my inferior and childish mind.

Friends, until you attain enlightenment the Spiritual Teacher is indispensable, therefore rely upon the holy Spiritual Guide.

Until you realize ultimate truth, listening is indispensable, therefore listen to the instructions of the Spiritual Guide.

Since you cannot become a Buddha merely by understanding Dharma, practice earnestly with understanding.

Avoid places that disturb your mind, and always remain where your virtues increase.

Until you attain stable realizations, worldly amusements are harmful, therefore abide in a place where there are no such distractions.

Avoid friends who cause you to increase delusions, and rely upon those who increase your virtue. This you should take to heart.

Since there is never a time when worldly activities come to an end, limit your activities.

Dedicate your virtues throughout the day and the night, and always watch your mind.

Because you have received advice, whenever you are not meditating, always practice in accordance with what your Spiritual Guide says.

If you practice with great devotion, results will arise immediately, without your having to wait for a long time.

If from your heart you practice in accordance with Dharma, both food and resources will come naturally to hand.

Friends, the things you desire give no more satisfaction than drinking sea water, therefore practice contentment.

Avoid all haughty, conceited, proud and arrogant minds, and remain peaceful and subdued.

Avoid activities that are said to be meritorious, but which in fact are obstacles to Dharma.

Profit and respect are nooses of the maras, so brush them aside like stones on the path.

Words of praise and fame serve only to beguile us, therefore blow them away as you would blow your nose.

Since the happiness, pleasure and friends you gather in this life last only for a moment, put them all behind you.

Since future lives last for a very long time, gather up riches to provide for the future.

You will have to depart leaving everything behind, so do not be attached to anything.

Generate compassion for lowly beings, and especially avoid despising or humiliating them.

Have no hatred for enemies, and no attachment for friends.

Do not be jealous of others' good qualities, but out of admiration adopt them yourself.

Do not look for faults in others, but look for faults in yourself, and purge them like bad blood.

Do not contemplate your own good qualities, but contemplate the good qualities of others, and respect everyone as a servant would.

See all living beings as your father or mother, and love them as if you were their child.

Always keep a smiling face and a loving mind, and speak truthfully without malice.

If you talk too much with little meaning you will make mistakes, therefore speak in moderation, only when necessary.

If you engage in many meaningless activities your virtuous activities will degenerate, therefore stop activities that are not spiritual.

It is completely meaningless to put effort into activities that have no essence.

If the things you desire do not come, it is due to karma created long ago, therefore keep a happy and relaxed mind.

Beware, offending a holy being is worse than dying, therefore be honest and straightforward.

Since all the happiness and suffering of this life arise from previous actions, do not blame others.

All happiness comes from the blessings of your Spiritual Guide, therefore always repay his kindness.

Since you cannot tame the minds of others until you have tamed your own, begin by taming your own mind.

Since you will definitely have to depart without the wealth you have accumulated, do not accumulate negativity for the sake of wealth.

Distracting enjoyments have no essence, therefore sincerely practice giving.

Always keep pure moral discipline, for it leads to beauty in this life and happiness hereafter.

Since hatred is rife in these impure times, don the armor of patience, free from anger.

You remain in samsara through the power of laziness, therefore ignite the fire of the effort of application.

Since this human life is wasted by indulging in distractions, now is the time to practice concentration.

Being under the influence of wrong views, you do not realize the ultimate nature of things, therefore investigate correct meanings.

Friends, there is no happiness in this swamp of samsara, so move to the firm ground of liberation.

Meditate according to the advice of your Spiritual Guide and dry up the river of samsaric suffering.

You should consider this well because it is not just words from the mouth, but sincere advice from the heart.

If you practice like this, you will delight me, and you will bring happiness to yourself and others.

I who am ignorant request you to take this advice to heart.

This is the advice that the holy being Venerable Atisha gave to Venerable Jangchub Ö.

The Three Principal Aspects of the Path

Homage to the venerable Spiritual Guide.

I shall explain to the best of my ability
The essential meaning of all the Conqueror's teachings,
The path praised by the holy Bodhisattvas,
And the gateway for fortunate ones seeking liberation.

You who are not attached to the joys of samsara,
But strive to make your freedom and endowment
  meaningful,
O Fortunate Ones who apply your minds to the path that
  pleases the Conquerors,
Please listen with a clear mind.

Without pure renunciation there is no way to pacify
Attachment to the pleasures of samsara;
And since living beings are tightly bound by desire for
  samsara,
Begin by seeking renunciation.

Freedom and endowment are difficult to find, and there is
　　no time to waste.
By acquainting your mind with this, overcome attachment
　　to this life;
And by repeatedly contemplating actions and effects
And the sufferings of samsara, overcome attachment to
　　future lives.

When, through contemplating in this way, the desire for
　　the pleasures of samsara
Does not arise, even for a moment,
But a mind longing for liberation arises throughout the day
　　and the night,
At that time, renunciation is generated.

However, if this renunciation is not maintained
By completely pure bodhichitta,
It will not be a cause of the perfect happiness of
　　unsurpassed enlightenment;
Therefore, the wise generate a supreme bodhichitta.

Swept along by the currents of the four powerful rivers,
Tightly bound by the chains of karma, so hard to release,
Ensnared within the iron net of self-grasping,
Completely enveloped by the pitch-black darkness of
　　ignorance,

Taking rebirth after rebirth in boundless samsara,
And unceasingly tormented by the three sufferings—

Through contemplating the state of your mothers in
    conditions such as these,
Generate a supreme mind [of bodhichitta].

But, even though you may be acquainted with renunciation
    and bodhichitta,
If you do not possess the wisdom realizing the way things
    are,
You will not be able to cut the root of samsara;
Therefore strive in the means for realizing dependent
    relationship.

Whoever negates the conceived object of self-grasping,
Yet sees the infallibility of cause and effect
Of all phenomena in samsara and nirvana,
Has entered the path that pleases the Buddhas.

Dependent-related appearance is infallible
And emptiness is inexpressible;
For as long as the meaning of these two appear to be
    separate,
You have not yet realized Buddha's intention.

When they arise as one, not alternating but simultaneous,
From merely seeing infallible dependent relationship,
Comes certain knowledge that destroys all grasping at
    objects.
At that time the analysis of view is complete.

Moreover, when the extreme of existence is dispelled by
    appearance,
And the extreme of non-existence is dispelled by emptiness,
And you know how emptiness is perceived as cause and
    effect,
You will not be captivated by extreme views.

When, in this way, you have correctly realized the essential
    points
Of the three principal aspects of the path,
Dear One, withdraw into solitude, generate strong effort
And quickly accomplish the final goal.

Colophon: Both texts were translated under the compassionate
guidance of Venerable Geshe Kelsang Gyatso Rinpoche.

Glossary

Alertness A mental factor that is a type of wisdom that examines our activity of body, speech and mind and knows whether or not faults are developing. See *How to Understand the Mind*.

Amitayus A Buddha who increases our lifespan, merit and wisdom. He is the Enjoyment Body aspect of Buddha Amitabha.

Analytical meditation See *Meditation*.

Anger A deluded mental factor that observes its contaminated object, exaggerates its bad qualities, considers it to be undesirable and wishes to harm it. See *How to Understand the Mind* and *How to Solve Our Human Problems*.

Asanga A great Indian Buddhist Yogi and scholar of the fifth century, author of *Compendium of Abhidharma*. See *Living Meaningfully, Dying Joyfully*.

Atisha (AD 982–1054) A famous Indian Buddhist scholar and meditation master. He was Abbot of the great Buddhist monastery of Vikramashila at a time when Mahayana Buddhism was flourishing in India. He was later invited to Tibet where he re-introduced pure Buddhism. He is the author of the first text on the stages of the path, *Lamp for the Path*. His tradition later became known as the "Kadampa Tradition." See *Joyful Path of Good Fortune* and *Modern Buddhism*.

Attachment A deluded mental factor that observes its contaminated object, regards it as a cause of happiness and wishes for it. See *Joyful Path of Good Fortune* and *How to Understand the Mind*.

Avalokiteshvara "Chenrezig" in Tibetan. The embodiment of the compassion of all the Buddhas. See *Living Meaningfully, Dying Joyfully*.

Beginningless time According to the Buddhist worldview, there is no beginning to mind, and so no beginning to time. Therefore, all sentient beings have taken countless previous rebirths.

Bodhisattva grounds These ten grounds are the realizations of Superior Bodhisattvas. See *Ocean of Nectar*.

Brahma A worldly god. See *Ocean of Nectar*.

Buddha's bodies A Buddha has four bodies—the Wisdom Truth Body, the Nature Body, the Enjoyment Body and the Emanation Body. The first is Buddha's omniscient mind; the second is the emptiness, or ultimate nature, of his or her mind; the third is his subtle Form Body; and the fourth, of which each Buddha manifests a countless number, are gross Form Bodies that are visible to ordinary beings. The Wisdom Truth Body and the Nature Body are both included within the Truth Body, and the Enjoyment Body and the Emanation Body are both included within the Form Body. See *Joyful Path of Good Fortune*.

Channel wheel "Chakra" in Sanskrit. A focal center where secondary channels branch out from the central channel. Meditating on these points can cause the inner winds to enter the central channel. See also **Channels**. See *Clear Light of Bliss*, *Modern Buddhism* and *Mahamudra Tantra*.

Channels Subtle inner passageways of the body through which subtle drops flow moved by inner winds. See *Clear Light of Bliss*, *Modern Buddhism* and *Mahamudra Tantra*.

Completion stage Highest Yoga Tantra realizations developed in dependence upon the inner winds entering, abiding and dissolving within the central channel through the force of meditation. See *Tantric Grounds and Paths* and *Modern Buddhism*.

Concentration A mental factor that makes its primary mind remain on its object single-pointedly. See *Joyful Path of Good Fortune* and *Meaningful to Behold*.

Contentment Being satisfied with one's outer and inner conditions, motivated by a virtuous intention.

Correct belief A non-valid cognizer that realizes its conceived object. See *How to Understand the Mind*.

Dakinis Female Tantric Buddhas and those women who have attained the realization of meaning clear light. Dakas are the male equivalent. See *The New Guide to Dakini Land*.

Deity "Yidam" in Tibetan. A Tantric enlightened being.

Demon See *Mara*.

Desirous attachment See *Attachment*.

Dharma Protector An emanation of a Buddha or a Bodhisattva, whose main function is to eliminate obstacles and gather all necessary conditions for pure Dharma practitioners. Also called "Dharmapala" in Sanskrit. See *Heart Jewel*.

Direct perceiver A cognizer that apprehends its manifest object. See *How to Understand the Mind*.

Discrimination A mental factor that functions to apprehend the uncommon sign of an object. See *How to Understand the Mind*.

Dualistic appearance The appearance to a mind of an object together with the appearance to that mind of the object's inherent existence. See *The New Heart of Wisdom*.

Emanation Animate or inanimate form manifested by Buddhas or high Bodhisattvas to benefit others.

Emanation Body See *Buddha's bodies.*

Enjoyment Body See *Buddha's bodies.*

Equanimity Generally speaking, a balanced mind free from strong attachment and aversion. See *Joyful Path of Good Fortune.*

Faith A naturally virtuous mind that functions mainly to oppose the perception of faults in its observed object. There are three types of faith: believing faith, admiring faith and wishing faith. See *Joyful Path of Good Fortune*, *Modern Buddhism* and *How to Understand the Mind.*

Feeling A mental factor that functions to experience pleasant, unpleasant or neutral objects. See *How to Understand the Mind.*

Foe Destroyer "Arhat" in Sanskrit. A practitioner who has abandoned all delusions and their seeds by training on the spiritual paths, and who will never again be reborn in samsara. In this context the term "Foe" refers to the delusions.

Form Body See *Buddha's bodies.*

Fortunate Eon The name given to this world age. It is so called because one thousand founding Buddhas will appear during this eon. Buddha Shakyamuni was the fourth and Buddha Maitreya will be the fifth. An eon in which no Buddhas appear is called a "Dark Eon."

Fourth Deliverer Refers to Buddha Shakyamuni. See also *Fortunate Eon.*

Generation stage A realization of a creative yoga prior to attaining the actual completion stage, which is attained through the practice of bringing the three bodies into the path, in which one mentally generates oneself as a Tantric Deity and one's surroundings as the

Deity's mandala. Meditation on generation stage is called a "creative yoga" because its object is created, or generated, by correct imagination. See *Mahamudra Tantra*, *Modern Buddhism* and *Tantric Grounds and Paths*.

Generic image The appearing object of a conceptual mind. A generic image, or mental image, of an object is like a reflection of that object. Conceptual minds know their object through the appearance of a generic image of that object, not by seeing the object directly. See *The New Heart of Wisdom* and *How to Understand the Mind*.

Geshe A title given by the Kadampa monasteries to accomplished Buddhist scholars. Contracted form of the Tibetan "ge wai she nyen," literally meaning "virtuous friend."

Geshe Chekhawa (AD 1102–1176) A great Kadampa Bodhisattva who composed the text *Training the Mind in Seven Points*, a commentary to Geshe Langri Tangpa's *Eight Verses of Training the Mind*. He spread the study and practice of training the mind throughout Tibet. See *Universal Compassion*.

Gods Beings of the god realm, the highest of the six realms of samsara. See *Joyful Path of Good Fortune*.

Guide to the Bodhisattva's Way of Life A classic Mahayana Buddhist text composed by the great Indian Buddhist Yogi and scholar Shantideva, which presents all the practices of a Bodhisattva from the initial generation of bodhichitta through to the completion of the practice of the six perfections. For a translation, see *Guide to the Bodhisattva's Way of Life,* and for a full commentary see *Meaningful to Behold*.

Guru yoga A special way of relying upon our Spiritual Guide in order to receive his or her blessings. See *Great Treasury of Merit* and *Heart Jewel*.

Gyalwa Ensapa (AD 1505–1566) A great Yogi and Mahamudra lineage Guru. See *Great Treasury of Merit.*

Hearer One of two types of Hinayana practitioner. Both Hearers and Solitary Conquerors are Hinayanists but they differ in their motivation, behavior, merit and wisdom. See *Ocean of Nectar.*

Heart Sutra One of several *Perfection of Wisdom Sutras* taught by Buddha. Although much shorter than the other *Perfection of Wisdom Sutras*, it contains explicitly or implicitly their entire meaning. Also known as the *Essence of Wisdom Sutra*. For a translation and full commentary, see *The New Heart of Wisdom.*

Hell realm The lowest of the six realms of samsara. See *Joyful Path of Good Fortune.*

Hero/Heroine A Hero is a male Tantric Deity embodying method, and a Heroine is a female Tantric Deity embodying wisdom. See *The New Guide to Dakini Land.*

Heruka A principal Deity of Mother Tantra who is the embodiment of indivisible bliss and emptiness. See *Essence of Vajrayana* and *Modern Buddhism.*

Hinayana Sanskrit for "Lesser Vehicle." The Hinayana goal is to attain merely one's own liberation from suffering by completely abandoning delusions. See *Joyful Path of Good Fortune.*

Humility A virtuous mental factor whose main function is to reduce deluded pride.

Hungry spirits Beings of the hungry spirit realm, the second lowest of the six realms of samsara. See *Joyful Path of Good Fortune.*

Imprint There are two types of imprint: imprints of actions and imprints of delusions. Every action we perform leaves an imprint on the mind, and these imprints are karmic potentialities to experience certain effects in the future. The imprints of delusions remain even after the delusions themselves have been abandoned, like the smell of garlic lingers in a container after the garlic has been removed. Imprints of delusions are obstructions to omniscience, and are completely abandoned only by Buddhas.

Indra A worldly god. See *The New Heart of Wisdom*.

Inner winds Special subtle winds related to the mind that flow through the channels of our body. Our body and mind cannot function without these winds. See *Mahamudra Tantra, Modern Buddhism* and *Clear Light of Bliss*.

Jangchub Ö Nephew of the eleventh century Tibetan king, Yeshe Ö. Together they underwent many hardships to invite the great Indian Buddhist master Atisha to Tibet, Yeshe Ö giving his life in the process. As a result of this selfless kindness, a revival of a pure Buddhadharma occurred throughout Tibet. This Buddhadharma became known as "Kadampa Buddhism," and continues to flourish to this day throughout the world. See *Joyful Path of Good Fortune* and *Modern Buddhism*.

Je Tsongkhapa (AD 1357–1419) An emanation of the Wisdom Buddha Manjushri, whose appearance in fourteenth-century Tibet as a monk, and the holder of the lineage of pure view and pure deeds, was prophesied by Buddha. He spread a very pure Buddhadharma throughout Tibet, showing how to combine the practices of Sutra and Tantra, and how to practice pure Dharma during degenerate times. His tradition later became known as the "*Gelug*," or "*Ganden Tradition*." See *Heart Jewel* and *Great Treasury of Merit*.

Kadampa A Tibetan word in which "Ka" means "word" and refers to all Buddha's teachings, "dam" refers to Atisha's special Lamrim instructions known as the "stages of the path to enlightenment," and "pa" refers to a follower of Kadampa Buddhism who integrates all the teachings of Buddha that they know into their Lamrim practice. See also **Kadampa Tradition**. See *Modern Buddhism*.

Kadampa Tradition The pure tradition of Buddhism established by Atisha. Followers of this tradition up to the time of Je Tsongkhapa are known as "Old Kadampas," and those after the time of Je Tsongkhapa are known as "New Kadampas." See also **Kadampa.**

Khedrubje (AD 1385–1438) One of the principal disciples of Je Tsongkhapa, who did much to promote the tradition of Je Tsongkhapa after he passed away. See *Great Treasury of Merit*.

Lamrim Tibetan, literally meaning "stages of the path." A special arrangement of all Buddha's teachings that is easy to understand and put into practice. It reveals all the stages of the path to enlightenment. For a full commentary, see *Joyful Path of Good Fortune* and *The New Meditation Handbook*.

Lineage A line of instruction that has been passed down from Spiritual Guide to disciple, with each Spiritual Guide in the line having gained personal experience of the instruction before passing it on to others.

Lineage Gurus The line of Spiritual Guides through whom a particular instruction has been passed down.

Mahamudra Sanskrit, literally meaning "great seal." According to Sutra, this refers to the profound view of emptiness. Since emptiness is the nature of all phenomena it is called a "seal," and since a direct realization of emptiness enables us to accomplish the great purpose—complete liberation from the sufferings of samsara—it is also called "great." According to Secret Mantra, "great seal" is the union of spontaneous great bliss and emptiness. See *Mahamudra Tantra*, *The Oral Instructions of Mahamudra*, *Clear Light of Bliss* and *Great Treasury of Merit*.

Mahayana Sanskrit for "Great Vehicle," the spiritual path to great enlightenment. The Mahayana goal is to attain Buddhahood for the benefit of all sentient beings by completely abandoning delusions and their imprints. See *Joyful Path of Good Fortune* and *Meaningful to Behold*.

Maitreya The embodiment of the loving kindness of all the Buddhas. At the time of Buddha Shakyamuni he manifested as a Bodhisattva disciple in order to show Buddha's disciples how to be perfect Mahayana disciples. In the future he will manifest as the fifth founding Buddha.

Mala A rosary used to count recitations of prayers or mantras.

Mantra Sanskrit, literally meaning "mind protection." Mantra protects the mind from ordinary appearances and conceptions. See *Mahamudra Tantra* and *Tantric Grounds and Paths*.

Mara Sanskrit for "demon," and refers to anything that obstructs the attainment of liberation or enlightenment. There are four principal types of mara: the mara of the delusions, the mara of contaminated aggregates, the mara of uncontrolled death and the Devaputra maras. Of these, only the last are actual sentient beings. See *The New Heart of Wisdom*.

Meaning clear light A very subtle mind that realizes emptiness directly without a generic image. See *Mahamudra Tantra* and *Clear Light of Bliss*.

Meditation A mind that concentrates on a virtuous object, and a mental action that is the main cause of mental peace. There are two types of meditation—analytical meditation and placement meditation. When we use our imagination, mindfulness and powers of reasoning to find our object of meditation, this is analytical meditation. When we find our object and hold it single-pointedly, this is placement meditation. There are different types of object. Some, such as impermanence or emptiness, are objects apprehended by the mind. Others, such as love, compassion and renunciation, are actual states of mind. We engage in analytical meditation until the specific object that we seek appears clearly to our mind or until the particular state of mind that we wish to generate arises. This object or state of mind is our object of placement meditation. See *The New Meditation Handbook* and *Joyful Path of Good Fortune*.

Mental factor A cognizer that principally apprehends a particular attribute of an object. There are fifty-one specific mental factors. Each moment of mind comprises a primary mind and various mental factors. See *How to Understand the Mind*.

Merit The good fortune created by virtuous actions. It is the potential power to increase our good qualities and produce happiness.

Method Any spiritual path that functions to ripen our Buddha lineage. Training in renunciation, compassion and bodhichitta are examples of method practices.

Milarepa (AD 1040–1123) A great Tibetan Buddhist meditator and disciple of Marpa, celebrated for his beautiful songs of realization.

Mindfulness A mental factor that functions not to forget the object realized by the primary mind. See *How to Understand the Mind* and *Meaningful to Behold*.

Naga A non-human being not normally visible to humans. Their upper half is said to be human, their lower half serpent. Nagas usually live in the oceans of the world but they sometimes inhabit land in the region of rocks and trees. They are very powerful, some being benevolent and some malevolent. Many diseases, known as "naga diseases," are caused by nagas and can only be cured through performing certain naga rituals.

Nagarjuna A great Indian Buddhist scholar and meditation master who revived the Mahayana in the first century AD by bringing to light the teachings on the *Perfection of Wisdom Sutras*. Nagarjuna's extraordinary life and works were prophesied by Buddha Shakyamuni. See *Ocean of Nectar*.

Negated object See *Object of negation*.

Non-conceptual mind A cognizer to which its object appears clearly without being mixed with a generic image. See *How to Understand the Mind*.

Nyungnay A fasting and purification retreat in conjunction with Eleven-faced Avalokiteshvara.

Object of negation An object explicitly negated by a mind realizing a negative phenomenon. Also known as "negated object." See *The New Heart of Wisdom*.

Observed object Any object upon which the mind is focused. See *How to Understand the Mind*.

Obstructions to liberation Obstructions that prevent the attainment of liberation. All delusions, such as ignorance, attachment and anger, together with their seeds, are obstructions to liberation. Also called "delusion-obstructions."

Obstructions to omniscience The imprints of delusions, that prevent simultaneous and direct realization of all phenomena. Only Buddhas have overcome these obstructions.

Offering to the Spiritual Guide "Lama Chopa" in Tibetan. A special Guru yoga of Je Tsongkhapa in which our Spiritual Guide is visualized in the aspect of Lama Losang Tubwang Dorjechang. It is a preliminary practice for Vajrayana Mahamudra. For a translation and full commentary, see *Great Treasury of Merit*.

Ordinary being Anyone who has not realized emptiness directly.

Perfection of Wisdom Sutras Sutras of the second turning of the Wheel of Dharma in which Buddha revealed his final view of the ultimate nature of all phenomena—emptiness of inherent existence. See *The New Heart of Wisdom* and *Ocean of Nectar*.

Placement meditation See *Meditation*.

Pratimoksha Sanskrit for "personal liberation." See *The Bodhisattva Vow*.

Primary mind A cognizer that principally apprehends the mere entity of an object. Synonymous with consciousness. There are six primary minds: eye consciousness, ear consciousness, nose consciousness, tongue consciousness, body consciousness and mental consciousness. Each moment of mind comprises a primary mind and various mental factors. A primary mind and its accompanying mental factors are the same entity but have different functions. See *How to Understand the Mind*.

Profound path The profound path includes all the wisdom practices that lead to a direct realization of emptiness and ultimately to the Truth Body of a Buddha. See *Joyful Path of Good Fortune* and *Ocean of Nectar*.

Prostration An action of showing respect with body, speech or mind. See *Joyful Path of Good Fortune* and *The Bodhisattva Vow*.

Pure Land A pure environment in which there are no true sufferings. There are many Pure Lands. For example, Tushita is the Pure Land of Buddha Maitreya, Sukhavati is the Pure Land of Buddha Amitabha and Dakini Land, or Keajra, is the Pure Land of Buddha Vajrayogini and Buddha Heruka. See *Living Meaningfully, Dying Joyfully* and *Heart Jewel*.

Realization A stable and non-mistaken experience of a virtuous object that directly protects us from suffering.

Renunciation The wish to be released from samsara. See *Joyful Path of Good Fortune*.

Root mind The very subtle mind located at the center of the heart channel wheel. It is known as the "root mind" because all other minds arise from it and dissolve back into it. See *Mahamudra Tantra*.

Secret Mantra Synonymous with Tantra. Secret Mantra teachings are distinguished from Sutra teachings in that they reveal methods for training the mind by bringing the future result, or Buddhahood, into the present path. Secret Mantra is the supreme path to full enlightenment. The term "Mantra" indicates that it is Buddha's special instruction for protecting our mind from ordinary appearances and conceptions. Practitioners of Secret Mantra overcome ordinary appearances and conceptions by visualizing their body, environment, enjoyments and deeds as those of a Buddha. The term "Secret" indicates that the practices are to be done in private, and that they can be practiced only by those who have received a Tantric empowerment. See *The Oral Instructions of Mahamudra*, *Mahamudra Tantra, Modern Buddhism* and *Tantric Grounds and Paths*.

Seed of delusion The seed of a delusion is the potentiality for that delusion to arise; it is the substantial cause of the delusion. Until we have finally abandoned a delusion, the seed of that delusion will remain within our mind, even when the delusion itself is not manifest. Seeds of delusions can be eradicated only by the wisdom directly realizing emptiness. See *How to Understand the Mind*.

Sentient being Any being who possesses a mind that is contaminated by delusions or their imprints. Both "sentient being" and "living being" are terms used to distinguish beings whose minds are contaminated by either of the two obstructions from Buddhas, whose minds are completely free from these obstructions.

Shantideva (AD 687–763) A great Indian Buddhist scholar and meditation master. He composed *Guide to the Bodhisattva's Way of Life*. See *Meaningful to Behold* and *Guide to the Bodhisattva's Way of Life*.

Six realms There are six realms of samsara. Listed in ascending order according to the type of karma that causes rebirth in them, they are the realms of the hell beings, hungry spirits, animals, humans, demi-gods and gods. The first three are lower realms or unhappy migrations, and the second three are higher realms or happy migrations. See *Joyful Path of Good Fortune* and *The New Meditation Handbook*.

Solitary Conqueror One of two types of Hinayana practitioner. See also ***Hearer***.

Spiritual Guide "Guru" in Sanskrit, "Lama" in Tibetan. A Teacher who guides us along the spiritual path. See *Joyful Path of Good Fortune* and *Great Treasury of Merit*.

Subsequent valid cognizer A completely reliable cognizer whose object is realized in direct dependence upon a conclusive reason. See *How to Understand the Mind*.

Subtle mind There are different levels of mind: gross, subtle and very subtle. Subtle minds manifest when the inner winds gather and dissolve within the central channel. See also ***Root mind***. See *Clear Light of Bliss* and *Mahamudra Tantra*.

Superior seeing A special wisdom that sees its object clearly, and that is maintained by tranquil abiding and the special suppleness that is induced by investigation. See *Joyful Path of Good Fortune* and *The Oral Instructions of Mahamudra*.

Sutra The teachings of Buddha that are open to everyone to practice without the need for an empowerment. These include Buddha's teachings of the three turnings of the Wheel of Dharma.

Tantra See ***Secret Mantra***.

Tara/Arya Tara A female Buddha who is a manifestation of the ultimate wisdom of all the Buddhas. "Arya" means "Superior," and "Tara" means "Liberator" or "Rescuer." Because she is a wisdom Buddha, and a manifestation of the completely purified wind element, Tara is able to help us very quickly.

Three principal aspects of the path The realizations of renunciation, bodhichitta and the wisdom realizing emptiness. See *Joyful Path of Good Fortune.*

Tranquil abiding A concentration that possesses the special bliss of physical and mental suppleness that is attained in dependence upon completing the nine mental abidings. See *Meaningful to Behold, Joyful Path of Good Fortune* and *The Oral Instructions of Mahamudra.*

Trijang Rinpoche, Vajradhara (AD 1901–1981) A special Tibetan Lama of the twentieth century. Also known as "Dorjechang Trijang Rinpoche" and "Losang Yeshe."

Truth Body See *Buddha's bodies.*

Union Refers to the Union of No More Learning, which is synonymous with full enlightenment.

Vajradhara The founder of Vajrayana, or Tantra. He is the same mental continuum as Buddha Shakyamuni but displays a different aspect. Buddha Shakyamuni appears in the aspect of an Emanation Body, and Conqueror Vajradhara appears in the aspect of an Enjoyment Body. See *Great Treasury of Merit.*

Vajradharma The manifestation of the speech of all the Buddhas. He looks like Conqueror Vajradhara, except that his body is red. See *The New Guide to Dakini Land.*

Vajrapani The embodiment of the power of all the Buddhas. He appears in a wrathful aspect, displaying his power to overcome outer, inner and secret obstacles.

Vajrayana The Secret Mantra vehicle. See also *Secret Mantra.*

Vajrayogini A female Highest Yoga Tantra Deity who is the embodiment of indivisible bliss and emptiness. She is the same nature as Heruka. See *The New Guide to Dakini Land.*

Valid cognizer A cognizer that is non-deceptive with respect to its engaged object. There are two types: inferential valid cognizers and direct valid cognizers. See *The New Heart of Wisdom* and *How to Understand the Mind*.

Vast path The vast path includes all the method practices from the initial cultivation of compassion through to the final attainment of the Form Body of a Buddha. See *Joyful Path of Good Fortune*.

Vinaya Sutras Sutras in which Buddha principally explains the practice of moral discipline, and in particular the Pratimoksha moral discipline.

Wisdom A virtuous, intelligent mind that makes its primary mind realize its object thoroughly. A wisdom is a spiritual path that functions to release our mind from delusions or their imprints. An example of wisdom is the correct view of emptiness. See *The New Heart of Wisdom* and *How to Understand the Mind*.

Worldly concerns, the eight The objects of the eight worldly concerns are happiness and suffering, wealth and poverty, praise and criticism and good reputation and bad reputation. They are known as "the eight worldly concerns" because worldly people are constantly concerned with them, wanting some and trying to avoid others. They are also known as "the eight worldly dharmas." See *Joyful Path of Good Fortune*.

Wrong awareness A cognizer that is mistaken with respect to its engaged, or apprehended, object. See *How to Understand the Mind*.

Wrong view An intellectually-formed wrong awareness that denies the existence of an object that it is necessary to understand to attain liberation or enlightenment—for example, denying the existence of enlightened beings, karma or rebirth. See *Joyful Path of Good Fortune*.

Yidam See *Deity.*

Yogi/Yogini Sanskrit terms usually referring to a male or a female meditator who has attained the union of tranquil abiding and superior seeing.

*B*ibliography

*V*enerable Geshe Kelsang Gyatso Rinpoche is a highly respected
meditation master and scholar of the Mahayana Buddhist tradition
founded by Je Tsongkhapa. Since arriving in the West in 1977,
Venerable Geshe Kelsang has worked tirelessly to establish pure
Buddhadharma throughout the world. Over this period he has
given extensive teachings on the major scriptures of the Mahayana.
These teachings provide a comprehensive presentation of the
essential Sutra and Tantra practices of Mahayana Buddhism.

Books

The following books by Venerable Geshe Kelsang Gyatso Rinpoche
are all published by Tharpa Publications.

The Bodhisattva Vow. A practical guide to helping others. (2nd ed.,
1995)
Clear Light of Bliss. A Tantric meditation manual. (3rd ed., 2014)
Essence of Vajrayana. The Highest Yoga Tantra practice of Heruka
body mandala. (1997)
Great Treasury of Merit. How to rely upon a Spiritual Guide. (2nd
ed., 2016)
Guide to the Bodhisattva's Way of Life. How to enjoy a life of great
meaning and altruism. (A translation of Shantideva's famous
verse masterpiece.) (2002)
Heart Jewel. The essential practices of Kadampa Buddhism. (2nd
ed., 1997)

How to Solve Our Human Problems. The four noble truths. (1st American ed., 2007)

How to Understand the Mind. The nature and power of the mind. (4th ed., 2014)

Introduction to Buddhism. An explanation of the Buddhist way of life. (1st American ed., 2008)

Joyful Path of Good Fortune. The complete Buddhist path to enlightenment. (2nd ed., 1995)

Living Meaningfully, Dying Joyfully. The profound practice of transference of consciousness. (1999)

Mahamudra Tantra. The supreme Heart Jewel nectar. (2005)

Meaningful to Behold. Becoming a friend of the world. (5th ed., 2007)

Modern Buddhism. The path of compassion and wisdom. (2nd American ed., 2015)

The New Eight Steps to Happiness. The Buddhist way of loving kindness. (3rd American ed., 2017)

The New Guide to Dakini Land. The Highest Yoga Tantra practice of Buddha Vajrayogini. (3rd ed., 2012)

The New Heart of Wisdom. Profound teachings from Buddha's heart (An explanation of the *Heart Sutra*). (5th ed., 2012)

The New Meditation Handbook. Meditations to make our life happy and meaningful. (2nd American ed., 2013)

Ocean of Nectar. The true nature of all things. (1995)

The Oral Instructions of Mahamudra. The very essence of Buddha's teachings of Sutra and Tantra. (2nd ed., 2016)

Tantric Grounds and Paths. How to enter, progress on and complete the Vajrayana path. (1994)

Transform Your Life. A blissful journey. (2nd American ed., 2015)

Universal Compassion. Inspiring solutions for difficult times. (4th ed., 2002)

Sadhanas and Other Booklets

Venerable Geshe Kelsang Gyatso Rinpoche has also supervised the translation of a collection of essential sadhanas, or ritual prayers for spiritual attainments, available in booklet or audio formats.

Avalokiteshvara Sadhana. Prayers and requests to the Buddha of Compassion.

The Blissful Path. The condensed self-generation sadhana of Vajrayogini.

The Bodhisattva's Confession of Moral Downfalls. The purification practice of the *Mahayana Sutra of the Three Superior Heaps*.

Condensed Essence of Vajrayana. Condensed Heruka body mandala self-generation sadhana.

Condensed Long Life Practice of Buddha Amitayus.

Dakini Yoga. The middling self-generation sadhana of Vajrayogini.

Drop of Essential Nectar. A special fasting and purification practice in conjunction with Eleven-faced Avalokiteshvara.

Essence of Good Fortune. Prayers for the six preparatory practices for meditation on the stages of the path to enlightenment.

Essence of Vajrayana. Heruka body mandala self-generation sadhana according to the system of Mahasiddha Ghantapa.

Feast of Great Bliss. Vajrayogini self-initiation sadhana.

Great Liberation of the Father. Preliminary prayers for Mahamudra meditation in conjunction with Heruka practice.

Great Liberation of the Mother. Preliminary prayers for Mahamudra meditation in conjunction with Vajrayogini practice.

The Great Mother. A method to overcome hindrances and obstacles by reciting the *Essence of Wisdom Sutra* (the *Heart Sutra*).

A Handbook for the Daily Practice of Bodhisattva and Tantric Vows

Heartfelt Prayers. Funeral service for cremations and burials.

Heart Jewel. The Guru yoga of Je Tsongkhapa combined with the condensed sadhana of his Dharma Protector.

The Hundreds of Deities of the Joyful Land According to Highest Yoga Tantra. The Guru Yoga of Je Tsongkhapa as a Preliminary Practice for Mahamudra.

The Kadampa Way of Life. The essential practice of Kadam Lamrim.

Keajra Heaven. The essential commentary to the practice of *The Uncommon Yoga of Inconceivability.*

Lay Pratimoksha Vow Ceremony.

Liberating Prayer. Praise to Buddha Shakyamuni.

Liberation from Sorrow. Praises and requests to the Twenty-one Taras.

Mahayana Refuge Ceremony and Bodhisattva Vow Ceremony.

Medicine Buddha Prayer. A method for benefiting others.

Medicine Buddha Sadhana. A method for accomplishing the attainments of Medicine Buddha.

Meditation and Recitation of Solitary Vajrasattva.

Melodious Drum Victorious in all Directions. The extensive fulfilling and restoring ritual of the Dharma Protector, the great king Dorje Shugden, in conjunction with Mahakala, Kalarupa, Kalindewi and other Dharma Protectors.

The New Essence of Vajrayana. Heruka body mandala self-generation practice, an instruction of the Ganden Oral Lineage.

Offering to the Spiritual Guide (*Lama Chopa*). A special way of relying upon a Spiritual Guide.

Path of Compassion for the Deceased. Powa sadhana for the benefit of the deceased.

Pathway to the Pure Land. Training in powa—the transference of consciousness.

Powa Ceremony. Transference of consciousness for the deceased.

Prayers for Meditation. Brief preparatory prayers for meditation.

Prayers for World Peace.

A Pure Life. The practice of taking and keeping the eight Mahayana precepts.

Quick Path to Great Bliss. The extensive self-generation sadhana of Vajrayogini.

Request to the Holy Spiritual Guide Venerable Geshe Kelsang Gyatso from his Faithful Disciples.

The Root Tantra of Heruka and Vajrayogini. Chapters One & Fifty-one of the *Condensed Heruka Root Tantra*.

The Root Text: Eight Verses of Training the Mind.

Treasury of Wisdom. The sadhana of Venerable Manjushri.

The Uncommon Yoga of Inconceivability. The special instruction of how to reach the Pure Land of Keajra with this human body.

Union of No More Learning. Heruka body mandala self-initiation sadhana.

The Vows and Commitments of Kadampa Buddhism.

Wishfulfilling Jewel. The Guru yoga of Je Tsongkhapa combined with the sadhana of his Dharma Protector.

The Yoga of Buddha Amitayus. A special method for increasing lifespan, wisdom and merit.

The Yoga of Buddha Heruka. The brief self-generation sadhana of Heruka body mandala & Condensed six-session yoga.

The Yoga of Buddha Maitreya. Self-generation sadhana.

The Yoga of Buddha Vajrapani. Self-generation sadhana.

The Yoga of Enlightened Mother Arya Tara. Self-generation sadhana.

The Yoga of Great Mother Prajnaparamita. Self-generation sadhana.

The Yoga of Thousand-armed Avalokiteshvara. Self-generation sadhana.

The Yoga of White Tara, Buddha of Long Life.

To order any of our products please visit www.tharpa.com or contact your nearest Tharpa Office (see page 349).

Study Programs of Kadampa Buddhism

*K*adampa Buddhism is a Mahayana Buddhist school founded by the great Indian Buddhist Master Atisha (AD 982–1054). His followers are known as "Kadampas." "Ka" means "word" and refers to Buddha's teachings, and "dam" refers to Atisha's special Lamrim instructions known as "the stages of the path to enlightenment." By integrating their knowledge of all Buddha's teachings into their practice of Lamrim, and by integrating this into their everyday lives, Kadampa Buddhists are encouraged to use Buddha's teachings as practical methods for transforming daily activities into the path to enlightenment. The great Kadampa Teachers are famous not only for being great scholars, but also for being spiritual practitioners of immense purity and sincerity.

The lineage of these teachings, both their oral transmission and blessings, was then passed from Teacher to disciple, spreading throughout much of Asia, and now to many countries throughout the Western world. Buddha's teachings, which are known as "Dharma," are likened to a wheel that moves from country to country in accordance with changing conditions and people's karmic inclinations. The external forms of presenting Buddhism may change as it meets with different cultures and societies, but its essential authenticity is ensured through the continuation of an unbroken lineage of realized practitioners.

Kadampa Buddhism was first introduced into the West in 1977 by the renowned Buddhist Master Venerable Geshe Kelsang Gyatso Rinpoche. Since that time, he has worked tirelessly to spread Kadampa Buddhism throughout the world by giving extensive teachings, writing many profound texts on Kadampa Buddhism and founding the New Kadampa Tradition–International Kadampa Buddhist Union (NKT-IKBU), which now has over a thousand Kadampa Buddhist Centers and branches worldwide. Each Center offers study programs on Buddhist psychology, philosophy and meditation instruction, as well as retreats for all levels of practitioner. The emphasis is on integrating Buddha's teachings into daily life to solve our human problems and to spread lasting peace and happiness throughout the world.

The Kadampa Buddhism of the NKT-IKBU is an entirely independent Buddhist tradition and has no political affiliations. It is an association of Buddhist Centers and practitioners that derive their inspiration and guidance from the example of the ancient Kadampa Buddhist Masters and their teachings, as presented by Venerable Geshe Kelsang.

There are three reasons why we need to study and practice the teachings of Buddha: to develop our wisdom, to cultivate a good heart and to maintain a peaceful state of mind. If we do not strive to develop our wisdom, we will always remain ignorant of ultimate truth—the true nature of reality. Although we wish for happiness, our ignorance leads us to engage in non-virtuous actions, which are the main cause of all our suffering. If we do not cultivate a good heart, our selfish motivation destroys harmony and good relationships with others. We have no peace, and no chance to gain pure happiness. Without inner peace, outer peace is impossible. If we do not maintain a peaceful state of mind, we are not happy even if we have ideal conditions. On the other hand, when our mind is peaceful, we are happy even if our external conditions are unpleasant. Therefore, the development of these qualities is of utmost importance for our daily happiness.

Venerable Geshe Kelsang, or "Geshe-la" as he is affectionately called by his students, has designed three special spiritual programs for the systematic study and practice of Kadampa Buddhism that are especially suited to the modern world—the General Program (GP), the Foundation Program (FP) and the Teacher Training Program (TTP).

GENERAL PROGRAM

The General Program provides a basic introduction to Buddhist view, meditation and practice that is suitable for beginners. It also includes advanced teachings and practice from both Sutra and Tantra.

FOUNDATION PROGRAM

The Foundation Program provides an opportunity to deepen our understanding and experience of Buddhism through a systematic study of six texts:

1. *Joyful Path of Good Fortune*—a commentary to Atisha's Lamrim instructions, the stages of the path to enlightenment.

2. *Universal Compassion*—a commentary to Bodhisattva Chekhawa's *Training the Mind in Seven Points*.

3. *The New Eight Steps to Happiness*—a commentary to Bodhisattva Langri Tangpa's *Eight Verses of Training the Mind*.

4. *The New Heart of Wisdom*—a commentary to the *Heart Sutra*.

5. *Meaningful to Behold*—a commentary to Venerable Shantideva's *Guide to the Bodhisattva's Way of Life*.

6. *How to Understand the Mind*—a detailed explanation of the mind, based on the works of the Buddhist scholars Dharmakirti and Dignaga.

The benefits of studying and practicing these texts are as follows:

(1) *Joyful Path of Good Fortune*—we gain the ability to put all Buddha's teachings of both Sutra and Tantra into practice. We can easily make progress on and complete, the stages of the path to the supreme happiness of enlightenment. From a practical point of view, Lamrim is the main body of Buddha's teachings, and the other teachings are like its limbs.

(2) and (3) *Universal Compassion* and *The New Eight Steps to Happiness*—we gain the ability to integrate Buddha's teachings into our daily life and solve all our human problems.

(4) *The New Heart of Wisdom*—we gain a realization of the ultimate nature of reality. By gaining this realization, we can eliminate the ignorance of self-grasping, which is the root of all our suffering.

(5) *Meaningful to Behold*—we transform our daily activities into the Bodhisattva's way of life, thereby making every moment of our human life meaningful.

(6) *How to Understand the Mind*—we understand the relationship between our mind and its external objects. If we understand that objects depend on the subjective mind, we can change the way objects appear to us by changing our own mind. Gradually we will gain the ability to control our mind and in this way solve all our problems.

TEACHER TRAINING PROGRAM

The Teacher Training Program is designed for people who wish to train as authentic Dharma Teachers. In addition to completing the study of fourteen texts of Sutra and Tantra, which include the six texts mentioned above, the student is required to observe certain commitments with regard to behavior and way of life, and to complete a number of meditation retreats.

A Special Teacher Training Program is also held at KMC London, England, and can be studied at the center or by correspondence. This special meditation and study program consists of six courses spread over three years based on the books of Venerable Geshe Kelsang: *How to Understand the Mind; Modern Buddhism*; *The New Heart of Wisdom*; *Tantric Grounds and Paths;* Shantideva's *Guide to the Bodhisattva's Way of Life* and its commentary, *Meaningful to Behold;* and *Ocean of Nectar.*

All Kadampa Buddhist Centers are open to the public. Every year we celebrate Festivals in many countries throughout the world, including the US and England, where people gather from around the world to receive special teachings and empowerments and to enjoy a spiritual vacation. Please feel free to visit us any time!

For further information about NKT-IKBU study programs or to find your nearest center, visit www.kadampa.org or contact:

US NKT-IKBU Office
Kadampa Meditation Center
New York
47 Sweeney Road
Glen Spey, NY 12737
USA

Phone: 845-856-9000
Toll free: 877-523-2672
Fax: 845-856-2110

Email: info@kadampanewyork.org
Website: www.kadampanewyork.org

NKT-IKBU Central Office
Conishead Priory
Ulverston
Cumbria, LA12 9QQ
England

Tel: 01229-588533

Email: info@kadampa.org
Website: www.kadampa.org

Tharpa Publications Worldwide

Books from Tharpa Publications are currently published in English (American and British), Chinese, French, German, Italian, Japanese, Portuguese and Spanish. Most languages are available from any Tharpa Publications office listed below.

Visit us at www.Tharpa.com or contact your local office for more information.

United States
Tharpa Publications US
47 Sweeney Road
Glen Spey, NY 12737
USA
Phone: 845-856-5102
Toll-free: 888-741-3475
Fax: 845-856-2110
E-mail: info.us@tharpa.com
www.tharpa.com/us

United Kingdom
Tharpa Publications UK
Conishead Priory
Ulverston
UK
Cumbria, LA12 9QQ
Phone: +44 (0)1229-588599
E-mail: info.uk@tharpa.com
www.tharpa.com/uk

Asia
Tharpa Asia
1/F Causeway Tower
16-22 Causeway Road
Causeway Bay
HONG KONG
Phone: (852) 2507 2237
E-mail: info.asia@tharpa.com
www.tharpa.com/hk-en

Australia
Tharpa Publications Australia
25 McCarthy Road
Monbulk, VIC 3793
AUSTRALIA
Phone: +61 (0) 3 9756 7203
E-mail: info.au@tharpa.com
www.tharpa.com/au

Brazil

Editora Tharpa Brasil
Rua Artur de Azevedo 1360
Pinheiros, 05404-003
São Paulo - SP
BRAZIL
Phone: +55 (11) 3476-2330
E-mail: contato.br@tharpa.com
www.tharpa.com.br

France

Editions Tharpa
Château de Segrais
72220 Saint-Mars-d'Outillé
FRANCE
Phone/Fax: +33 (0)2 43 87 71 02
E-mail: info.fr@tharpa.com
www.thatpa.com/fr

Japan

Tharpa Japan
KMC Tokyo
E-mail: info@kadampa.jp
www.kadampa.jp

Canada

Tharpa Publications Canada
631 Crawford St.
Toronto, ON, M6G 3K1
CANADA
Phone: 416-762-8710
Toll-free: 866-523-2672
Fax: 416-762-2267
E-mail: info.ca@tharpa.com
www.tharpa.com/ca (English)
www.tharpa.com/ca-fr (French)

Germany

Tharpa-Verlag Deutschland
Mehringdamm 33, Aufgang 2
10961 Berlin
GERMANY
Phone: +49 (030) 43055666
E-mail: info.de@tharpa.com
www.tharpa.com/de

Mexico

Editorial Tharpa Mexico
Enrique Rébsamen No. 406
Col. Narvate, C.P. 03020
México, D.F.
MEXICO
Phone: +01 (55) 56 39 61 86
Phone/Fax: +01 (55) 56 39 61 80
E-mail: info.mx@tharpa.com
www.tharpa.com/mx

Portugal

Publicações Tharpa Portugal
Rua Moinho do Gato, 5
Várzea de Sintra
2710-661 Sintra
PORTUGAL
Phone: +351 219231064
E-mail: info.pt@tharpa.com
www.tharpa.pt

Spain

Editorial Tharpa España
Calle Manuela Malasaña No 26
28004 Madrid
SPAIN
Phone: +34 917 55 75 35
E-mail: info.es@tharpa.com
www.tharpa.com/es

Republic of South Africa

Tharpa South Africa
26 Menston Rd.
Dawncliffe,
Westville, 3629, KZN
REP. OF SOUTH AFRICA
Phone: +27 (0)72 551 3429
Fax: +27 (0)31 266 0096
E-mail: info.za@tharpa.com
www.tharpa.com/za

Switzerland

Tharpa Verlag Schwiez
Mirabellenstrasse 1
CH-8048 Zürich
SWITZERLAND
Phone: +41 44 401 02 20
Fax: +41 44 461 36 88
E-mail: info.ch@tharpa.com
www.tharpa.com/ch

Index

The letter "g" indicates an entry in the glossary.

B

C

E

Further Reading

If you enjoyed *The New Eight Steps to Happiness*, the following books and meditation CD will help deepen your understanding and practical experience of Buddhism and meditation. *Ask your favorite bookseller for these products or order online at www.tharpa.com/us*

Books

MODERN BUDDHISM
The Path of Compassion and Wisdom

By developing and maintaining compassion and wisdom in daily life, we can transform our lives, improve our relationships with others and look behind appearances to see the way things actually exist. In this way we can solve all our daily problems and accomplish the real meaning of our human life. With compassion and wisdom, like the two wings of a bird, we can quickly reach the enlightened world of a Buddha. The free eBook and PDF are available at www.emodernbuddhism.com

HOW TO SOLVE OUR HUMAN PROBLEMS
The Four Noble Truths

This inspiring book shows how Buddha's popular teaching on the Four Noble Truths can help us solve basic human problems such as dissatisfaction and anger, and provides a profound illumination of our human experience and our potential for deep inner freedom.

THE NEW MEDITATION HANDBOOK
Meditations to Make our Life Happy and Meaningful

Discover the inner peace and lightness of mind that comes from meditation. Twenty-one meditations explain step-by-step how to develop increasingly beneficial states of mind, that together form the entire Buddhist path to enlightenment.

INTRODUCTION TO BUDDHISM
An Explanation of the Buddhist Way of Life

An ideal guide for everyone interested in Buddhism and meditation. This book presents the central principles behind the Buddhist way of life, such as meditation and karma, as tools for developing qualities such as inner peace, love and patience.

Meditation CD

MEDITATIONS FOR A KIND HEART
The Healing Power of Cherishing Others

These three guided audio meditations help listeners put the teachings from *The New Eight Steps to Happiness* into practice. Meditations on Cherishing Others, Taking Away Suffering and Giving Happiness are each 10–13 minutes. The CD includes a full-color, 16-page booklet that explains the five stages of meditation. Also in this series are *Meditations for Relaxation* and *Meditations for a Clear Mind*.

VISIT OUR WEBSITE
tharpa.com/us

See our complete selection of books,
guided meditations and artwork

Learn more about Buddhism and meditation

Find a meditation class near you
(there are over 250 Kadampa centers and branches
across the US, and 1,200 around the world)

FOLLOW US ONLINE
facebook/tharpaus · twitter.com/tharpaus

For inspiring quotes, photographs, video and
information on new products and special offers.

THARPA PUBLICATIONS
47 Sweeney Road
Glen Spey, NY 12737
info.us@tharpa.com
(845) 856-5102 or (888) 741-3475